PRAISE FOR
MYTHS OF MANAGĊ_ _

'This book is so true, so sensible and so snappily written, I wish I had written it myself. If every business person read it, all managerial stupidity would wither away.' **Lucy Kellaway, Associate Editor and Work and Career Columnist,** *Financial Times*

'I consider myself to be reasonably sophisticated, rather subtle in my thinking processes. Hence, I am almost horrified that I can find absolutely nothing in *Myths of Management* with which I disagree. Sure, I might have said this or that a bit differently, with an emphasis on X instead of Y. But in the end, I buy the act. You may well not go 44 for 44 in assessing the authors' arguments, but I do offer a guarantee. You will be challenged 44 times, and it's almost impossible to imagine that you will get anything other than a sky-high return on investment from reading, and seriously reflecting on, virtually every page in the book. Bonus: It's fun to read. I suspect that you will, as I did, chuckle many a time at the degree to which you've fallen into one of the traps Stefan Stern and Cary Cooper expose.' **Tom Peters, leading management guru and co-author of *In Search of Excellence***

'Stefan Stern and Cary Cooper have summarized all the daft things I have seen written about management into one place and then dispatched them as myths by providing great common-sense insights in plain English which we can understand. For anyone wanting to manage – that is, creating the conditions for others to succeed – this is a must-read book.' **Sir Ian Cheshire, Chairman of Debenhams and former CEO of Kingfisher plc**

'The business of management is crucial, but prone to myth. In this fascinating book, Stefan Stern and Cary Cooper bring wit and courage to show what it takes to go beyond the hype and to become an insightful, and perhaps even brilliant, manager.' **Lynda Gratton, Professor of Management Practice, London Business School**

'Reports of the death of management are hugely exaggerated. We still do it – poorly – and we still need better insight how to do it well. Stefan Stern and Cary Cooper have exhumed and exorcized some of the deadlier myths still haunting corporate boardrooms and do a terrific job identifying vital ways to do the true hard work of managing.' **Margaret Heffernan, writer, business leader and consultant**

'If we want to improve the productivity of the economy, what happens within organizations is key. Leadership and management are both important. Yet for decades we have worshipped leadership (leading to excessive pay for many CEOs) and undervalued management. In this brilliant book, Stefan Stern and Cary Cooper debunk the myths that have encouraged bad practices. As the authors argue, open, humble, inclusive, listening leadership and management are essential – and they can be learned. Read this cracker of a book!' **Vicky Pryce, former Joint Head of UK Government Economic Service**

'Management matters – but is misunderstood. In this book, two very experienced observers skilfully take apart common misconceptions about the theory and practice of management. Their clear thinking helps us to discover how good management can positively make organizations more productive and satisfying work places. This is a timely and provocative book. It deserves to be widely read. **Rob Goffee and Gareth Jones, authors of *Why Should Anyone Be Led by You?***

'Stefan Stern and Cary Cooper have written a wonderful book to remind us of the basic, beyond-the-hype, essence of management. Purely and simply, it's about the people.' **Herminia Ibarra, Professor of Organizational Behaviour, London Business School**

Myths of Management

What people get wrong about being the boss

Stefan Stern and Cary Cooper

KoganPage

First published in Great Britain and the United States in 2018 by Kogan Page Limited

2nd Floor, 45 Gee Street	c/o Martin P Hill Consulting	4737/23 Ansari Road
London	122 W 27th St, 10th Floor	Daryaganj
EC1V 3RS	New York, NY 10001	New Delhi 110002
United Kingdom	USA	India

www.koganpage.com

ISBN   978 0 7494 8023 3
E-ISBN   978 0 7494 8024 0

British Library Cataloguing-in-Publication Data

A CIP record for this book is available from the British Library.

Library of Congress Cataloging-in-Publication Data

Names: Stern, Stefan, author.
Title: Myths of management : what people get wrong about being the boss / Stefan Stern and Cary Cooper.
Description: 1st Edition. | New York, NY : Kogan Page Ltd, [2018] | Series: Business myths | Includes bibliographical references and index.
Identifiers: LCCN 2017041128 (print) | LCCN 2017033876 (ebook) | ISBN 9780749480240 (ebook) | ISBN 9780749480233 (pbk.) | ISBN 9780749480240 (eISBN)
Subjects: LCSH: Management. | Communication in management. | Executive ability.
Classification: LCC HD31 (print) | LCC HD31 .S69256 2018 (ebook) | DDC 658–dc23
LC record available at https://lccn.loc.gov/2017033876

Typeset by Integra Software Services, Pondicherry
Print production managed by Jellyfish
Printed and bound by Page Bros, Norwich, UK.

In memory of Diana J Stern (1935–2014),
a mother, a manager and a Mensch

SFDS

I would like to dedicate this book to two of my management mentors, who are no longer with us, Professor Sir Roland Smith and Professor Fred Massarik (UCLA)

CLC

CONTENTS

Acknowledgements x

Introduction 1

Myth 1   **There is one right way to lead or manage** 5

Myth 2   **It's tough at the top** 9

Myth 3   **Long hours will lead to success** 12

Myth 4   **It's important not to show vulnerability or doubt** 16

Myth 5   **It's lonely at the top** 20

Myth 6   **You need to be the smartest person in the room** 24

Myth 7   **Hierarchy is finished** 27

Myth 8   **Consistency is essential** 31

Myth 9   **Only hire people who will fit in** 33

Myth 10   **Leadership is more important than management** 37

Myth 11   **You have to pay top dollar to get the right person** 41

Myth 12   **Annual appraisals help you manage performance** 45

Myth 13   **Information must be controlled and limited** 49

Myth 14   **... but women don't really want top jobs** 53

Myth 15   **Leaders are born, not made** 57

Myth 16   Your first 100 days in a new job are make or break 61

Myth 17   You have to know everything that is going on 65

Myth 18   Heroic leaders can change entire organizations on their own 69

Myth 19   The boss with the best strategy wins 72

Myth 20   It is not possible to work flexibly in senior roles 76

Myth 21   Pay must be kept confidential 80

Myth 22   Psychology is psychobabble and there's no need or place for it 82

Myth 23   The robots are coming to take your job 86

Myth 24   Leadership must be transformational 91

Myth 25   Conformity leads to success 95

Myth 26   Feelings are soft and for losers 99

Myth 27   Keep your distance if you want respect 102

Myth 28   Be yourself – it's all about authenticity 106

Myth 29   Date of birth is destiny 110

Myth 30   People are motivated by money 114

Myth 31   Fear works and 'engagement' is unnecessary 118

Myth 32   The business case will always prove persuasive 122

Myth 33   There's nothing wrong with the business, there's just a few rotten apples 126

Myth 34   We have woken up to the problems caused by prejudice 130

Myth 35   **All the power resides at the top** 132

Myth 36   **People will learn if you explain things to them clearly** 136

Myth 37   **You must keep up with all the new management ideas and give them a try** 139

Myth 38   **You've got to talk like a real, serious, grown-up business person. Learn the jargon** 143

Myth 39   **You can't manage people if you can't see them** 147

Myth 40   **Who needs employees anyway? Get with the gig economy** 151

Myth 41   **People hate change** 155

Myth 42   **Big data will fix everything** 159

Myth 43   **A cool office will make everybody more creative** 163

Myth 44   **There are only 44 things to get wrong** 166

Appendices: Fireside chats with prominent management thinkers
  1   *Charles Handy* 171
  2   *Eve Poole* 177
  3   *Henry Mintzberg* 180
  4   *Herminia Ibarra* 184
  5   *Laura Empson* 189
  6   *Lynda Gratton* 195
  7   *Margaret Heffernan* 200
  8   *Rob Goffee and Gareth Jones* 207
  9   *Tom Peters* 214

References 219
Index 229

ACKNOWLEDGEMENTS

I am grateful to all the bosses I have worked for, the good ones, the brilliant ones, and the not necessarily completely flawless ones, for the examples they have given me to draw on for this book. I spent a year at the BBC in the mid-1990s, which was a crash course in office politics. I remember fondly my time at the Industrial Society shortly after, where I first got to grips with the idea and practice of management, and also met my great hero and mentor, the late Geoffrey Goodman. Rufus Olins made me features editor of *Management Today* magazine. I owe him for that important break. I lived through Web 1.0 with Pradeep Jethi and Simon Caulkin. And then the *Financial Times* took a chance on me, first as a freelance contributor, later as a columnist. I am grateful to the editor Lionel Barber and the dozens of superb colleagues I got to work with there. The *FT* is a class act, still. Robert Phillips and Richard Edelman were generous and imaginative employers. And the trustees of the High Pay Centre have been kind and patient and tolerant of my less than perfect management.

My co-author, Cary Cooper, has been a wonderful source of encouragement and support. Sadly I had a vacancy for a new Jewish mother, but Cary came through for me. This book would never have been written without his energy, enthusiasm and inspiration. I also thank my 95-year-old father for his great wisdom, temperament, maturity and insights. Kogan Page have been excellent to work with. They really know what they're doing.

Most of all I thank my wife, Rachel, and daughters, Josie and Rosa, who have learnt to put up with the grumpiness of a dad whose words weren't always flowing quite as well as they might have.

Stefan Stern

INTRODUCTION

Management matters. It's big stuff. Boring, sometimes, perhaps – but usually important. We need to take it seriously and get better at it.

Management is everywhere, all around us, but so often unseen. The train is late? Management. An operation is postponed? Management. A sudden, unexpected resignation? Management.

But it's not all bad news. A great new restaurant? Management. A successful drug trial for a new treatment? Management. Sporting triumph? Management. It's all management, all the time.

You've got two things to deal with at work: people and resources. If you can manage people and resources better than your competitors you will be fine. In the public and not-for-profit sectors resources may be constrained. So how you manage people becomes possibly even more important. It will certainly determine whether public services are provided effectively or not.

Management matters, a lot. To adapt the economist Paul Krugman's well-known observation on productivity: management isn't everything, but it is almost everything. So in case you were wondering: 'Why another book on management?' – that's why.

What's the big idea?

The authors of this book have been around for a bit. Between us we have around seven decades of experience of studying and thinking about work and how it gets done. We've had our share of good and bad bosses, and have on occasion been put in charge of a few things too. We have, as it were, been there and done that. That is why we can declare confidently, right at the outset, that there are absolutely no new ideas in this book.

Why should there be? People have been managed and led for centuries. The best-known formal codification of management practices, in the modern world, was produced over 100 years ago by F W Taylor, with his approach known as 'scientific management'. Several decades later Taiichi Ohno described Toyota's groundbreaking production system, which helped it to become the world's leading car manufacturer. And then there have been all those other management books…

Technology changes and business cycles come and go but human beings remain essentially the same. We adapt to change, and sometimes find new ways of doing things, but the fundamental building blocks of work – people, teams, leaders, tasks – do not really change. Beware if someone tells you they've had a new idea about how to manage people.

Just about managing

In his book *Reinventing Management* (2010), Julian Birkinshaw, professor of strategy and entrepreneurship at London Business School, observes that, while many organizations might have a defined business model, fewer have a management model, an understanding of the way in which they want management to be practised. There are some predictable consequences to this, unearthed by the vast World Management Survey (begun in 2002) and led by three economics professors: Nicholas Bloom, Raffaella Sadun and John Van Reenen.

In short, the survey has found that many businesses (over 8,000 have been studied) are simply not nearly as good at management as they think they are. As many as 79 per cent of organizations believed they were above average. But in fact only 15 per cent of US companies and fewer than 5 per cent elsewhere could really be said to be superior operators when measured against a management practices scale drawn up by the researchers. (The good news is that certain specific interventions, under the headings of targets, incentives and monitoring, have been shown to raise performance.)

In the UK (at least) we urgently need to raise our productivity. It has been unimpressive for far too long. If we want wages to rise (anyone against that?) we have to be more productive. That means raising our output per capita, through working more effectively. It means we need better management.

Conclusion? Management matters. QED.

What's the medium-sized idea?

This book is one in a series designed to explode a few myths. It has given us a chance to look again at some of those things that bosses may instinctively believe to be true but which simply aren't so. Is leadership more important than management? Do you really have to be the smartest person in the room? Are long hours the best way to achieve success? Is it OK to change your mind? And so on.

There are no footnotes to read, nor are there vast amounts of data to digest. While the book is not fact-free, this is really just what we think, based on years of studying management and considering what's going on.

And while there may not be a Big and Exciting New Idea here, there is at least one Reasonably Large Idea to wrestle with, and it is this: see it human. We are human beings, not yet (and not for a long time to come) made redundant by new technology and the advancing robot army. Jobs are changing, and working life is changing too. Human beings, however, are still around, and the task of management remains.

Management is about people: working with them, understanding them, encouraging them, stretching and developing them, inspiring them. Management means getting things done with people. That means our workplaces should be safe and civilized places where people are respected and can give of their best. We hope any readers who doubt this point will feel differently after getting to the end. And if you don't take our word for it, please also read and enjoy the 'fireside chats' (interviews) we have conducted with some of our favourite management thinkers, which we quote from extensively throughout and which can be read in full in the Appendices at the back of the book.

Getting things done

In the children's movie *The Boss Baby* (2017) there is an amusing moment when babies emerging from their production line (it's a kids' film, OK?) are tested to see where on earth (literally) they should be sent. If the babies laugh and gurgle when tickled they are sent to a happy and welcoming family. If they don't, a light with the word 'Management' on it flashes up and they are sent to work. (It's a joke probably aimed more at the accompanying grown-ups rather than the younger demographic.)

Still, it's a challenge. The word 'management' is a downer for too many people. Why did that understated and downbeat comedy show *The Office* become such a big smash and global phenomenon? Because we've all had bad bosses, and we've all suffered at the receiving end of bad management.

The last word, before we start, should go to Peter Drucker, the greatest management writer of them all. It is a warning to reject the myths of management and focus instead on what is truly effective. 'So much of what we call management', Drucker said, 'consists in making it difficult for people to work.'

May that be a lesson to you.

- MYTH 1 -

THERE IS ONE RIGHT WAY
TO LEAD OR MANAGE

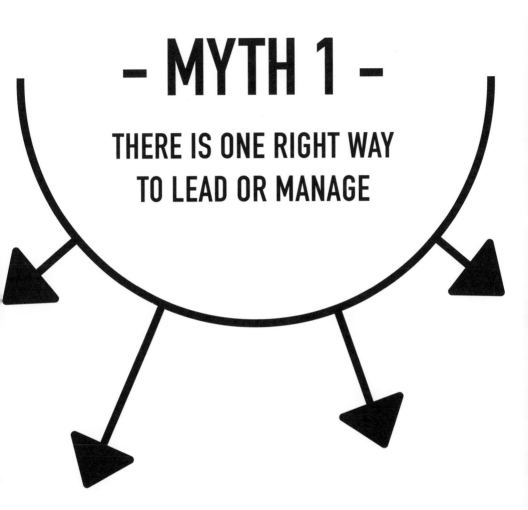

*Beware those who say they have 'cracked' leadership
and management for good.*

Wouldn't life at work be easier if there were simple solutions to our complicated problems? There would be so much less to think about. Less stress. Your repertoire of behaviour and choices would be that much smaller. You could carry on in the knowledge that leadership style A or management decision B would be all there was to it. Job done – literally.

This yearning for simplicity partly explains why you see all those management books at the airport offering seductive promises such as 'three steps to compete and win' or 'the right way to lead'.

But there is no one right way to lead or manage. People are different. Circumstances change. Businesses and organizations go through different life stages and cycles, as do the prevailing trading conditions. The competition may change the way they do things, requiring you to change too. Leaders and managers have to be able to adapt, just as they want their teams to adapt.

The idea that there might be only 'one right way' was challenged by Paul Hersey and Ken Blanchard (1969) nearly five decades ago. They developed the idea of 'situational leadership' – a more adaptive and flexible way of considering the task of leaders and managers.

People at work need both direction and support, in varying degrees. Hersey and Blanchard argued that, depending on who you were working with and when, at least four different types of subtly varying behaviour were required.

Initially, while starting out on a task or a project, a team might need quite a lot of direction – this is 'telling'. As the nature and demands of the task become clearer, a bit less direction and a bit more support is needed. There is more two-way communication going on – this is 'selling'.

Once work is truly under way, more of the decision making is shared and teams carry on almost autonomously – with even less direction, even more support – this is 'participating'. And when responsibility for the work has been fully taken on by the team virtually no direction is needed, only interested but detached support is required – this is 'delegating'.

The psychologist Rob Davies has compared this, not entirely seriously, to a reductive description of how to play golf (conversation with authors). A golfer has only four different types of shot to play: hit the ball a long way, hit it a short way, hit the ball from the grass, or hit it from sand. (Keen amateur golfers may object that their experience of the game throws up rather more variety, and less linear progress, in their struggles on the course.)

But the point is the same. One management or leadership size, or style, will not fit all situations. This is one of the reasons that Rob Goffee and Gareth Jones, authors of the essential *Why Should Anyone Be Led by You?* (2006), argue that the simple instruction to 'be yourself' is inadequate advice to any aspiring boss. They add the qualifier 'with skill'. You need what they call 'situation-sensing skills' to judge how (and how much) you need to intervene in any situation (see also Myth 28 on authenticity).

Good role models, bad role models

Why, though, are we still so susceptible to the idea that one type of leader or manager may have 'cracked it' once and for all, and that all the rest of us need to do is try to imitate and emulate that person? It is partly that appeal of the simple solution: 'all you need to know'. (We should remember, however, the view usually attributed to the American journalist H L Mencken, that for every complicated problem there is a solution that is simple, neat and wrong.)

As Phil Rosenzweig of IMD in Lausanne has also argued, in his book *The Halo Effect* (2007), we can be tempted to believe the myths (or simple stories) that organizations tell themselves and the outside world about how they have succeeded, stories which in turn are spread and sustained by journalists and business academics.

Thus CEO A or B is said to have embodied an ideal leadership style and approach *for all times*. Be more like Sir Terry Leahy or Steve Jobs or Lou Gerstner, it is said, and all will be well. But this is bad advice.

Leaders and businesses succeed at a given time, for a limited period. But there are no permanent victories, and no single way of leading and managing that will always work. Indeed, temporary success so often leads businesses to think, mistakenly, that they have less reason to change what they are doing. Tesco is just the latest formerly dominant player that has had to rethink completely how it operates, when only a few years ago the company (and its management) was regarded as infallible. The point about Jim Collins' book *Good to Great* (2001) was not that his exemplar companies had worked out the timeless secret of success, rather that in a given period of time they had made important changes that led to success.

As the writer Eve Poole tells us in our interview with her (Appendix 2), leadership is not static. 'It is a craft skill, and it requires daily practice... the work I have done suggests that real leaders know this, and work with it, seeking out opportunities to hone their skills in order to future-proof their leading.' Dr Poole calls this process 'leadersmithing'.

'Leadersmithing... establishes the recipe for top leadership and sets out ways to learn this either through weekly exercises or by seeking out exposure to critical incidents under pressure, to cement the learning and enable consistent and sustained performance under pressure in the future', she says. 'It is about layering on experiences, deliberately rather than at the hand of fate, to develop the character and muscle memory to lead in the full range of situations likely to occur in the future.'

'Why you should be more like me'

Tolstoy's famous line about families – that while happy ones are more or less alike, unhappy ones are unhappy in their own particular way – does not apply to businesses and organizations. The happy ones are unique too. This is why there can never be one right way to lead or manage in any context. The former global managing partner of McKinsey, Ian Davis, once made this point well in a conversation with the authors. 'All generalizations about business are wrong', he said. And when you consider how many businesses his firm has studied over the years, this seems like a useful (and, unusually, cheap) piece of advice. You have to try to understand the situation you find yourself in now, and operate in the way that the situation demands.

Indeed, Davis once also brilliantly summed up what is wrong with those piles of brash business books piled up at the airport* that promise to reveal the secrets of superstar business leaders. Whatever the official title of the book was, the true sub-heading was really: 'Why you should be more like me' (conversation with authors). But no matter how many black polo-neck jumpers you buy you will never be Steve Jobs. Don't try to be more like them. Be more like you. It's all you've got, after all.

Note

*   Of course, if you have bought this book at an airport, thank you.

- MYTH 2 -

IT'S TOUGH AT THE TOP

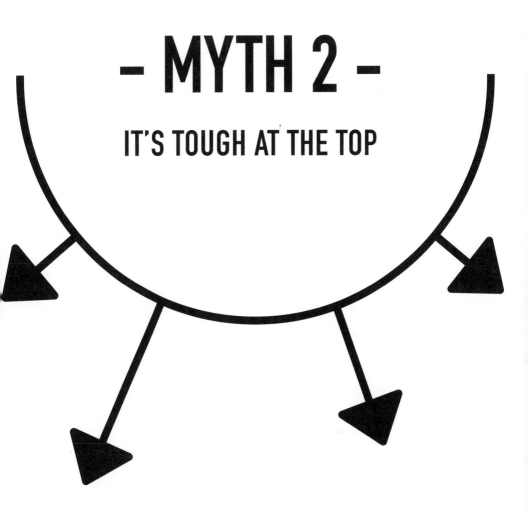

The self-serving talk of how hard it is to be a leader ignores the stresses and pressures faced by the rest of the workforce.

Beware the chief executive who tells you, as many do, that 'letting go of people' is the toughest thing they ever have to do. They probably don't really mean it. In a world where human beings have become 'headcount', and cost savings and efficiencies are a permanent top agenda item, the idea that CEOs might be squeamish about making cuts is pretty fanciful. Restructurings and redundancies are the order of the day, sometimes unavoidably. Save your sympathy for those on the receiving end of those decisions.

It is easy for bosses to console themselves with the thought that few people appreciate how tough their job is. The buck stops with them, it is true. They may get paid the most, by far, but they will take the blame if and when things go wrong. It is their reputation that is on the line.

But consider the ways in which it really isn't tough at the top. First, you have a lot of help on offer, for much of the time permanently on call. It's not just the number of personal assistants. Colleagues, whose future career prospects will depend on the judgements you form about them, will be only too keen to help out too.

All logistical challenges in your life will be taken care of. You will travel in comfort and stay in luxurious accommodation. You will be listened to carefully. You will get to speak first, and last, to sum up the conversation and offer your conclusion ahead of everybody else's. You will get to choose which tasks you want to carry out when, and which tasks you can happily delegate. You will have much more autonomy than anyone else in the business.

It's tough in the middle, and at the bottom

Sir Michael Marmot's lengthy 'Whitehall studies' (1991) – research into the health and well-being of civil servants – have found that it is officials working at lower levels in the hierarchy, and not at the top, who face the greatest stress, and are most at risk of suffering serious health problems.

The study of those people with low 'job control' found that they were four times more likely to die of a heart attack than those with high 'job control'. They also appeared to be more likely to suffer from other stress-related conditions such as cancer, stroke and gastrointestinal disorders.

In other words, it is not tough at the top. It is tough in the middle and at the bottom. 'The high-status person has a lot of demand,' Marmot has written, 'but he or she has a lot of control, and the combination of high demand and low control is what's stressful.' More junior staff may also enjoy much less 'social participation': their networks are smaller and less powerful, so it is harder for them to influence their situation. Increasingly, with the bifurcation in the labour market, there are, crudely, a smallish number of really good (and well-paid) jobs at the top, a moderate (but reduced) number of stressful if moderately satisfying jobs in the middle, and a lot of uncertain and badly paid jobs at the bottom. And that's where the going really is tough.

Get real

In his book *The Leader on the Couch* (2006), Professor Manfred Kets de Vries of the INSEAD business school quotes one CEO who was prepared to admit (in the privacy of a seminar room): 'Every day when I go into the office I have the ability to make the lives of my 10,000 employees either miserable or positive. It doesn't take very much to go either way.'

This, at least, is an honest assessment. And it confirms the extent to which the real challenges of working life are to be found out there on the shop floor or in middle management, and not in the hushed boardrooms, corner offices or corridors of power.

Realizing this should influence every leader's or manager's approach. How much autonomy or freedom to operate are you giving your people? Do they have to keep asking for permission to carry out even the simplest tasks?

Have you recognized the pressures that they are under – for example, the fact that in the part of business where they work their resources may be limited, unlike in the more serene setting at the top? Bluntly, being on much lower incomes will also impose unavoidable pressures on your more junior colleagues. Do you have any idea how the cost of living affects them? Do you know what it's like to use crowded public transport at the busiest times of the day? It's not as nice as being driven in a limo, you know.

Entitled

As the pay and conditions of the world's 'super-managers' have taken off – as detailed by Thomas Piketty in his important work *Capital in the Twenty-first Century* (2014) – many have been left behind, economically and in other ways. And this has had dramatic political consequences, such as the UK's Brexit vote, the election of Donald Trump and the rise of populist parties elsewhere in Europe and beyond. Business leaders may not like these developments, but they have in part been provoked by bosses who misguidedly see themselves as misunderstood or underappreciated, even as they enjoy wonderful pay, terms and conditions.

Bosses have conveyed an unattractive sense of entitlement, with their claims to be rare and special talent that deserves to be treated differently. Excessive pay is only one symbol of this, but it is no doubt the most powerful one. Believing yourself to be worth such a vast multiple of the pay of the average worker in the business says a lot about that you and the ethos of the business generally. As one former FTSE 100 CEO has admitted: 'We win the lottery every year.' That doesn't sound too bad, does it?

If you really think it's tough at the top, try living and working down at the bottom for a bit.

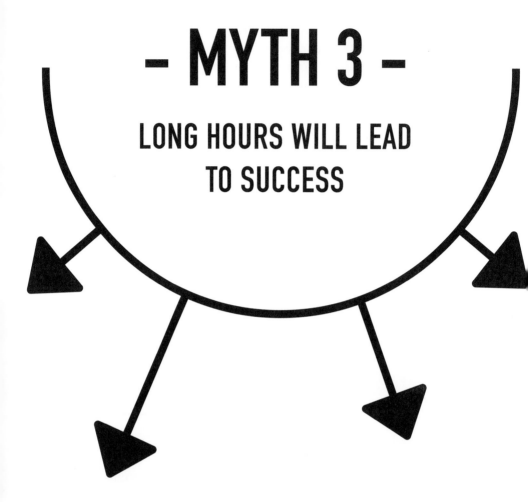

– MYTH 3 –

LONG HOURS WILL LEAD TO SUCCESS

By all means put in some long hours when necessary. But know that you have to stop and live your life. Get some balance back.

First in, last out. Some bosses believe that they have to set an example with their time-keeping. And that means showing up early and staying late. The problem is that this may not be a very good example to set. Being present but not productive – 'presenteeism' – is no real use to anyone. And intimidating colleagues into staying late just for show is even worse.

It is not just an 'Anglo-Saxon' problem. The Japanese even came up with a word, *karōshi*, which means 'death from overwork'. Staying late and just sitting by the window (they have a phrase for that too), mainly because your boss hasn't gone home yet, has long been a symptom of many Japanese workplaces. (A Japanese government panel has suggested that employee overtime should be kept to under 100 hours a month, with an annual limit of 720 hours (The Japan Times, 2017). Even this huge number is proving hard to enforce.) Yet in Germany working late would normally be seen as a sign that you were simply being inefficient. You should be embarrassed that you are still in the office, not proud.

Persistently flat UK productivity does not point to there being many benefits to a long-hours culture either. Being 20 per cent less productive than the French, for example, is the equivalent of the Brits still going in to work on Friday when the French have already started a long weekend. Is that success? (Clue: it isn't.)

Why don't you want to go home?

Creating a workaholic culture is not the answer to our productivity problem, or good for our mental health. The PR firm Lansons studied the UK workforce in a 2015 study called, reasonably enough, *Britain at Work*, a survey of over 2,000 employees. It showed that many people are doing a large amount of unpaid overtime, with 61 per cent saying they regularly work beyond their contracted hours. In 2017 the TUC calculated that UK workers did 2.1 billion unpaid hours in the previous year, worth over £6,000 a head on average, or nearly £34 billion in total. But if we are working so hard, why aren't we productive? Lower productivity means people don't get paid as much as they could. They are putting in the time but not getting the results in any sense.

When we consistently work long hours our health and well-being suffer. We become tired and are less able to come up with creative solutions to problems, which in turn has a negative impact on our performance. We enter a vicious circle. Many of us compensate for sluggish performance by putting in even more hours, which eventually leads to increased levels of pressure, mistakes or poor decisions, and even worse performance. Home and family life inevitably suffers too.

Health is wealth

In the past, the main causes of long-term sickness absence were things such as back pain and other musculoskeletal disorders. Today, stress, depression and anxiety are the illnesses keeping people out of work. Or keeping them present, but not adding any value.

According to the *Britain at Work* survey, 30 per cent of workers don't feel they have enough time to do their job effectively, and 18 per cent say they are often too tired to do their job properly. The UK is trapped in a long-hours, low-productivity culture. We assume that working more hours at full capacity is the answer to our productivity slump, when actually it's part of the cause. If we really want to improve productivity we need to change our attitudes and understand that this is not a healthy, productive or sustainable way of working in the long term.

Are all those meetings necessary? Do you have to go on so many trips, taking you away from home for extended periods? Do there have to be so many social functions in the evenings or even at weekends? These are questions managers should be asking.

Breaking the long-hours culture

If we want people's behaviour to change, there has to be a credible signal from the top that long hours are neither needed nor desired. And that signal has to be transmitted right through the organization. This means recruiting managers who aren't just technically competent but who are good at managing others. Too often we see people who aren't cut out for it promoted into management positions. This is because many organizations don't hire managers based on their people skills, but on their technical skills or their bottom-line output in a previous job (without knowing what damage they left in their wake).

When recruiting managers we need to take their interpersonal skills into account, and consider how capable they are of managing and building relationships with their colleagues.

Britain needs leaders with the ability to speak to employees in a language they can relate to; engaged leaders who can build trust, cultivate flexible cultures and give their staff more manageable workloads, with achievable deadlines and the autonomy to work in a way that makes sense to them.

For many, managing a team becomes even more difficult when workers' personal lives overflow into their jobs. Most line managers are not trained to deal with challenging conversations around troubles at home, feeling depressed or anxious, or problematic relationships at work – the stuff of life. We have to get better at this too.

Organizations need to ensure their managers are equipped with the skills to be able to handle these conversations, and to prioritize so-called 'soft skills' much higher on the recruitment agenda. Until this happens we won't see significant improvements in the UK's productivity. Creating a workaholic culture is not the answer. Nor is it good for the health of working people. As Woody Allen put it: 'I don't want to achieve immortality through my work. I want to achieve it by not dying.'

'Tell me, what is it you plan to do with your one wild and precious life?'

There is no need here to repeat the line about what never gets said by anyone on their deathbed. We all know the joke, but find it hard to act on its message. Of course, economics – cash – plays a part in this. But it is possible to avoid getting trapped in a job you hate just to keep enough money coming in. This is something that many under-40s in particular seem to have grasped. They have seen their parents make that mistake and they don't want to repeat it.

Work matters. It provides structure and meaning, as well as income. People want to make a purposeful contribution. But until they are better led and managed, too many will be on a depressing, fruitless treadmill. The task for leaders and managers is to show how long hours at work can do more harm than good, and that sometimes the best thing you can do is go home.

CREDIT This myth is a reproduction of an article first appearing in the October 2015 issue of *HR* magazine. Reproduced with kind permission from *HR* magazine.

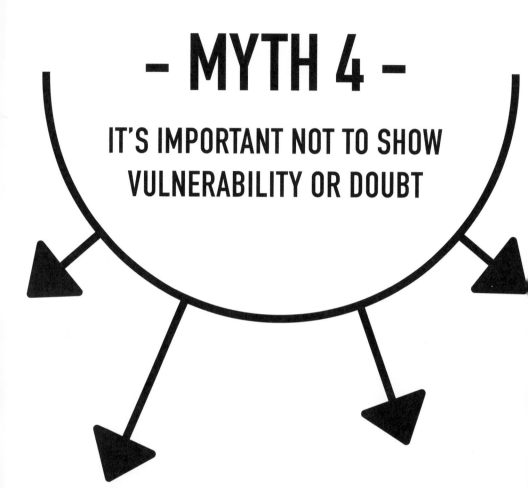

- MYTH 4 -

IT'S IMPORTANT NOT TO SHOW VULNERABILITY OR DOUBT

John Wayne is dead. In the 21st century it is OK for bosses not to be certain, to share concerns and ask for help.

In October 1980, Margaret Thatcher, leader of the Conservative Party and prime minister for the previous year and a half, went down to her party's annual conference in Brighton under severe political pressure. Unemployment was rising fast and inflation was still in double digits. Mrs Thatcher's government was deeply unpopular, and many observers expected her to change course and moderate her policies.

Instead, she said this: 'To those waiting with bated breath for that favourite media catchphrase, the U-turn, I have only one thing to say: You turn if you want to. The lady's not for turning!'

The delegates, and onlooking media, were delighted. The phrase stuck, so much so that even now, almost four decades later, the idea of performing a 'U-turn' (in the United States they call it 'flip-flopping') is still seen as politically disastrous. You just don't do it. Leaders are supposed to be strong and decisive. They never change their minds.

Margaret Thatcher, Britain's first female prime minister, was a remarkable figure. Whether you approved of what she achieved in office or not, her place in history is assured. But this famous soundbite decrying the U-turn has been a disaster for leadership and management. This is one of the most enduring management myths of all: that, regardless of the situation, you stick to your guns, betray no weakness or doubt, and press on, full steam ahead, in all circumstances. Never take a step back. U-turn if you want to... be a loser.

But this mythical mantra does not even accurately describe Mrs Thatcher's record in office. Yes, she led a successful battle against the miners during their strike in 1984/85, but she had in fact flinched from combatting them three years earlier when the odds favoured the union. She was capable of talking tough publicly while finessing her position in private. That is the real world. But myths can prove popular and long-lasting.

Macho is not mucho

Stale and outdated notions of what it means to lead and manage continue to undermine performance. It may have become a cliché to declare the death of 'command and control management', but it has been a long time in the dying. Top-down management can still dominate, and make severe, counterproductive demands on staff. A survey of over 3,500 senior managers conducted by the Chartered Institute for Personnel and Development in October 2015 found that 29 per cent have to 'compromise their principles' to meet the current needs of the business. And 20 per cent said they have to compromise their principles to keep their boss happy.

The case for a more open and inclusive style of management, as opposed to a rigid and dictatorial one, is simply made. When millions of people were employed to perform relatively simple, repetitive tasks in a more heavily manufacturing-dominated economy, the job of managers consisted to a large extent of simply hitting production targets. F W Taylor's 'scientific management', based on efficient processes and 'time and motion' disciplines, was all you needed.

Now, with services forming by far the largest part of the modern, mature economy (in the UK they are around 80 per cent of the economy), the human factor has become more important. We need people at work to be able to think and respond sensitively and creatively to what customers want. You can't really bully that behaviour out of people on an ongoing basis. So managers need to be more human too: open, not closed; in touch, not remote; communicative, not silent; and yes, at times even vulnerable, revealing doubts, not 'flawless'.

Professor Henry Mintzberg (see Appendix 3) is clear: 'Management is plain old-fashioned personal engagement. Nothing fancy, nothing sophisticated. Just people who care, and get involved, and know what's going on. They're sympathetic to other human beings, not "human resources"… You know, when you see someone who is a natural in the job it's the most natural thing in the world, doing what they do.'

Frailty, thy name is… everybody

The psychologist Daniel Goleman popularized the term 'emotional intelligence' in the mid-1990s. It can be understood in a number of ways, but at its heart – pun intended – it has to do with understanding and working with your own and colleagues' emotional responses to the world. That means, for example, recognizing when you are uncertain or have doubts, when you cannot utter bold and unequivocal instructions to your team.

In *Why Should Anyone Be Led by You?* (2006), Rob Goffee and Gareth Jones argued that trying to be a macho, doubt-free boss was a misguided undertaking. 'Leaders should let their weaknesses be known', they wrote. 'By exposing a measure of vulnerability, they make themselves approachable and show themselves to be human.'

Strong men, weak performance

Around the world an array of 'strong men' hold the reins of power – Trump (United States), Putin (Russia), Erdogan (Turkey), Xi Jinping (China), Duterte (Philippines). They impress their supporters, and make their opponents tremble. But how well are they doing, really? What long-term problems are being built up? What state will their countries be in when they leave office? We would draw the wrong lesson from their temporary, apparent success if we thought their style and methods should be brought into the workplace.

Even Mrs Thatcher, so dominant for so many years in the UK, met a miserable end politically, her legacy still controversial and fought over. And in the aftermath of her leadership the Conservative Party imploded, eventually remaining out of office for 13 years, only finally winning a majority again in 2015, 23 years after its last big win in 1992.

Clint, not Maggie

If it's role models we are looking for, Hollywood offers us something slightly better than the 'real world' of politics. Inspector Harry Callahan of the San Francisco homicide division – 'Dirty Harry', played by Clint Eastwood, gives us some useful advice in the second movie of the series, *Magnum Force* (1973).

Fighting corruption and dishonesty all around him, Harry keeps his cool. He outwits his enemy, who has overreached himself, and emerges triumphant again. And his verdict on his defeated opponent? 'A man's got to know his limitations', he says.

Clint is right. Don't pretend to be someone you are not, or that you are free of all doubt and uncertainty. It is OK to change your mind and change direction when the situation demands it. You can even ask for help if you need to. That's not weakness – it's strength.

– MYTH 5 –

IT'S LONELY AT THE TOP

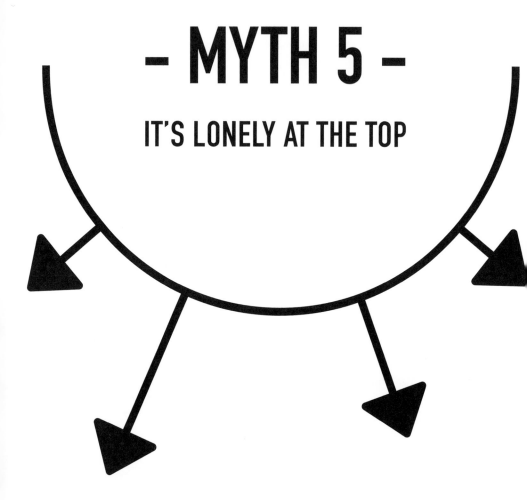

It is time to reach out, not hunker down, when they put you in charge.

'Trust no one, my friend, no one!' This is how Herod Agrippa warns the young (and future emperor) Claudius in the BBC adaptation of Robert Graves' history about the rise of the unlikely Roman leader (Wise, 1976). 'Not your most grateful freedman. Not your most intimate friend. Not your dearest child. Not the wife of your bosom. Trust no one!'

Those who see life and work as a tournament in which success can come only at the expense of others will probably find that advice persuasive. And doubtless there are workplaces where trust levels are low and it is every man or woman for him- or herself.

But low-trust environments are inefficient. You waste too much time playing politics and looking over your shoulder. You do not know which colleagues you can truly rely on. A lack of trust puts up the cost of doing business, as the Nobel prize winner Oliver Williamson has shown (Nobel Prizes and Laureates, 2009).

This is not controversial or hard to understand. And yet one of the most enduring myths of management is that it is, and must be, lonely at the top. The big decisions sit with you alone, it is said. You cannot take people into your confidence, because you do not know if confidences will be respected. Worse – what if they are out to get you? Share and tell them as little as possible. Knowledge is power. This sort of insecurity lies behind that nice old gag about how to approach succession planning: that on getting to the top you must search the organization high and low to find your most likely successors – and destroy them.

Only the lonely

Bosses should not be taking big decisions on their own. Ideas should be discussed and tested before being carried out. That's not just good corporate governance, it is common sense. Peter Drucker said that there should not be agreement at the top until there had been disagreement. In other words: there has to be debate before you can move on. That is hard to do on your own, inside your own head, without talking to anybody else. The myth of the lonely leader laying down the law without consulting colleagues first is old-fashioned and needs to be dismantled.

Partnerships – law or accountancy firms, and management consultancies – sometimes offer an enlightening alternative to the lone-gun leadership model. Partnerships may take longer to reach an agreed decision through their practice of consulting and re-consulting with partners. But when they take a decision and commit to a future path it is more likely to be a soundly based choice. After the downturn that followed the global financial crisis in 2008, hitherto hugely successful partnerships such as the legal firm Allen & Overy and the retailer John Lewis faced the unprecedented need to push through redundancies. Both did so with the minimum of fuss and disruption to the business, partly on account of the consultative nature of the leadership that was on offer in these two very different organizations. These were tough decisions, but they were not lonely ones. Many people had contributed their thoughts and points of view.

Laura Empson, a professor at Cass Business School in London and an expert on professional service firms, puts it nicely: 'If you think it's lonely at the top you are not doing it right.' (See our 'fireside chat' with Laura in Appendix 5.)

Trust me

The antidote to loneliness is trust. And people will only be able to prove that they are trustworthy if you first show them that they are trusted. You have to give trust to get it back. You have, in that sense, to take a risk to break out of the loneliness trap.

You also have to seek out people who have views different from your own. One way of apparently dealing with loneliness is to bring in people who will agree with you. But that is a bad way of trying to feel part of something bigger. It will lead only to staleness and a lack of creativity. Reaching out to others must mean genuinely seeking those who are not like you, who bring something different to the conversation. Hunkering down on your own is bad enough. But pretending to yourself and others that you are open to outside voices, while really only looking for yes-men and yes-women, is even worse.

It's a team sport

Leadership is a team sport. You need other people on your team to help you do it. This is literally true in the real world of sport. Even those stars who seem to achieve things on their own are usually dependent on many other people. Tennis players are forever staring up at their coaches and members of the entourage (which may include physiotherapists, fitness gurus, nutritionists and psychologists) for inspiration. Golfers talk to their caddy the whole way round the course. No one need ever have to feel lonely out there. The same is true for managers at work.

Grasp this point and so much about leading and managing people will become easier. You are not on your own. You can ask for help. You can and should challenge your thinking with other people's perspectives. You are not supposed to come up with all the answers by yourself.

Even that 'rock star' of Wall Street, Jamie Dimon of J P Morgan, says he needs the advice and support of trusted colleagues. At an event at Harvard Business School a few years ago he was discussing his view of leadership, and performed a bit of myth-busting of his own.

'They tell you that you've always got to have at least one close colleague who will tell you the truth', Dimon said. 'Well, if you've only got one guy in 10 who will tell you the truth you should fire the other nine!' (Stern, 2008).

If you are feeling lonely at the top you are not doing it right. Open your door, get out of your office, talk to others, seek help and advice. Let the outside world in if you want to become a better boss.

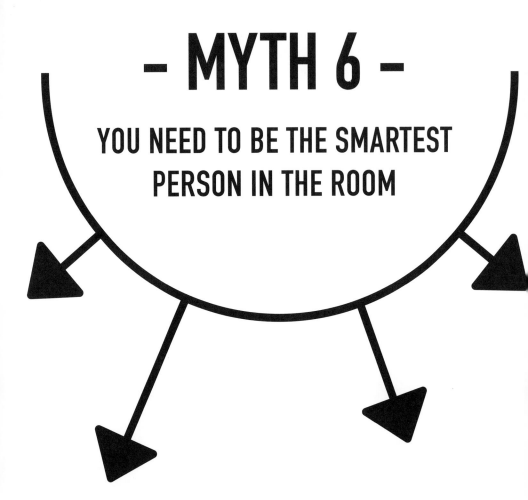

– MYTH 6 –

YOU NEED TO BE THE SMARTEST PERSON IN THE ROOM

*It is not about being the brainiest. It's about hiring good
people and trusting them to get on with the job.*

There is a cry you sometimes hear when the boss has had enough of all the
whingeing and the carping: 'OK, if you think you're so smart, why don't
you try running this place?' The complaint is based on the premise that the
person in the top job must also somehow be the cleverest. Leaders get the
big bucks, it is felt, because they are so smart. But this does not follow at all.
All the wisdom does not reside in the most senior positions. The clever thing
for managers to do is recognize where the talent lies and pass on as much of
the work as possible in that direction.

The deferential view of leadership holds that the best ideas come from the
top. The word strategy derives from the Greek word for a military general

(see Myth 19). So it's understandable if managers feel under pressure to be the source of inspiration. And from the employee's point of view it's a lot easier as a team member to slump in your chair and wait for the boss to tell you what to do.

But the really smart leader recognizes that he or she is almost certainly not the smartest person around. This takes unfashionable humility. This is not how business leaders are usually seen or portrayed. Success will come, however, when everyone's abilities can be drawn upon and, in the best sense of the word, exploited.

Knowing what you don't know

In his 2017 letter to shareholders, Amazon founder and chief executive Jeff Bezos revealed the combination of intelligence married with humility which has helped build the company's remarkable success. Now, Bezos is a pretty smart guy. But he does not pretend to know everything, nor claim to be the know-all who must have ultimate authority on any big decision.

Bezos emphasized the importance of being disciplined about how you come to a decision. 'Most decisions should probably be made with some-where around 70 per cent of the information you wish you had', he wrote. 'If you wait for 90 per cent, in most cases, you're probably being slow' (Bezos, 2017). So that's the first point: you can't know everything, no matter how smart you may think you are. Sometimes you just need to get on with it, and if it turns out the decision isn't a very good one, adjust and adapt.

And then he went on to make a fascinating point about how to make decisions work on their merits, and not allow hierarchy or misguided defer-ence to kill things off.

Disagree and commit

'Use the phrase "disagree and commit"', Bezos advised. 'This phrase will save a lot of time. If you have conviction on a particular direction even though there's no consensus, it's helpful to say, "Look, I know we disagree on this but will you gamble with me on it? Disagree and commit?" By the time you're at this point, no one can know the answer for sure, and you'll probably get a quick yes.

'This isn't one way. If you're the boss, you should do this too. I disagree and commit all the time. We recently greenlit a particular Amazon Studios original [TV production]. I told the team my view: debatable whether it would be interesting enough, complicated to produce, the business terms aren't that good, and we have lots of other opportunities. They had a completely different opinion and wanted to go ahead. I wrote back right away with "I disagree and commit and hope it becomes the most watched thing we've ever made." Consider how much slower this decision cycle would have been if the team had actually had to convince me rather than simply get my commitment.

'Note what this example is not: it's not me thinking to myself "well, these guys are wrong and missing the point, but this isn't worth me chasing." It's a genuine disagreement of opinion, a candid expression of my view, a chance for the team to weigh my view, and a quick, sincere commitment to go their way. And given that this team has already brought home 11 Emmys, 6 Golden Globes and 3 Oscars, I'm just glad they let me in the room at all!'

Remember you are human

It is natural to want to lead, to rise up the corporation, and to have one's talents recognized. Ambition can be healthy. And if you genuinely have something to offer as a leader, it would be wrong to deprive others of your abilities.

But success is a bad teacher. It can confirm in the eyes of the successful that they are supremely gifted and that their instincts are more or less infallible. It is at this point that lingering humility can slip away, to be replaced by the dangerous conviction that you really are the smartest person in the room.

In this book we are trying to show that leadership and management matter, but not because of the supreme individual gifts of the leader; rather, it is the skill of coordinating and promoting the abilities of others that is most important. Managers are crucial because of what they encourage and allow others to do. It is everybody else who is smart, not just the boss.

And for those still hung up on the idea of being seen as 'the smartest guys in the room', remember that this phrase became well known after the collapse of Enron, the once apparently heroic, but ultimate doomed energy company, which collapsed in 2001. Sometimes you can try too hard to be smart and end up looking pretty stupid, at best.

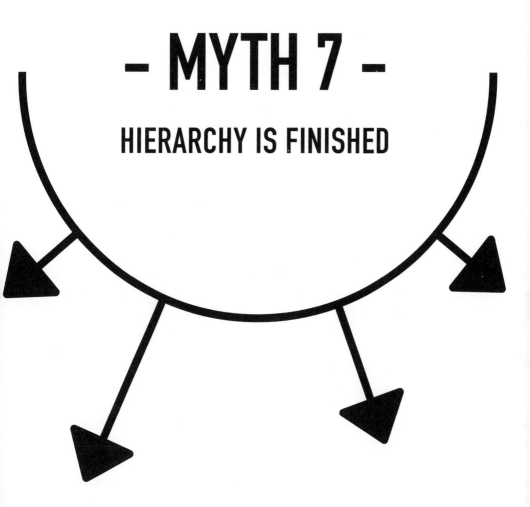

– MYTH 7 –

HIERARCHY IS FINISHED

When one person meets another, a hierarchy is instantly formed.
(Professor John Hunt (1937–2015), London Business School)

In the 1960s they had a phrase for it: 'Don't trust anyone over 30.' It summed up an attitude to authority which was, to say the least, disrespectful, and at times wholly cynical. What on earth could those grey-haired idiots have to teach us? They were senior operatives in a failed system, 'superiors' and therefore not to be trusted. They were the enemy.

Diluted just a little, a similar attitude took hold inside some businesses and organizations. A multi-tiered, rigid hierarchy may have made sense in a more formal and socially restrictive world. But that was yesterday's story, baby. We were all equal now – or heading that way. Who was anyone to boss me around? Hierarchy was in trouble. It was time to smash it, or at least severely undermine it.

The critics of hierarchy made some good points. Job rank alone should not automatically confer authority, nor be seen as a sign that a certain job-holder necessarily possesses superior abilities. Respect has to be earned. What is more, the sort of talented, creative people you might want to employ and see flourish do not expect to be told what to do, or obey some sort of organizational pecking order. 'If clever people have one defining characteristic, it is that they do not want to be led', as Rob Goffee and Gareth Jones argued in their book *Clever: Leading your smartest, most creative people*.

With the coming of the recession of the early 1980s the attack on hierarchy was supported by the prevailing economic circumstances. The wide-scale redundancies brought about by deindustrialization and 'downsizing' could be justified by the argument that unnecessary staff tiers could be swept away. And, this being management, a new buzzword was coined: 'delayering'. In plain English this involved massive job cuts. But bosses could present these job cuts in part as an attempt to simplify the hierarchy. It could be portrayed as a progressive thing to do.

Even today, the quest for the truly 'flat', non-hierarchical business model persists. The concept of 'holacracy' has been much talked about in recent years. Emerging from the IT sector, the idea is that a 'holarchy' – a flat network of self-managing, self-governing teams – can replace the formal top-down hierarchy. As with most management fads, the claims made for it have been overdone, and the few success stories have either been short-lived or not necessarily all that they seemed or were presented as being.

More interesting, and persuasive, is a company like W L Gore, the high-tech textile and fibre manufacturing firm. Here there are no formal job titles, limited (perhaps non-existent) hierarchy, just small teams of expert people working collaboratively and agreeing what needs to be done. Authority is earned but not strictly categorized. As one Gore employee told Professor Gary Hamel (as described in his 2007 book *The Future of Management*): to find out if you are regarded as a leader at Gore, call a meeting and see if anyone shows up.

But W L Gore's culture is unique, established by its founder in the 1950s. It is a privately owned business, not having to respond to the demands of impatient shareholders. This is not a model that a mature or more conventional business could easily adopt.

Nature abhors a vacuum

'When one person meets another, a hierarchy is instantly formed.' This was an observation made by the late Professor John Hunt of London Business School. It was (for the time) an almost countercultural and certainly a provocative statement to make. This was not the spirit of the egalitarian, anti-elitist mood that had arisen in the 1960s and '70s.

But Hunt had a point. Whether we like it or not, hierarchies tend to get established in any workplace, formally and/or informally. Consider the subtle and often largely hidden power relationships that exist in professional service firms such as legal or accountancy practices. Partnerships may look pretty 'flat' from the outside. There may be a senior partner and a managing partner working in an apparently non-hierarchical manner with colleagues. But some partners will be more equal than others. Highly trusted (or high fee-earning) colleagues may have unofficial but undoubted 'position power' in the firm. It may be unspoken, and no job title will point to the hierarchy involved. But it will be there all the same. Jeffrey Pfeffer, professor at Stanford's graduate school of business, agrees. 'Hierarchy is a fundamental structural principle of all organizational systems', he has written (2013). It is 'here to stay'.

Progression and the career ladder

But there's something else slightly unfashionable that needs to be said about hierarchy: it's actually quite a good thing. The delayering of the 1980s and '90s has had several negative consequences. It is not just the vast loss of jobs, bad though that was. The removal of tiers of management has created teams and divisions that are too big for anyone to manage. (John Garnett at the Industrial Society used to say that a team of 12 people was about the right size: 'Good enough for Our Lord, good enough for anybody else.')

While people used to mock the pettiness of multi-tiered organizations, with too much emotional energy being wasted worrying about each little step up to the next rung, the old career ladder did at least provide a sense of progression and structure in working life. Now, sitting in broad-banded and vast divisions, many employees have lost sight of a meaningful career path. The step up to the next formal level of management is much bigger, dauntingly so in many cases. This in part reflects the now familiar 'hollowing out' of businesses, with some middle management tasks being replaced by new technology, leaving mainly lower-skilled work for badly paid employees at the bottom, with a few super-managers getting paid super salaries at the top. A more hierarchical structure, with more tiers, would help deal with the disorientation and disillusionment that the loss of hierarchy has brought about.

Back to the future?

To be clear: this is a not a reactionary or conservative cry for a return to rigid class hierarchies, or even less social mobility and the unthinking forelock tugging of the old order. That was all bad and had to go. Indeed, so much more needs to be done to open up businesses and organizations to more potential employees. In that sense the old hierarchy did and does have to be dismantled.

Younger workers, the famous millennials for example, may find hierarchy weird and unreasonable. They may not assume that older colleagues know more or should be listened to. They don't 'know their place', to the occasional frustration of their grey-haired managers. This is a good challenge to the 'grown-ups' to make sure they earn respect and are worth listening to. But endless disruption from below upsets the workplace for everyone. A cohesive team will accept that someone (or some idea or purpose) is in charge, and work with that.

When some employers got rid of hierarchical layers they got rid of a healthy career path too. They should have been more careful about what they were wishing for. A healthy and successful organization will always have a hierarchy, just one in which everyone can succeed and fulfil their potential.

– MYTH 8 –

CONSISTENCY IS ESSENTIAL

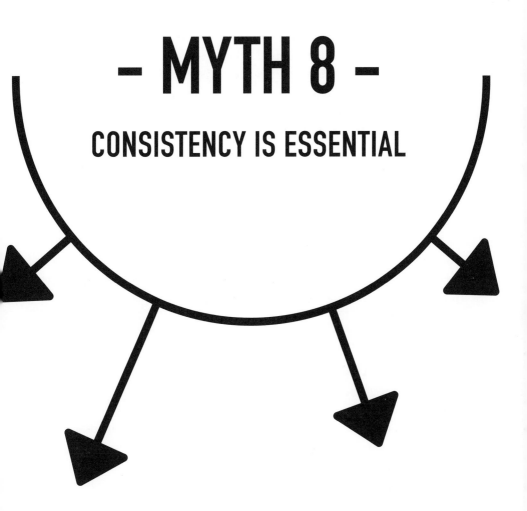

Management is not a job for a one-trick pony. Situations
will change and you must adapt to deal with them.

Only the insecure never change their minds. Life moves on. Situations alter. In business, the competition may do something unexpected. In the public sector, policy (and budgets) may shift. There is nothing wrong in abandoning a former position or view. It may be necessary to do so. If the ship is heading for the rocks you should change course, and maybe even perform a complete about-turn. Even if you are emotionally invested in a course of action or a way of doing things, you may first have to spot and then acknowledge your biases, and 'move on'.

We have already discussed how the U-turn (or 'flip flop') has come to be seen as the worst form of managerial indecisiveness (see Myth 4). But it is worth saying a little more about the false god of consistency. The urge to be consistent is understandable. It looks like solidity, and might reassure colleagues. Vacillation and mood swings will not inspire confidence. Consistency may also represent fairness: treating people in the same way regardless of their seniority or status, for example.

There is a place for consistency: consistency of purpose. But in trying to achieve an objective your strategy and tactics will have to change depending on the circumstances. When promoted to a new role your repertoire of behaviour will have to grow. That is not inconsistency – it is development. If nature had been consistent, evolution would never have happened. Life is adaptation and change, not consistency.

In the commercial world consistency can kill. Kodak may have displayed consistency in persevering with ageing film technology when the world was going digital, and the UK's Woolworths retail chain may have tried to preserve a previously successful formula. Both suffered as a result of their consistency.

Words to the wise

The writer Ralph Waldo Emerson famously wrote, in his essay *Self-Reliance* of 1841, that: 'A foolish consistency is the hobgoblin of little minds, adored by little statesmen and philosophers and divines.' It can take courage to admit you need to do things differently, but it is stupid to pretend otherwise when change is needed. It is cowardly to hide behind consistency when you ought to be doing things differently.

The best-known critique of consistency appears to be, sadly, a partially invented or misremembered quote: the remarks usually attributed to the economist John Maynard Keynes. He said, or perhaps didn't: 'When the facts change I change my mind. What do you do, sir?'

No one has found a written document or verbatim report of Keynes uttering precisely those words. But it doesn't really matter who did or did not come up with it – the sentiment is correct. It is the perfect answer for any manager accused of being inconsistent. We need fact-based and reality-based management, not one that is based on myths. On that point at least we should be consistent.

– MYTH 9 –

ONLY HIRE PEOPLE WHO WILL FIT IN

*Uniformity is death. Look for people who are different
and will add something to your team.*

'Is he one of us?' Mrs Thatcher used to ask about people she was going to meet or work with for the first time. She wanted to know if someone was 'on side'. Cohesion matters, of course. When we talk about teamwork we usually have in mind a picture of harmony, a world in which like-minded people find it relatively easy to collaborate and be effective.

And yet, ahead of another hiring decision or recruitment drive, asking if potential joiners are 'one of us' is perhaps the worst possible thing to do. People who fit in easily are not necessarily the ones you want at all.

Think this one through. It may seem sensible, natural even, to pick another person just like you, or who reminds you of existing members of the team. Some bosses love it when a 'mini-me' walks in for a job interview. They have an immediate affinity with the candidate, who seems familiar, comes from a similar background, and so on.

But how would hiring someone so similar add something to what you already have? There is a fast-changing and increasingly diverse world out there. Customers would like some affinity with the people who serve them, too. Variety is the spice of business life.

At the top of the company a lack of diversity can be even more problematic. It has taken the imposition of quotas (or the threat of imposition) to shake up the old boys' network which so many boardrooms have come to represent. 'What on earth do we need a woman for?' has long been the unspoken question. 'We've never had one before. This isn't their sort of place. Why change a winning formula?' This is the self-serving and closed thinking that keeps everything just the way it is. Which suits… some people – those already safely installed at the top.

But top teams where everyone 'fits in', which are mono-cultural and lacking in diversity of all kinds, are going to be home to groupthink and a narrow outlook. It will all be too cosy, and not sharp enough. There will be no challenge to authority. And that is how smallish problems grow, eventually becoming crises.

Seductive similarity

Unconscious bias can lead us to reject people who are different, and instead favour the familiar. This is one reason why interview panels should contain a mix of people – men and women, people from different backgrounds or of different ages – to try to prevent unwitting favouritism. As the psychologist Binna Kandola argues (conversation with authors), simply reminding an interview panel before they start work that they should try hard to be fair and be alert to unconscious biases may help them do a better job.

There are perhaps one or two exceptions to the idea that difference must be actively sought out. A senior member of staff at *The Economist* was once asked what explained their remarkable success. 'I would say it is down to the tremendous lack of diversity', he declared, to a rather startled, largely American audience (witnessed by authors). You are not supposed to say things like that. But our *Economist* hack was being slightly mischievous, true to the spirit of his employer. The staff of the 'newspaper' (as they insist on calling it) may hire a lot of Oxbridge graduates from middle- and upper-middle-class backgrounds. But to survive and flourish at the title they then have to go on to display an open, critical mind and a broad range of interests. The apparent surface-level uniformity conceals a hive of active and varied minds.

Culture club

Maybe 'fitting in' is simply a misconceived notion, if it implies uniformity and turgid steadiness. The management guru Gary Hamel has bemoaned the common desire to seek 'alignment' at work (conversation with authors). Why would you do that? To stop new ideas from emerging? To suppress disputes that need to come to the surface?

The insurer Hiscox prides itself on its less-than-conventional image, with its offices filled with 'challenging' modern art, and staff members who go on adventurous holidays. Its UK managing director, Steve Langan, told *Director* magazine in January 2016: 'What we like are people with individualistic points of view doing their own thing – there's a countercultural thread here.' Indeed, the firm commits to 'reinvent ourselves every year' (Koch, 2016).

Hiscox's CEO, Bronek Masojada, says it is a good idea for a company's culture to be difficult for new recruits to get to know. In other words: you don't want people to be able to fit in too easily. The fact that it takes time for people to get to know and understand the business is a positive sign. Your culture will by definition be hard to copy, and the people who stay will understand it in a way competitors never will.

Different is good

The journalist A A Gill, who died in December 2016, argued that the most interesting people were often the 'misfits'. 'The interesting adults are always the school failures, the weird ones, the losers, the malcontents', he said. 'This isn't wishful thinking. It's the rule' (Gill, 2012).

And yet it can take some nerve to seek out difference, to avoid the obvious or clichéd candidate, to resist the temptation to settle for a quiet life. There is a paradoxical tension at work here: we want team spirit and cohesion, and yet we don't want everyone to be the same. We want people to be complementary but varied. There's a reason why this is one of the most famous gags in Monty Python's *Life of Brian*:

Brian: You've got to think for yourselves! You're all individuals!

Crowd: Yes! We're all individuals!

Brian: You're all different!

Crowd: Yes, we are all different!

Man in crowd: I'm not...

The crowd: Shhhh!

The man in the crowd did not fit in, but maybe he had the right idea. Get him to send in his CV.

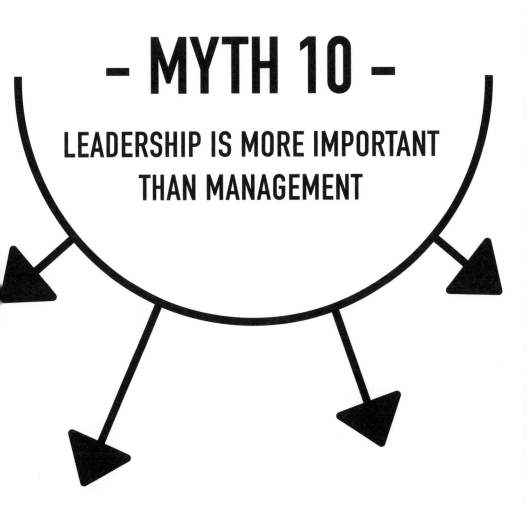

– MYTH 10 –

LEADERSHIP IS MORE IMPORTANT THAN MANAGEMENT

The traditional either/or debate – 'which is more important, leadership or management?' – is tedious and unhelpful. We need both.

Managers deserve at least some sympathy. Not only do they get blamed for almost everything that ever goes wrong, regardless of whether it's their fault or not, but they are permanently wrestling with what you might call a branding issue. They face a rival in the world of work, a cooler, sleeker presence that induces deference and, at times, hushed respect. The problem is simply stated: what is banal, petty, quotidian *management* when compared with muscular, dynamic, heroic *leadership*? Why be a boring old manager when you could be a leader?

Forty or fifty years ago, when memories of dictatorships – and the Second World War they led to – were still fresh, it is unlikely that the idea of leadership would have been held up as such an unqualified good. People were worried about *Führerprinzip* for good reason. True, President Kennedy had swept aside some memories of the past with his remarkable inauguration speech in 1961: 'The torch has been passed to a new generation of Americans – born in this century, tempered by war, disciplined by a hard and bitter peace, proud of our ancient heritage.' But even his brief period in office was not unblemished. Scepticism and nervousness about leaders and leadership survived through another two decades.

From the 1980s onwards, leaders and leadership began to regain some of their lustre. Recession in the early 1980s encouraged the emergence of ruthless, decisive 'downsizers' (also known as 'corporate killers') such as Jack Welch at GE, who grabbed the opportunity offered by economic crisis to make sweeping changes – cuts – to their businesses. On the world stage, the Reagan/Thatcher axis provided political cover for such actions, and reinforced the fashion for tough leadership.

'Business process re-engineering' – BPR – was the tough guy's approved method, placing an emphasis on the need for an unflinching approach to leading organizations. 'If they [employees] are complaining it's a sign you are making progress' was the watchword. Leaders were back in vogue.

'Adding value for shareholders'

Also around this time, and related to the resurgence of 'strong' leaders, the stock market preference for chief executives who got share prices up fast grew in intensity. CEOs were there to drive companies hard and 'add value' to shareholders. Business leaders who may have taken a more balanced view of their company's purpose and looked to the longer term were not rated as highly as the dealmakers and swashbucklers who 'made things happen'. Lords Hanson and White got quite close to grabbing the prize corporate jewel that was ICI in 1991. The predatory lords were resisted, but ICI was never the same again, eventually committing to that same 'shareholder value' ethos which ultimately proved a dead end. (The company was finally acquired by the Swedish AkzoNobel in 2008.[*])

I blame the management

Managers, meanwhile, were… what, exactly? Unglamorous, trivial, small, as opposed to big picture. And middle managers were even worse, an unnecessary layer of stodge to be swept away. 'Delayering' as a concept was predicated in part on the idea that the all-knowing leader at the top had little need of managers to implement his (usually his) 'vision'. The leader merely deemed that things would happen, as the Canadian academic Professor Henry Mintzberg put it (Thinkers 50, 2011).

Leaders thought big and managers acted small. Leaders, it was said, do the right thing whereas managers merely did things right. A thick black line was drawn between leadership and management as disciplines. When John (now Lord) Birt left his job as director-general of the BBC, it was said that under him the organization had been 'over-managed and under-led'. The time had come for leadership, which his successor Greg Dyke would provide. That he did, brilliantly in some ways, but chaotically, perhaps, in others. The BBC was now over-led and under-managed. The dichotomy had struck again.

Avoid false choices

Time for a quick game of 'would you rather...?' Would you rather work for a boss who can lead but not manage, or for a boss who can manage but not lead? There is only one sensible answer to this question. It is 'neither'. We need bosses who can do both. President Bill Clinton advises us to 'avoid false choices'. He is right. And choosing to be either a manager or a leader is one such false choice.

Those 'useless' middle managers that were got rid of – what did they do again? Well, it was that old-fashioned but invaluable task of supervision. Not in an intrusive or menacing sense: supervision is a central management task; simply paying attention to people and what they do. Showing that you care. Organizations today may be leaner, but they are meaner too. And where are we falling down in particular? In basic areas such as customer service, skills development and consequent increased productivity, all things that boring old managers are there (or should be there) to worry about.

Charles Handy tells us (see Appendix 1) that it is systems that need to be managed above all. But we shouldn't treat people as 'things'. 'People need to be led, or cajoled, or involved, or other words that give you some form of independence, some choice', he says. 'Whereas in management, if you start treating people as things, if you slot them into little holes where they have to do as they're told, they are part of the system then and that's why they don't like it... people don't understand that, they think their job is to bring people into line, to manage the behaviour of people, and I just think that's counterproductive. By all means change the conditions in which they work. But please don't try to change them.'

We don't need another hero

We have bought too heavily into the myth of the heroic, lonely leader, the brilliant soloist who by sheer force of personality and charisma makes things happen on his or her own. In the media and financial markets we talk about vast businesses through the personality of the CEO, as if one human being alone can determine the fate of a company operating in dozens of countries with tens or even hundreds of thousands of employees and countless product lines. It is a fairy-tale notion of business. Fairy tales can be charming. But they should not be taken as a literal guide to living for grown-ups.

Henry Mintzberg has it right. 'The narcissistic view of leadership has taken organizations off the rails', he has said. Leadership is important. It is vital. But it is a team sport. And a leader without good managers is nothing.

For too long we have worshipped leaders, often incorrectly as it later turned out, and failed to value management properly. We need to bring back a proper sense of proportion, valuing leadership and management appropriately, and equally. That is how we will get the job done.

Note

* John Kay has written brilliantly on the sad decline and eventual fall of ICI. There is more here (2003) https://www.johnkay.com/2003/02/13/the-high-cost-of-icis-fall-from-grace/ and here (2014) https://www.johnkay.com/2014/05/07/drug-companies-are-built-in-labs-not-boardrooms.

- MYTH 11 -

YOU HAVE TO PAY TOP DOLLAR TO GET THE RIGHT PERSON

The so-called 'market for talent' is not efficient. Its prices are not reliable. Some people simply ask for too much, and shouldn't get it.

Jim Collins, the management guru, has a good question for leaders: what are you in it for? In fact it's a good question for anyone drawing a (largeish) salary. Why are you doing what you do? Is it really just to see a (necessarily) big lump of cash land in your bank account every month? Maybe it is.

We all have to make a living, and life can be expensive. There is no shame in wanting to be comfortable. But when that line of thinking is extended too far into the recruitment process, employers can come unstuck. Suddenly, it seems, only a certain large amount of cash will be enough to attract the people you think you want. Nobody any good will come for less, it will be said.

But that is wrong. Indeed, once you start using big, fat carrots as your main way of attracting people to work for you, don't be surprised if you find a queue of greedy donkeys heading towards your door. If they come mainly for a big pay cheque they will leave just as easily when an even bigger one is offered. Our thinking (if we can call it that) on high pay has really got stuck in a rut, and is weighed down with myths and misconceptions.

When enough is not enough

Time was, and it was not a very long time ago, it was simply not considered respectable for a boss to be paid vastly more than the people who worked for him or her. The banker J P Morgan, who was no softie, declared that he did not support lending money to any business where the highest-paid employee received more than 20 times the pay of the lowest paid. He felt that this would be an unstable situation. It was possible in those circumstances that bosses would essentially be in it for themselves.

This view on the danger of excessive pay gaps was shared by Peter Drucker, the management writer. 'I have often advised managers that a 20–1 salary ratio between senior executives and rank-and-file white-collar workers is the limit beyond which they cannot go if they don't want resentment and falling morale to hit their companies', he wrote in an essay in 1984.

As recently as the late 1990s, the average FTSE 100 chief executive was getting paid around 45 times what the average worker in the business received. That was clearly excessive by previous standards. But 20 years later it looks like relative restraint. Now that ratio has tripled to around 130:1. And this after an era of outsourcing in which many lower-paid jobs are no longer formally on the company payroll, allowing the average pay figure to rise.

Have bosses got three times better at their jobs in the past two decades? Has the job got three times harder? No, and no. Ah, but perhaps these businesses are much bigger than they used to be, what with globalization and all. Does that justify the bigger pay packets?

Again, no. As Sir Philip Hampton, the former chairman of Sainsbury's and the Royal Bank of Scotland, and now chair at GlaxoSmithKline, has said, the bigger the business, arguably the less credit should go to the CEO (quoted in High Pay Centre, 2015). Why? Because there is so much more infrastructure in place, and so many more senior executives and managers taking more of the important day-to-day decisions.

But these CEOs are exceptional people, are they not? Rare beasts. Of course they can command big salaries. Well, this too is a convenient story to tell, if you are a CEO (or a wannabe one). We obsess so much about a few supposedly heroic leaders – who are often later revealed to have been less than heroic and decidedly normal (see Myth 18) – that we seem to think that anyone with the job title of CEO must somehow share some of that magic. It is a self-serving delusion that CEOs and aspiring CEOs must be paid massive sums. But this attitude fuels a pay ratchet which influences pay in the rest of the business and in wider society (including the public sector) too, damaging all of us.

Trickle down

It is not the 'politics of envy' or 'class war' that leads to these criticisms of excessive pay. It is about efficiency as well as fairness. Some people are simply being paid too much. They are not, to adapt the L'Oréal slogan, worth it. A recent 10-year study at the Lancaster University Management School found at best only a 'negligible' link between the mediocre performance of businesses and the vast pay packages on offer at the top.

By acquiescing in this apparently unstoppable process through which top pay rises ever higher, we make things worse. The 1 per cent (and 0.1 per cent) soar further and further out of sight. The votes for President Trump and Brexit in part reflect protest and outrage at these excesses (and of course CEO pay in the United States is even higher). Wealth has not 'trickled down'. But a harmful attitude to wealth and inequality has.

If this attitude of 'grab as much as you can' spreads through an organization, or a society, we are all harmed. We should worry much more about the contribution senior executives make, not what they take out. Indeed, why is it that some super-rich execs feel the need to 'put something back' later on in their careers? Is it, perhaps, that they realize they have taken too much in the first place?

Rewarding work

So closing that pay gap, using published pay ratios to apply pressure, is a good idea. But fundamentally we need to dispense with the notion that only vast salaries will attract the right people. Money really isn't everything. It is a poor way of attracting, retaining and motivating people (see Myth 30). So relax about that person who won't get out of bed for less than X million. Let them stay in bed. Your business or organization will perform better with people who really want to be there, who are fairly but not excessively paid, and for whom it is the work itself, and not the pay cheque, that matters most of all.

– MYTH 12 –

ANNUAL APPRAISALS HELP YOU MANAGE PERFORMANCE

Management should be an ongoing conversation, not a once-a-year round-up of good and bad things. Get rid of appraisals.

There's a reason why it is sometimes called the 'annual reprisal' interview. But even if your organization refers to it more euphemistically as a 'performance review', the chances are that this remains a heavily bureaucratic, counterproductive activity which most colleagues have lost faith in. They are still being done, inevitably. But for how much longer?

The annual performance review is a relic from a vanishing world. More rigidly structured businesses and hierarchies created jobs with more predictable requirements. It seemed like a good idea to measure performance under a number of limited headings, which in turn encouraged the repetition of similar tasks. That is what work felt like, after all.

Waiting a year to discuss how this work had been carried out reflected the annual financial reporting cycle of the business as a whole. And of course it tied the measurement of that performance into any bonus or 'performance-related pay' incentive scheme.

But this is part of what is wrong with annual performance reviews of this kind. There is an incentive to game the system, for both employer and employee. Employees may be tempted to alter their behaviour to hit targets – possibly quite arbitrary or even harmful ones – in order to win a bonus (as was seen in the scandal at Wells Fargo bank in 2016). Employers, meanwhile, may be tempted to set unreasonably 'stretching' targets to ensure that bonus pay-outs are limited, and that managers themselves look like hard taskmasters who do not pay out too easily. But the damaging effect on employees' morale of impossibly hard-to-achieve targets is obvious. Not that this stops them from being set, of course.

Wrong goals, wrong method

Work has changed. Collaborative teamworking is even more important than it used to be. Projects may be short-lived experiments rather than extended grand plans. Teams may be formed and reformed rapidly. Hierarchies are flatter (if not gone altogether – see Myth 7). For all these reasons, separating out the individual contribution of one worker and measuring it against individual targets is a much less straightforward task than it used to be.

If work has changed, then management has to change too. The need for supervision has not gone away. But instead of an annual or semi-annual assessment, management needs to become something more like an ongoing (if interrupted) conversation. There need to be regular tweaks on the dial, not an annual tapping of a dusty barometer.

Many big employers have recognized this. Microsoft, Accenture, Deloitte, Gap, even GE – home of an aggressive 'forced ranking' system – have all either dropped or reformed their annual employee ranking procedures.

Arup, the engineering firm, was ahead of the game on this. Its performance management system used to invite colleagues to name four main objectives they wanted to achieve in the year ahead. The problem was, the firm realized, that by limiting this list to four, there would never be a fifth or sixth achievement. The boxes on the form and the bureaucracy were limiting performance, not managing it. The fixed number of objectives has been dropped. Now for Arup colleagues the sky – not unreasonably in their line of business – is the limit.

People, not robots

Automation is changing a great deal at work, but as long as human beings are still being employed we need to adopt management practices that acknowledge the realities of human nature. In fact it is not merely human nature that needs to be recognized, but animal instincts. As the consultant Charles Jacobs noted in his book *Management Rewired* (2009), Homo sapiens and the chimpanzee are 98 per cent alike in terms of their biology. We should understand that some of our responses, to threats and to 'authority', may have quite a lot in common with those of our primate cousins.

'Whether we're a chimpanzee or a corporate employee, we don't like being controlled by others', Jacobs wrote. Some rigid management approaches are 'more suited to forms of life lacking the ability to think'.

Chimps don't like being told off, and nor do we. 'Feedback' is hard to take, as well as sometimes being hard to give. It is human (animal) nature to focus on the negative bits and forget about whatever good news may have been offered. Jacobs recommended abandoning traditional appraisals. Instead, 'employees should set their own objectives, critique their own performance and, if there is a performance shortfall, determine what corrective action needs to be taken', he argued.

Go for growth

Carol Dweck, a professor in psychology at Stanford University, has popularized the concept of the 'growth mindset', a resilient personality trait that welcomes challenges and is able to learn from (and not be permanently disheartened by) failure (Dweck, 2006). Its opposite is a 'fixed mindset', which holds that improvement is unlikely, and the best thing to do is to try to avoid mistakes.

When viewed in the context of these two categories, the standard appraisal mechanism can be seen as reinforcing a fixed mindset, severely limiting the potential of employees to achieve more. While ostensibly about managing performance, it in fact serves to keep people in a box and limits what they could actually do. Far better to erase the rigid lines on the appraisal form and set people free to be creative and take some risks.

See it human

You wouldn't save up all your 'feedback' to a partner in a relationship for a once-a-year truth-telling session. Why then do some businesses and organizations still do this? It may seem efficient, on the surface. But it is a cop-out. Management means paying attention and making interventions at the right time, not drawing up a list of criticisms to be delivered in one go after an extended wait.

The UK, like many other mature economies, faces a challenge to raise its productivity. Traditional performance management techniques are, ironically enough, doing nothing to help in that task. The most productive thing many employers could do would be to tear up the established performance management system and start again. You don't know what you might achieve until you try.

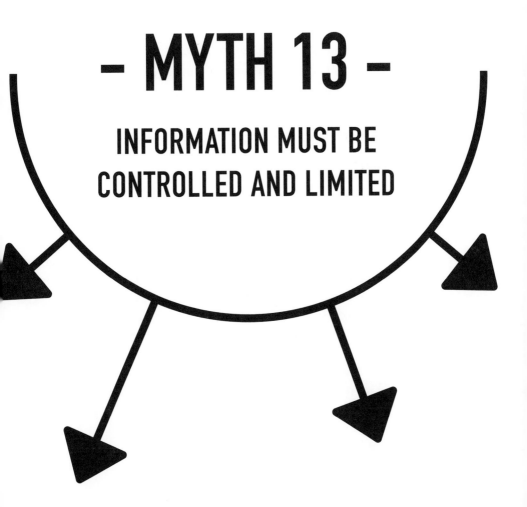

- MYTH 13 -

INFORMATION MUST BE CONTROLLED AND LIMITED

Lighten up. Tell the truth – there's less to remember that way. Secrecy is inefficient. Share, listen and learn from colleagues.

'Loose lips sink ships', wartime British citizens were told. It was a safer course of action to keep your mouth shut. Secrecy was vital to the nation's security. Information was released on a need-to-know basis. 'And you', the unspoken thought ran, 'do not need to know.'

The Second World War was followed by a Cold one, which lasted until the end of the 1980s. For decades the instincts of those at the top were for discretion, confidentiality, classified information, secrets. Business was not much different. Corporations are headed by 'chief executive officers', after all. Why wouldn't they adopt an approach to secrecy modelled by government and the military? Knowledge is power, the thinking ran, and authority arises from the control of knowledge exercised at the top. It wasn't just the key to the executive washroom that was dangled before the ambitious young professional, but access to valuable information. Manage your career wisely and a world of intriguing knowledge could be yours.

Pay no attention to that man behind the curtain

In this way information – real or imagined – became part of the currency and also the mythology of corporate life. This was the world of the Wizard of Oz before Dorothy's dog Toto pulled back the curtain. There was good stuff, powerful stuff, to find out about if you just stayed in with the right people. But for everybody else the curtains remained drawn.

Back in the real world, as the Cold War melted away, new technology helped perform a similar kind of unveiling to the one carried out by Toto. The internet connected people in new and powerful ways. It allowed – wanted – information to flow more freely. With the crumbling of traditional hierarchies (see Myth 7) and the waning of deference, employees were now equipped to ask for and expect much more information from senior colleagues. Traditional power relationships changed. Many of us are still struggling to adapt to these new conditions.

The media industries provide quite a good example of this. Where once anonymous, lofty correspondents and commentators offered up their insights to a supposedly grateful readership, and could hide behind the formidable architecture of the printed product, soon readers were e-mailing in questions and challenges directly or, even more scarily for the once powerful journalists, adding their own comments beneath articles in chat rooms or on other social media websites. Live TV or conference appearances are now accompanied by a real-time running commentary online. Information is not sacred or secret anymore. It is all (nearly all) out there. Views and opinions can be contested, and facts challenged.

Ten thousand chief executives

The people who work for you, whether in your office or remotely, are not the subservient, passive citizens of wartime. They have opinions and are ready to share them. They have ideas. But if you want information to flow 'up' to you then you are going to have to let it flow freely 'down' to them. Openness is vital. Some have called this new approach 'radical transparency'. And it makes a lot of sense.

Secrets are inefficient. Keeping things confidential wastes managers' time and does nothing to improve trust. Good ideas need light and oxygen. They won't grow in a vacuum or in a permanently sealed, darkened room.

If James Surowiecki was even half right in his 2004 book *The Wisdom of Crowds* then the organization that puts up barriers of secrecy around its information is making a big mistake. Employees meet the customers, do the actual work, see what is selling and what isn't, and know what the reputation of the business is like out there in the real world. They are a ready-made market-research team. You need to hear what they think, promptly.

But for that to happen, management has to make it clear that views are welcome and are actively sought, and that there will be no comeback for people who are delivering bad news. The opposite should be the case: why not have rewards for those who draw attention to things that aren't working well? There should be prizes for such 'whistleblowers', not punishment.

Nothing to lose

If this is all so obvious, why do so few managers behave in a truly transparent and open way? Some perhaps lack the confidence to do so. It may go against the grain where they work, or run counter to how they have built up their career so far. The tone is set from the top, of course. But leaderships that suppress information end up like the dictators of failing regimes just before their overthrow, waving at the crowds below and being surprised to be met by the sound of booing and, in extreme cases, gunfire. If you ignore the weak signals coming up to you at the top, you will be confronted by a much louder and more dramatic signal later on.

Even if you work in a less open culture, there will be things you can do to encourage greater openness and a better flow of information. Make your meetings informal. Allow people to speak up. Share your concerns and ask for help. Listen more than you talk. Dedicate time to make open and honest feedback happen. And make sure you take action on the matters that get brought up.

In the end, good management is all about this kind of reciprocity. John Garnett of the Industrial Society used to say: 'If you care about what they care about, they'll care about what you care about.' And the way you convince the people you manage that you care is to have a candid, free-flowing conversation with them. Try being human! What have you got to lose? You never know, it could work.

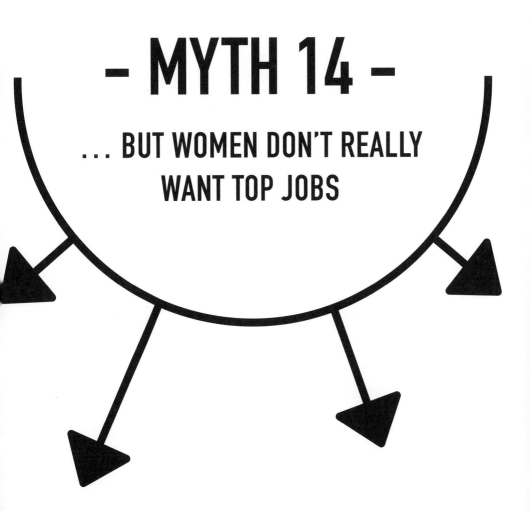

– MYTH 14 –

… BUT WOMEN DON'T REALLY WANT TOP JOBS

Organizations designed by men to be run by men will fail. Action is urgently needed to get more women into top jobs.

Those top tables and the seats of power: it's called an 'old boys' club' for a reason. Its members are old(-er), male, and usually white too, for that matter. It is an exclusion zone. Membership is restricted. Applications to join may be accepted, but should not actively be sought or expected by the wrong sort of person (you know who you are). It's simple, really. They are just looking for the right sort of chap. If that isn't you, bad luck.

This may all sound a bit clichéd, but there's a reason for that. It is true. Progress on shifting these power relationships at work has been numbingly slow. The most striking aspect of this is in the area of pay. Almost 50 years after the Equal Pay Act, average women's earnings in the UK are still around 18 per cent lower than men's.

The continuing gender pay gap, finally being addressed in the legislation over mandatory reporting, reflects these imbalances of power. Men have clung on to it for so long. It took the (very thinly veiled) threat of mandatory quotas to 'encourage' UK boardrooms finally to increase the number of women directors in recent years. Even this has been a partial and possibly even a pyrrhic victory. Yes, there are now more female directors around UK board tables – around the 25 per cent mark in the FTSE 100. But the overwhelming majority of these new posts are non-executive roles. There are still only a handful of women CEOs in the FTSE. And below board level there are few signs that top jobs will be filled by more women in the future. What is called (in one of the business world's most unfortunate phrases – see Myth 38) the 'talent pipeline' is hardly bursting with future female bosses, sadly.

Excuses, excuses

You will have probably heard all the arguments regularly offered up to explain the absence of women at the top before. But let's run through them one more time before dismissing them for good.

It is said that women don't always possess the same competitive 'alpha' instinct to conquer and lead. Getting to the top doesn't appeal to them in the same basic way that it does for men. But there are enough examples of successful and powerful women to disprove that. The problem here is that not enough opportunities are truly open to them.

Some people say that women choose to leave organizations, that they prefer running their own smaller set-up to remaining in the big leagues. But this is getting it the wrong way around. It's quite possible that capable women choose (or feel forced) to leave organizations, but this is mainly because they are rejecting the ethos and practices of the places where they work. They do not want to have to become what seems to be required to get to the top. So they leave to form a business more in keeping with their own values.

Above all, it is argued that women – mothers in particular – find it impossible to balance the demands of work and home. Something called a 'maternal instinct' somehow dilutes their ambition, as though it is not possible to be both fully committed at work while caring about family life at home (see Myth 20). This last point, the argument used most often, is simply preposterous.

Of course, caring and domestic responsibilities are rarely shared equally between male and female partners. Slowly – very, very slowly – that is changing. Fathers and mothers can now share their parental leave, and some are beginning to do so. But we are still miles away from a world of flexible working that works for everybody. Employers could and should do more to help. We will know we have made meaningful progress when we start seeing male executives being referred to as 'working fathers'.

By men for men

Male authors can say this without being accused of bias or special pleading. The problem here is men, not women. As Avivah Wittenberg-Cox, author of *How Women Mean Business*, has long argued, so many of the (often well-intentioned) interventions such as 'women's networks' or campaigns have been based on the assumption that there is something wrong with women themselves. If they could just change their attitude, or 'lean in' a bit harder, things would get a lot better for them, fast. But 'we don't need to fix the women!', as Avivah always says. It is the organizations that need fixing. And that means it is male attitudes that have to change.

Fight the power

'Monopolies are terrible things,' Rupert Murdoch is supposed to have once said, 'until you've got one.' For men and power it is the same thing. They have had it to themselves for a long time and are reluctant to give it up.

But they must. Bluster and prejudice will not do any longer. The majority of graduates are women; girls are doing better at school than boys, but once they get to work the men somehow (re-)assert control. And too many capable women somehow disappear. Too many men favour and promote other men, and reject women to whom they fail to relate or to understand. Male bosses may sometimes 'mentor' other women – ie they tell them what to do – but how often do they truly sponsor and support them? Not often enough, clearly. There is too much closed thinking. But employers urgently need to change to attract and retain the people they need.

This may start with equal pay. The consultants McKinsey say that the UK economy could be £150 billion bigger if the gender pay gap is closed by 2025 (Hunt et al, 2016). Money talks. This is one area where the bottom-line arguments may finally get the attention of even the most committed male chauvinist. The loss in output caused by the departure of women from the workplace, or their failure to reach positions of power and influence, is too costly to ignore any longer.

Move over, darling. Time to make way for women.

Note

* For an excellent summary of these and other related issues, see *Why Women Need Quotas* by Vicky Pryce (2015).

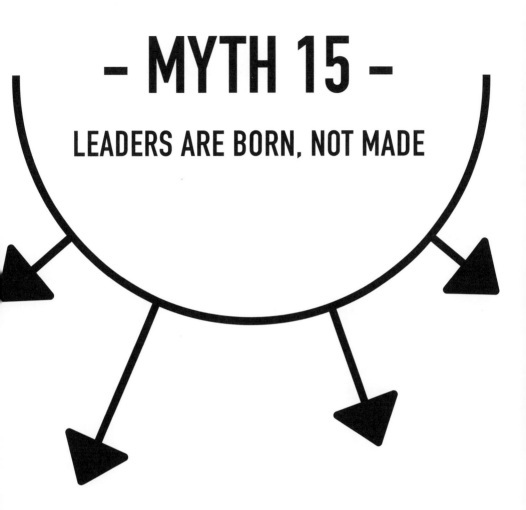

– MYTH 15 –

LEADERS ARE BORN, NOT MADE

Leadership skills are not a mystery, nor are they forever out of reach.
Anyone can learn to get better at it.

'Because I am blessed by my good brain, I tend to get to the answer rather quicker and more often than most people.' The words of the late Bob Horton, the forceful chairman of BP and later Railtrack, in an interview given to *Forbes* magazine in February 1992, embody that traditional belief which holds that some people are simply better suited to being leaders than many others. Horton's mixed record at BP, and frankly terrible one at Railtrack, do not necessarily support his claim of having possessed an unusually good brain or superior decision-making abilities. He did at least have the good grace to follow up his boast with the admission: 'That will sound frightfully arrogant.' On this point, at any rate, Horton was correct.

Leaders sometimes operate what used to be called a 'closed shop'. It can be a self-validating and self-congratulatory cohort. The fact that they have got to the top is proof that they possess the right stuff, and that others do not. Luck has apparently played no part in their rise. Indeed, they may suggest that lesser beings should forget about any prospect of achieving a similar advance. Leaders, you see, are born, not made. You've either got it or you haven't. And if you haven't got it you might as well forget it.

But this is nonsense. Most of us are capable of displaying at least some leadership skills at the right time, in different contexts. While corporate hierarchy may still have a bit more life in it than many imagine (see Myth 7), there are times when we need to ignore job titles and 'seniority' and let anyone who can do so take a lead.

Command and control

Assertive, forceful bosses sometimes think that they possess military-style qualities. They think that their directive approach is in keeping with the great generals of the past. But there's a secret about, for example, the British army, which often comes as a surprise. The thing is, they don't really believe in 'command and control' leadership. Or, at least, they see its severe limitations. At the Royal Military Academy Sandhurst, the British army's leadership training college, they have long taken a more sophisticated and nuanced view of leadership than that.

It all goes back to the First World War. When over-educated but out-of-touch young officers started telling young men to go over the top, they found to their horror and surprise that not everyone immediately agreed. It was dangerous out there, and not every officer had the authority to persuade or command.

A hundred years ago the army dealt with such objections brutally: insubordinates were shot. But in the aftermath of war there was a realization that not only had young soldiers been treated appallingly, but that there was something wrong with the way leaders had behaved. Command and control did not necessarily work in the heat of battle. You couldn't just tell people what to do, especially if their lives were in danger.

A more important and successful military role model was Field Marshal (William) Slim, leader of the 14th Army in the successful Burma campaign during the Second World War.

Leadership, Slim said, was 'plain you'. Speaking at the American Sandhurst, West Point, in 1950, Slim said: 'If I were asked to define leadership, I should say it is the projection of personality. It is the most intensely personal thing in the world because it is just plain you.' There is no mystique, no fake 'charisma' required to step up and lead. It is essentially a question of drawing on the qualities you have and revealing them to those you are trying to lead. There is no 'one right way' (see Myth 1).

There must have been something to Slim's approach. He led a multinational force, brought together in crisis and facing the formidable Japanese army in treacherous conditions, and succeeded. General Lord Dannatt, former chief of the general staff, has said of Slim: 'His quiet authority won the hearts of his soldiers. Slim may not have had the manpower and equipment that he would have liked, but he had the leadership, the intellect and the mature understanding of operational art to win in Burma and to inspire subsequent generations.'

Anyone can lead

The army has much to teach us. Soldiers are trained to recognize that, while there may be an officer in charge at the start of a battle or operation, that officer could get killed at any moment. Someone else will have to step up to replace them. That person could be you, plain you.

This battlefield lesson could be translated into the ostensibly more peaceful environment of the workplace. Why should 'the boss' have all the bright ideas? Anyone should be able to speak up. Anyone could come up with the new way of working or 'customer insight' that could make all the difference to the business.

It follows that 'leadership training' should be made available to staff at all levels, not just a lucky few at the top. Chronic productivity problems stem in part from a lack of genuine empowerment and skills development through the workforce, including the neglect of so-called leadership skills (which are in fact just normal people management skills – see Myth 10). This reflects the classic British mistake that has been made in secondary education for decades: worrying too much about those who are already doing well, and not worrying enough about those who have enjoyed fewer advantages and risk falling behind.

Some leaders love to spread and perpetuate myths about their special abilities. They worry more about their own PR than the success of the business they are supposed to be leading. They tell you that leaders are 'born, not made', and that others should know their place. They draw on this mythology when trying to justify their huge salaries (see Myth 11).

But leaders are not members of some obscure magical tribe. They are just people, plain you. Anyone can lead. Leaders are made, not born.

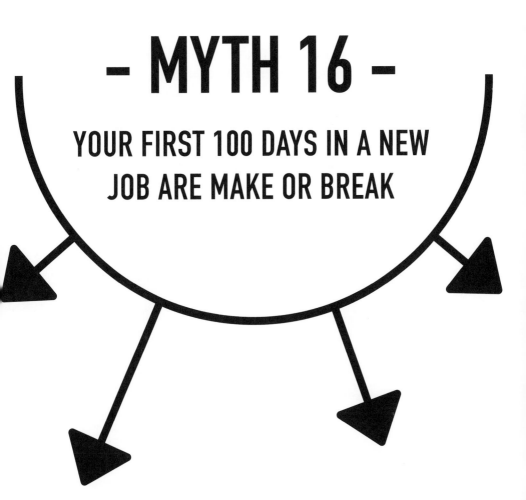

– MYTH 16 –

YOUR FIRST 100 DAYS IN A NEW JOB ARE MAKE OR BREAK

Let us begin anew… Together let us explore the stars, conquer the deserts, eradicate disease, tap the ocean depths, and encourage the arts and commerce… let [us] join in creating a new endeavour… a new world of law, where the strong are just and the weak secure and the peace preserved.

All this will not be finished in the first 100 days. Nor will it be finished in the first 1,000 days, nor in the life of this administration, nor even perhaps in our lifetime on this planet. But let us begin.
(Inaugural speech of John F Kennedy, 20 January 1961)

'Jack' Kennedy has proved a tough act to follow. (As the fictional President Jed Bartlet in *The West Wing* was to observe to his successor, Matt Santos, on the eve of the latter's inaugural speech: 'Yeah, Kennedy kind of screwed us with that one, didn't he?') As JFK spoke those words, the mythology surrounding his presidency had already begun to develop. But he, in turn, had been evoking another, no less distinguished leader, Franklin Roosevelt, who had also begun his term in office with a frenetic first 100 days of activity.

It might seem a bit arbitrary to claim that the 100-day deadline forms a meaningful landmark for any new leader. Surely the way things look on the 1,000th or even 5,000th day would tell you a lot more about how well someone has performed in a job. Too late. The label has stuck. All new leaders, particularly those in high-profile positions, face their own initial 100-day assessment, whether they like it or not.

Ask what you can do for your colleagues

Some of the problems experienced by new bosses in the first few weeks can be self-inflicted, arising from a failure to do basic homework. Steve Newhall at headhunters and leadership consultants Korn Ferry comments on how many leaders can be underprepared when they reach the next level in their careers (conversation with authors). He says that when 'parachuted into a situation, you have got to find out who the power brokers are pretty fast, and get to understand your relationships with key stakeholders. But if you are an insider, you face that other difficult challenge of managing people on Monday who were peers on the previous Friday.'

Quick wins

The authority on these tricky transitions to new senior roles is Michael Watkins, author of *The First 90 Days: Proven strategies for getting up to speed faster and smarter* (2003). In an interview with the LearnVest website (Bianchi, 2014) he explained some of his thinking on making the next step up and how people usually worry too much about the technical job skills while not paying enough attention to the company's politics and first impressions. 'What you do early on during a job transition is what matters most', Watkins said. 'Your colleagues and your boss form opinions about you based on limited information, and those opinions are sticky – it's hard to change their minds. So shape their impressions of you to the best of your ability.'

Big boss bootcamp

Preparing for this transition takes time, something you may not always have. But presuming that your promotion does not come completely out of the blue, what practical steps can a leader take to be ready to perform?

Thomas Neff and James Citrin, headhunters from Spencer Stuart, published their views on the matter a few years ago in their bluntly titled book *You're in Charge – Now What?* They argue that meticulous preparation is necessary to be effective on days 1 to 100. This means using the weeks before you start in the new role to do some systematic research.

'Meet with the smartest observers you can find – employees, alumni, customers, suppliers and analysts – to garner their insights', they suggest. 'Do not feel compelled to walk into your new role with a strategy already developed: it will be wrong, incomplete, and/or lack buy-in.' Intense preparation is required because, once you are 'in post', events and new responsibilities will come flying, and there may be little time to think clearly about the difficult decisions you now face.

And 100 days is not a long period in which to make an impact. 'Assuming that a new leader works six days a week and 14 hours a day,' Neff and Citrin assume, heroically, 'barely 1,200 hours are available through the course of the first 100 days. New leaders need to spend as much time as possible absorbing, listening, learning, establishing relationships and making decisions, and can't afford to waste a single hour.'

Get on with it?

New leaders face another choice: crudely, to go for hyperactivity, or instead to 'listen and learn' before committing to action. The context will inform the new leader's strategy. A crisis provides the justification for dramatic measures. And the first weeks may be the best time to do something radical, while colleagues and investors accept such steps are required.

But where there is no crisis, senior managers and other staff will be surprised to learn that their apparently healthy business needs some strong medicine, especially if it is to be administered by a new leader who will not have had time to conduct a proper diagnosis.

And yet markets seem to demand speedy and decisive action from corporate leaders, just as they also demand quarterly earnings guidance. This is the environment many new bosses find themselves in. And those next quarterly figures are always just 100 days away.

So yes, the first 100 days in a new job are important. But they are not make or break. Better to watch, learn and listen before diving in. Not everything will be broken. And vested interests will try to bend your ear. You will need time to weigh up all the evidence before acting decisively. This may take much longer than three months.

And never forget Allen Ginsberg's observation: 'It's never too late to do nothing at all.'

Steady as she goes

'Nothing prepares you; no job prepares you for the job of a CEO', Andrew Liveris, chief executive of Dow Chemical, once said, in an interview with the *Financial Times* (Freeland, 2007). You are scrutinized as never before. Existing colleagues start talking to you differently. Old enemies bury hatchets, and new friends and admirers you never knew you had suddenly appear. Your jokes, which in the past may have raised the odd smile, are now met with loud and apparently heartfelt laughter.

All these factors could bamboozle a new leader, and tempt him or her into taking precipitate action early on. So it is also worth remembering that at the end of JFK's first 100 days in office there was a little incident in Cuba at a place called the Bay of Pigs.

CREDIT This myth was adapted by Stefan Stern from his article First 100 days: a time to act and a time to wait and see, *Financial Times*, 3 July 2007.

- MYTH 17 -

YOU HAVE TO KNOW EVERYTHING THAT IS GOING ON

Control freakery is for tyrants. You cannot manage/run everything.
So delegate. Enough with the micromanaging.

When the chief executive of a vast financial institution sends an e-mail with the subject line 'Rogue biscuits', concerning the outrageous behaviour of catering staff in offering pink wafers to senior executives, you know that something has gone badly wrong. Whether or not this story – told, of course, about Fred Goodwin, the former CEO of the Royal Bank of Scotland – is 100 per cent true is almost beside the point (it was written up in *Masters of Nothing: The crash and how it will happen again unless we understand human nature* by two Conservative MPs, Matthew Hancock and Nadhim Zahawi, in 2011 and has not been challenged). Everything we have heard about life at RBS under Sir Fred (as he then was) suggests that micromanagement was rife. The morning management meeting – also known as the 'management beating', during which the boss could give senior colleagues an almighty grilling – points to the existence of a miserable culture under a leader who was ultimately out of control. It's an extreme example, for sure. But a necessary warning.

Bosses can't do it all on their own. Most realize this. And yet the instinct to micromanage, to show minimal trust, to demand control, to resist the idea of allowing others to take decisions – these things can be harder to let go of. Of course managers should set high standards and have high expectations. But without sensible delegation they will go mad. Just as the sports coach at the side of the pitch cannot make every pass or hit every ball, so a manager has to let others get on with the business in hand.

Keep me informed

Managers, like stock markets, do not like surprises, especially unpleasant ones. So information should not be hoarded or guarded like a state secret. But the flow of information has to be managed. We should not overwhelm our colleagues with too much noise and (supposed) 'data'. The control panel of the Spitfire fighter plane from the Second World War contained a vast number of dials and other instrumentation, all of which doubtless proved useful for certain specific tasks. But in the heat of battle there would not have been time to look at more than the most crucial indicators.

Good managers will make it clear what they need to know and when, but not demand too much detail all of the time. Openness and transparency can help: it saves everybody else's time. It is more efficient not to have to worry about which bit of information has dribbled out and which has been kept secret. Where there is openness and shared purpose you need fewer meetings and fewer formal exchanges of information. People just know what they are supposed to be getting on with, and how.

Find the messenger, and *don't* shoot him

Another reason to allow and encourage information to flow freely is that you might help prevent scandal or catastrophe that way. 'Good communication is the smoke detector for incubating crises', as Anthony Fitzsimmons and Derek Atkins in their recent book *Rethinking Reputational Risk:*

How to manage the risks that can ruin your business, your reputation and you (2017).

But just how little has been learned on this point, in the financial sector in particular, was revealed by a depressing episode at Barclays Bank in 2016.* The bank's chief executive, Jes Staley, twice used internal security staff to try to identify an anonymous whistleblower who had contacted the board through a supposedly secure communications channel.

The complaint, in the form of two letters, concerned a new senior hire to the bank, a former colleague of Staley's in the United States. On the second occasion that the CEO tried to unmask the whistleblower, a US law enforcement agency was also deployed. But in that same year of 2016, the bank had appointed a board-level 'whistleblower's champion', Mike Ashley (not the sports goods retailer), who had signed off this statement in the annual report:

> As champion, I have specific responsibility for the integrity, independence and effectiveness of the Barclays' policies and procedures on whistleblowing, including the procedures for protecting employees who raise concerns from detrimental treatment. During 2016, I recorded a video message to all employees Group-wide, highlighting my role as Whistleblower's Champion and raising awareness of the policies and procedures we have in place.

So: Barclays will protect its whistleblowers' anonymity, right? Staley, however, had felt the accusations against the new colleague were unfair. In an internal e-mail to staff Staley explained:

> In my desire to protect our colleague... I got too personally involved in this matter. My hope was that if we found out who was sending these letters we could try and get them to stop the harassment of a person who did not deserve that treatment. Nevertheless, I realise that I should simply have the compliance function handle this matter, as they were doing. This was a mistake on my part and I apologise for it.

The legal firm employed to investigate this affair, Simmons and Simmons, reported that the CEO had behaved 'honestly but mistakenly', which is a fine example of the skilful way a professional services firm can earn their fees without upsetting their client too much.

The serious point is this: after the financial crisis of 2007/08, bank bosses should be concerned that those bringing wrongdoing to light feel able to do so without the fear that they might be harming their own career prospects. Anonymity must be respected. But when a CEO himself launches a campaign to identify a whistleblower, a very troubling message is being sent out. And that message is: keep your mouth shut, if you know what's good for you. This is not how we need bank employees, indeed any employee, to feel.

Let it go, let it go

Life is too short – managerial life, anyway – to try to find everything out and attempt to attain perfect knowledge of all that is going on. It can't be done. You will have to delegate. You will have to trust other people. You will be pleasantly surprised by what they can do for you, if you let them. In any case, people cannot be trustworthy unless you trust them.

Only small people become micromanagers.

Note

* There is good coverage of the Barclays whistleblower case here: https://www.theguardian.com/business/live/2017/apr/10/barclays-boss-investigated-over-attempts-to-unmask-whistleblower-live.

– MYTH 18 –

HEROIC LEADERS CAN CHANGE ENTIRE ORGANIZATIONS ON THEIR OWN

We have fallen for the myth of the heroic, lonely leader, the brilliant soloist doing it all by themselves. Leadership is a team sport.

Can Dave Lewis save Tesco? Will Bob Dudley turn BP around? Journalists and financial analysts ask these questions, and headline writers dutifully stick them at the top of the page. But the questions are absurd. We really should stop asking them.

Consider an international business employing tens of thousands, perhaps hundreds of thousands of people. Who is actually doing the work? On whose contribution does success depend? The exaggerated focus on one person at the top ignores the fact that there are country managers, divisional heads and a senior executive team, all reporting to a board of directors, which sits above the lot of them. In any case, no big decision should be taken by a chief executive on his or her own. Good corporate governance requires that checks and balances are applied, in particular by the board.

So why do we persist with this fairy-tale notion that one human being can apparently determine the fate of a vast corporation single-handedly? To some extent we are struggling with the legacy of the 19th-century writer Thomas Carlyle, who famously declared: 'The history of the world is but the biography of great men.' Movies and popular history have singled out individuals for praise and credit rather than movements, geo-political trends or the work of unknown masses. It's just easier, as well as superficially more attractive, to put it all down to one person.

Bertolt Brecht, the German playwright, mischievously set the record straight in his poem 'Fragen eines lesendes Arbeiters' ('Questions from a worker who reads books'). In it an innocent reader is struck by the grand statements made by the history books about famous figures from the past, prompting him to question whether Alexander the Great conquered India all on his own, or whether Caesar didn't even have a cook with him when he defeated the Gauls. For every great leader, he realizes, there are many more stories and supporters enabling him.

Match of the day

The media prefers to tell stories through people – it's what journalists are taught as trainees. 'News is people', as the great newspaper editor Sir Harry Evans said. And in the world of sport this tendency is even more pronounced. Consider the TV coverage of football, for example. One camera remains fixed on the manager's face in the dug-out, trying to capture every burst of emotion or reaction to events on the pitch. And yet the manager doesn't make a single tackle or score a single goal. The players do that. The real work is happening out there on the field of play. But in the eyes of the public, the manager's personality is all. Can José Mourinho save Manchester United? No, not on his own, but working with the players he and they could. But if that question exaggerates the importance of a manager with 20 or 30 people, how misguided is it to think that one CEO can 'turn around' the fate of a business with tens of thousands of staff?

You are not on your own

As with football, leadership really is a team sport. By definition, if you don't have any followers you cannot be a leader. But it goes deeper than that. Until followers choose to work with you and interact with you, there is a hole where leadership should be. 'It takes two to make leadership happen', as Laura Empson, a professor at Cass Business School, London, says (see Appendix 5).

Some business leaders are prepared to admit this. Lee Scott, a former CEO of Walmart, once told the *Financial Times* (Birchall, 2008): 'I don't run the company... as a CEO if you have to get up every morning and tell them what to do, then you've got the wrong people in the jobs.'

CEOs tend to fall into one of two camps: those who emphasize all the work they have done and downplay the contribution made by colleagues, and those who rather want to describe how able some of the people they work with are. The latter category is more convincing.

It is not, or shouldn't be, 'lonely at the top' (see Myth 5). It is not unwise to 'betray uncertainty' to colleagues, or reveal a temporary lack of confidence because you think you cannot really completely trust people around you. Loners may think they have to keep some of their innermost thoughts to themselves. But that's a mistake. Everyone needs support, everyone needs a few trusted advisers, and mentors, to do the job, especially if it is a high-pressure one. And if you feel you cannot trust the people around you, it is probably time to get a new top team. Rather than feeling isolated, good leaders will be plugged into rewarding relationships both inside and outside the business.

'Transformational' leadership

Our excessive focus on CEOs, to the exclusion of other questions, has led us astray. It partly explains people's weakness for the overblown concept of 'transformational leadership' (see Myth 24). Lasting change takes time to achieve, and requires the work of many people. Beware the leader who arrives to start a new job telling everybody that he (it usually will be a he) is going to 'transform' the business simply by being there.

Let the press and the analysts wallow in their delusion that one person is running the company, 'turning it around' or 'saving it' all on their own. Behind the scenes, and unnoticed by many (but not by a good CEO), important work is being carried out. If you are a boss, reach out to colleagues for help. And if you are not in charge, be a constructive follower to help make your boss a better leader.

CREDIT This myth is an adapted version of an article first appearing in the summer 2016 issue of *The In-House Lawyer* magazine. Reproduced with kind permission from Legalease Ltd.

- MYTH 19 -

THE BOSS WITH THE BEST STRATEGY WINS

Management is about getting things done. You need an aim but don't let a grand strategy tie you down.

Strategy. Such a lovely word, isn't it? From the Greek, *strategos*, meaning a general in the army. This word strategy conveys bigness and importance. Traditionally it means the plan that comes from on high, or the general's tent at any rate. Say it: s-t-r-a-t-e-g-y. You feel better already, don't you?

The economist John Kay (1998) was one of the first to poke fun at the grandiosity of the cult of strategy. Strategy is really a synonym for 'expensive', he pointed out. So 'this is a strategic acquisition' means 'we are going to pay far too much for this thing', while 'we are strategy consultants' means 'our fees are very high'.

Strategy in business was really invented – popularized, at least – by the elite management consultancy firms. Before the 1960s, not many business leaders even talked very much about strategy: they had business plans, and decided how to allocate capital. But firms such as McKinsey and the Boston Consulting Group elevated planning into something far more daunting – this was strategy. And, as John Kay intimated, strategy was something you could build a mystique around and charge a lot more money for.

What is strategy, anyway?

A lot of hot air and vagueness gets offered up in the name of strategy. But as Richard Rumelt explained in *Good Strategy, Bad Strategy: The difference and why it matters* (2011), you first have to understand what it is you are really trying to do.

Strategy is not a 'superficial restatement of the obvious combined with a generous sprinkling of buzzwords', he wrote. Rather it is 'a coherent plan to tackle a defined problem'.

Rumelt makes several other observations:

- Good strategy is rare. Many organizations that claim to have a strategy do not. Instead, they have a set of performance goals. Or, worse, a set of vague aspirations.

- 'Bad strategy' occurs when there is bad doctrine, when hard choices are avoided, and/or when leaders are unwilling or unable to define and explain the nature of the challenge.

- The poorer a firm's resource base, the more it must depend upon adroit and clever coordination of actions.

- Competitors do not always respond quickly, nor do customers always see the value of an offering. Good strategy anticipates and exploits inertia.

- Changes in technology, law, costs and buyer tastes are normally beyond the control of any competitor, but they can be harnessed. (In other words – luck really matters.)

Intelligent strategy, as Roger Martin and A G Lafley point out in their book *Playing to Win* (2013), involves making good choices. You have to choose when you must compete head-on, when it would be better to collaborate, and when you should leave the (battle)field to others.

And Henry Mintzberg, professor at McGill university in Montreal (see our 'fireside chat' with him in Appendix 3), has also provided scepticism about waffly strategies for years. In his book *The Rise and Fall of Strategic Planning* (1994) he dismissed 'the pronouncement of platitudes – ostensible strategies that no one has any intention of implementing, even if that were possible'.

In his later work *Strategy Bites Back* (co-authored with Joe Lampel and Bruce Ahlstrand, 2004), Mintzberg criticized strategies for being 'standard, generic, uninspiring'. 'Strategy doesn't only have to position, it has to inspire', he wrote. 'So an uninspiring strategy is really no strategy at all.'

Ali C

A perhaps surprising entrant into this world of strategy is Alastair Campbell, the former director of communications for Tony Blair. But New Labour was of course a highly successful election-winning machine for several years, and at the heart of that success lay a pretty disciplined approach to strategy.

Campbell (2012) has set out nine rules to observe in the execution of strategy:

1 OST is my first rule: objective, strategy, tactics. Get these the wrong way around and you are in trouble.

2 It is not a strategy unless it is written down.

3 Developing a strategy is about having arguments, not avoiding them.

4 Strategy is a team game and works best when everyone from the boardroom down to reception supports it.

5 The best strategies can be written as a word, phrase, paragraph, page, speech and book.

6 Good strategy is based on thorough analysis and understanding.

7 Good strategy is about action, not theory.

8 Communications are a means to an end – think about the business goal, not just the communications goal.

9 The best strategies are consistent, but have flexibility to adapt.

... It's the way that you do it

So, get the strategy right and all will be well, yes? Well, no. Campbell is right to say that 'good strategy is about action, not theory'. In fact we should really say that it is the execution of strategy that is most important of all. ('Even good ideas must sooner or later degenerate into work', as Peter Drucker said.)

It is better to carry out an average strategy well than a good strategy badly. And of course 'strategy' is sometimes just too grand and heavy a label to describe the everyday business of carrying out tasks and getting things done. As Herb Kelleher, the founder of Southwest Airlines, said: 'Strategy is over-rated and doing stuff is under-rated. Our strategy? Doing stuff.'

Bottom up and top down

Campbell makes one other crucial point. Strategy is a team game that needs support at all levels. It follows that the best way to develop strategy is to involve people at all levels. We are misled by that original Greek sense of the word strategy, something that comes only from the top. But a lofty plan made on high and deposited on an organization in a supposedly finished state will not belong to the rest of the workforce. It will be just another set of words handed down to employees with no comeback expected or allowed. And that will not work. There will be no buy-in from the people who most of all need to believe in it – the people who are going to do the work.

It is time to lighten up a bit about the heavy business of strategy. The world is changing fast. You have to adapt. Strategies will have to be adjusted and rewritten. And, in the end, it's what you do and how you do it that counts. It doesn't really matter what the strategy is called.

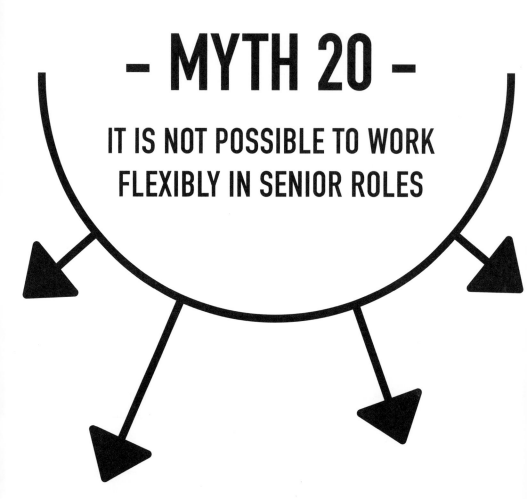

– MYTH 20 –

IT IS NOT POSSIBLE TO WORK FLEXIBLY IN SENIOR ROLES

The 100 hours a week job is not normal, and not a goal to aim for.
Flexibility makes it possible for more people to give of their best.

Lead from the front. This is what new bosses are often told to do. Set an example. Get in early, leave late. Make it clear you expect others to do so too. Keep the office fires burning.

Sometimes you do have to put in those long hours. But as we have already argued, long hours in themselves do not guarantee success (see Myth 3). Indeed, it may be counterproductive to stay at work in the hope that physical presence will somehow bring forth miracles, even if you are already beyond tired. Sometimes you really should just go home.

The lingering prejudice that showing up is all and going home is weak is taking a very long time to die. It may never completely disappear. There is still guilt and embarrassment in the air when people apologize for leaving the workplace 'early', no matter what the cause of that departure is. You may still hear jokey calls of 'Half day, then?' or 'Thanks for dropping in' as you head to the door.

The office is not a prison, at least it shouldn't be. And yet many seem reluctant, or feel unable, to attend to some other important non-work task during office hours. A survey for the www.workingmums.co.uk website (2016) showed that 18 per cent of women had been forced to leave their jobs when flexible working was not made possible. Caring responsibilities cannot be ducked. Another survey of 2,000 UK employees for the Red Letter Days for Business consultancy (2015), called *Lack of flexibility is killing UK productivity*, found that highly engaged staff were able to work much more flexibly, including working from home, than those who were much less engaged.

The example leaders should be setting is working flexibly themselves. Fortunately there is more of this going on than you might think.

Flexible working works, at the top too

In 2017, *Management Today* magazine published an extended feature on 'power part-timers', a list of 50 senior people who prove that it is not necessary to stay shackled to the office desk for one of those 100-hour weeks (Saunders, 2017). A selection of individuals from this feature makes the point powerfully.

There is Liz Brown, head of group corporate development at Dixons Carphone, the FTSE 100 electrical goods retailer. She works four days a week, even though she has been set a target of generating an extra £1 billion in 'shareholder value', ie getting the share price up.

There is Ingrid Cope, senior legal adviser at Pernod Ricard in the UK, part of the world's second-largest drinks business. She is a member of the senior management team... and works three and a half days a week.

There is Arpad Cseh, executive director in the infrastructure team of UBS Asset Management, providing financial advice to clients worldwide, working on two infrastructure funds valued at over $2 billion. He does this two and a half days a week. The rest of the time he works on a climate change initiative.

There is Katie Garrett, senior project manager in Goldman Sachs' technology division. She works four days a week. In 2014, she was made senior engineer, a title reserved for the most influential vice presidents in the firm's technology division.

There is Dawn Heath, a partner at Freshfields Bruckhaus Deringer, the magic circle legal firm. She works four days a week, one of those from home. She was Freshfields' first UK lawyer – and only the second globally – to be elected to the partnership on a part-time arrangement.

And there is Rob Symington, co-founder of Escape the City, a 'global community' with 250,000 members. He works two days a week on the business, which has £1 million in turnover, advising professionals on starting new careers or rejuvenating their existing one.

The *Management Today* article also featured some senior-level job-sharers, senior civil servants, charity heads and HR directors who work three days each, again making it clear that flexibility at the top is not only doable but even advantageous – the 'two Mondays' effect, for example, can get the working week off to a strong start if both job-sharers work that day.

Nobody is indispensable

Sir Gerry Robinson, the former head of the Granada media and leisure business, used to say that he really only had about a dozen or so big decisions to make a year, and that as long as he got nine or ten of them right the company would be OK. He delegated a lot to colleagues, allowed them to get on with it, but told them quickly if he wasn't happy with what they were doing. He also said it should be perfectly possible for a CEO to finish by Friday lunchtime and be on the golf course that afternoon (he may not have been entirely serious on this last point).

But, in a long and highly successful business career, Sir Gerry did not put in the stupid, sadomasochistic hours that some consider necessary. He said he would rather do 8 good hours in the office than 12 tired ones (Davidson, 1995). He usually aimed to be out of the office well before six to get home to his family. And if he could do it, so can anybody else. Indeed, the smartphone and laptop allow work to come home with you whenever you like, in a way that wasn't possible 20 years ago.

This demand for constant presence, whether of the boss or of more junior colleagues, is ridiculous. When bosses insist on being ever-present it is often a sign of insecurity and underperformance (see the saga of Marissa Meyer at Yahoo, discussed in Myth 39).

This management myth is one of the most damaging of all and also one of the hardest to shake off. Bosses need to set themselves free. They could trust themselves and their colleagues to work more flexibly. The evidence suggests that both performance and employee well-being will rise. In particular, if you are serious about trying to offer an attractive career path to women there has to be more flexible working while women are still carrying out more caring responsibilities at home, whether with children or older relatives.

But the example must be set at the top. By all means don't expect anyone to work harder than you do. But make flexible working a reality for both you and the rest of your team and watch how your business really starts to hum.

– MYTH 21 –

PAY MUST BE KEPT CONFIDENTIAL

More openness means there's less to worry about. Transparency on pay may be a tough discipline but it will be worth it.

'I know you said we can't expect a pay rise this year,' says a character in an old cartoon, 'but couldn't you at least cut that bastard Jenkins' pay?'

Compare the market dot com. We all do it, even if we know we shouldn't. It is natural to want to know how well we are doing compared with others. But many bosses are wary of such comparisons. They think that they could be disruptive, creating disharmony at work. So they insist on keeping pay levels confidential as far as possible.

How differently things look in Scandinavia, where there is a centuries-old tradition of pay transparency. Tax returns are all accessible by the public, although a recent reform in Norway, whereby you receive notification that someone has been looking your details up, has put a slight dampener on the level of enquiries being made.

I'll show you mine if you show me yours

But this could never happen in Britain or the United States, could it? Well – think again. New legislation requiring the publication of gender pay-gap data will force companies to be more open about pay levels and the gap between people, men and women, carrying out similar tasks. In the UK, of course, the Equal Pay Act has been in place since 1970, yet pay equality is still a long way off.

But how about full transparency, and the complete disclosure of everybody's pay? Wouldn't that cause unnecessary aggro? That is not the view of John Mackey, founder and chief executive of the Whole Foods supermarket group. He introduced full transparency on pay over 30 years ago, just six years after starting the company. He did so for practical business reasons; Mackey believed that by sharing as much data as possible, including sales figures by store and by region, colleagues would have a better sense of how well the business was doing, and what they might need to do to progress.

'I'm challenged on salaries all the time', Mackey has said (Fishman, 1996). 'How come you are paying this regional president this much, and I'm only making this much?' I have to say, 'because that person is more valuable. If you accomplish what this person has accomplished, I'll pay you that, too.'

Let there be light

True, the transition from confidentiality to openness on pay may not be smooth. There may be a few unpleasant shocks. As Adrian Furnham, a professor in psychology at University College London, has written: 'Secrecy feeds conspiracy, but openness outrage and fury... the hottest issue is comparative pay and how it is calculated. Nothing angers people more than a perceived less deserving person who is paid more than you. Hence pay secrecy, which is always easier to deal with than transparency.'

Easier in the short term, yes. But secrecy has its costs too, in creating unnecessary bureaucracy which wastes managers' time, and in the establishment of exclusive cliques who are in the know, while others are kept in the dark. And that really is divisive. But if everyone is in the know there are fewer secrets to keep and more chance of a common purpose being shared.

So go on, flick the light switch, open up, share, and see how much better you might all work together.

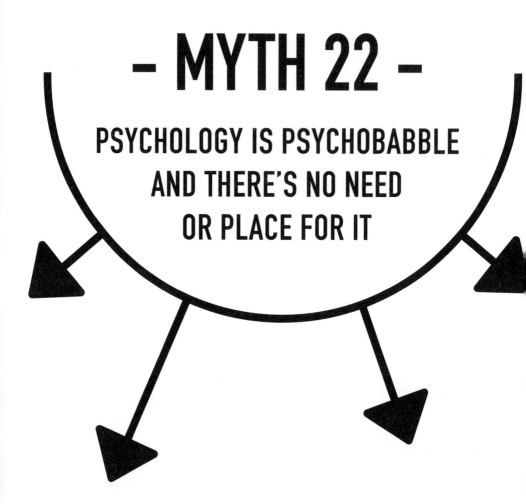

– MYTH 22 –

PSYCHOLOGY IS PSYCHOBABBLE AND THERE'S NO NEED OR PLACE FOR IT

We're human and we're complicated. Psychology can help. We need to lose our hang-ups and study how and why we behave the way we do.

The stiff upper lip has got a lot to answer for. Traditional British notions of reserve and control have proved to be enduring. This is not all bad. There is something to admire in those who maintain their dignity even under extreme pressure. We don't want our bosses to have wild mood swings or to be tempestuous in the office.

Yet only a hundred years ago British soldiers were still being shot for alleged cowardice when their mental trauma in the trenches was mistaken for a lack of backbone. It took decades for military and business leaders to recognize that the mind could get exhausted just as much as the body. The Roffey Park Institute, founded in Horsham, Sussex, just after the end of the

Second World War, was initially established as a rehabilitation centre, helping people with profound stress, anxiety and mental 'burn-out' to recover and prepare to return to work.

Psychology was, until relatively recently, something that should not be talked about in the workplace. It was all very well for excitable Continentals like that funny Dr Freud chap to prattle on about the darker corners and mysteries of the mind. But Brits as a rule did not need that sort of thing. Other people might have psychological issues. We would not. And anyone who wanted to start a discussion about such matters would be ignored, or silenced. This was not psychology, it was 'psychobabble'. It was an indulgence, unmanly, and not something respectable folk ought to be concerned with. Old-school managers did not want a workforce emoting and engaging in, as they saw it, Princess Diana-style 'disclosure'. Some subjects were best left undiscussed.

They've got an -ology

But psychologists know stuff. They carry out experiments and observe how people react. They study human behaviour and understand how and why we might do the things we do. They can sometimes predict how we will respond to different types of event or situation. This is useful information. And managers should be aware of it.

Consider just three powerful examples from the field.

Abraham Maslow (1908–1970; see profile by Emrich) helped us understand that human beings have a 'hierarchy of needs', starting with the basics of food and shelter at the bottom, then a need for safety, moving up through the need for love and belonging, a sense of esteem, and leading ultimately, to a desire for 'self-actualization' at the top. Managers should understand that capable people will be unlikely to perform well at work, fulfilling their potential, if they do not feel these essential needs are being met – if they are unable to speak freely and express themselves, for example.

Frederick Herzberg (1923–2000; see obituary by Feder, 2000) explained how human motivation must come from within. It cannot be commanded. 'If I kick my dog (from the front or the back), he will move', he wrote in a famous *Harvard Business Review* article (Herzberg, 1968). 'And when I want him to move again what must I do? I must kick him again.' This kind of 'kick in the ass' management produces movement, not motivation, Herzberg said. If certain 'hygiene factors' are not maintained at work – if pay levels are manifestly unfair, or if the treatment of workers is bad – then people will be demotivated. Intrinsic motivation comes from having a sense of achievement in the work, being properly recognized for it, or seeing that job (career) progression is possible. 'If you want people to do a good job,' Herzberg said, 'give them a good job to do'.

Martin Seligman (1942–; see profile by Positive Psychology Center) first explained how 'learned helplessness' could afflict those suffering with depression. People can get trapped in despair and negativity and see no way out. More happily, he later developed ideas under the heading of 'positive psychology', and has done much to spread the concept of well-being at work. Character strengths such as courage and temperance can be developed to help equip employees to cope with the pressures of work.

And so on. This is not psychobabble. This is good stuff.

The people people

Belatedly, managers (as well as the general public) have acquired a taste for psychology. It has become popular at last. Writers and academics such as Malcolm Gladwell, Daniel Pink, Dan Ariely and the Heath brothers (Dan and Chip) have helped disseminate psychological theories and research. In the UK one of this book's co-authors (Cary Cooper) has played a leading role in raising awareness of the damaging effects of stress and overwork (see Myth 3).

Finally it is OK to acknowledge that psychology matters and that we need to have a better grasp of it at work. Many company boards have been using psychometric tests as part of their selection process for years. They just haven't liked talking about it. Perhaps they should.

If bosses were more familiar with the concept of intrinsic motivation, for example, they would be less dumbfounded by the disappointing results from employee engagement surveys. If they knew about their colleagues' hierarchy of needs and desire for 'job enrichment' they would think harder about organizational structure, job design and the way work gets done. This all matters a lot.

The psychology (and mental health) of leaders can have a decisive impact on the success or otherwise of the business. So why do some people still shy away from a candid assessment of their and their colleagues' mental state? They may be nervous about what they might discover. But they need to know.

In his book *The Leader on the Couch* (2006), Manfred Kets de Vries, a professor at INSEAD, showed how useful a better understanding of bosses' psyches could be. 'Many management theories that explain how people make decisions in organisations are inadequate over-simplifications', he wrote. 'In fact, the apparently rational explanations for certain decisions often turn out to be fiction, rationalisations made after the fact... Like it or not, "abnormal behaviour" is more "normal" than most people are prepared to admit.'

– MYTH 23 –

THE ROBOTS ARE COMING
TO TAKE YOUR JOB

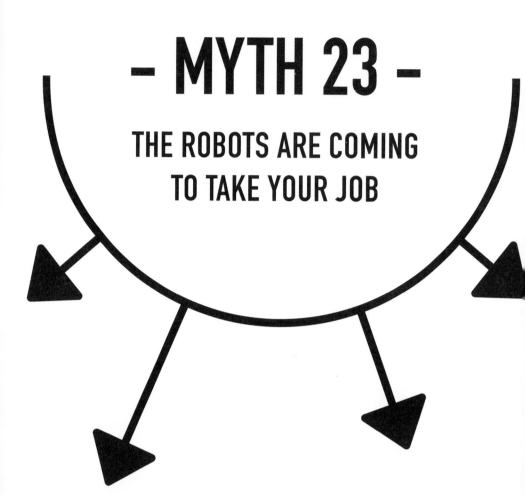

*We've been adapting to the arrival of new technology for centuries.
We always will. Don't fear the robots, work with them.*

Pick a number, any number. As many as 47 per cent of jobs in the United States are at risk of being automated in the next 20 years, according to two (much quoted) Oxford academics (Frey and Osborne, 2013). No, it's 38 per cent, say the consultants at PwC (Masunaga, 2017). No, no, it's only 9 per cent, says the OECD (Arntz, Gregory and Zierahn, 2016). And if you look at the US census form from 1950, only one occupation listed on it has actually been completely replaced by automation since then: lift attendant. We have always feared what the machines might do to us. And yet somehow human beings keep finding a way to be useful and fit in.

Which is not to say, of course, that there isn't a lot more automation coming, and that more tasks currently carried out by humans aren't going to be done by robots. And this process is creeping higher up the 'value chain', coming within reach of white-collar professionals. A computer might now be able to come up fast with a more or less usable translation of a foreign text (although it will almost certainly lack finesse and risks missing subtleties of meaning). Basic legal and accountancy tasks are well within the scanning capabilities of today's technology.

And then there's agriculture. In 2017, the *Financial Times* introduced its readers to Thorvald, a marvellous bit of robotic machinery developed in Norway. Currently still driven by an operator with a joystick, Thorvald can 'carry trays of strawberry plants to human pickers, sparing them miles of walking through vast fields', the *FT* reported (Chaffin, 2017). 'At night, he passes over plants with ultraviolet lights to kill mildew that might otherwise spoil as much as half the crop.'

Will farmers invest in little machine armies of Thorvalds, tending to their crops, pulling up vegetables and picking fruit at harvest time? It depends. People may still be a cheaper option, for quite a long time. And a better option too: while Thorvald might be able to yank up some carrots, for example, soft fruit present a far tougher challenge. Pål Johan From, the Norwegian engineer who developed Thorvald, told the *FT*: 'I would say it's 10 to 20 years before we can make a robot that can pick [a strawberry] at the same speed as a human... Raspberries are even harder.'

Still, it is clear that machines can and will do more and more. So have humans had it? Hardly. We are still in charge, usually. We tell machines what to do. (And when machines or algorithms do take over, if only temporarily, the effects can be disturbing. When London's Borough Market was subjected to a terrorist attack in June 2017, the 'dynamic pricing' model used by Uber, the taxi firm, sprang into action, sending prices spiking upwards until human beings intervened to stop the computers from trying to make more money while people were trying to get home fast. It is not good enough, as the guru Ben Hammersley has said, for managers to shrug and declare that 'The algorithm made me do it.')

Yes, machines can learn to be quicker and cleverer, and be very useful while they are at it. But essentially they are still doing what they have been programmed, by humans, to do. Peter Drucker may have been being unduly (and uncharacteristically) harsh when he said, in 1967 admittedly, that 'the computer is a moron', but you know what he meant.

Professor Laura Empson, an expert on professional services firms (PSFs) at Cass Business School, tells us (see full interview in Appendix 5) that some of the fears about machines replacing professionals are overdone. 'Technology is never a substitution for brilliant people', she says. 'Technology, typically, has been a substitution for essentially routinized tasks, and there is a lot of extremely routine work that is done within a lot of these [PSF] firms, though they may be reluctant to acknowledge that. It's one of the reasons they need to Hoover up so many graduate recruits every year.

'Technology can replace that. But when you as a chief executive face a hostile takeover, if you want to raise billions of dollars to fund your expansion, or when you are worried you might be up in front of the SEC for some bad accounting practices, you are not going to ask a computer for the answer.'

People as robots

In fact, the worrying point is not so much that robots are becoming more like humans, but rather that too much low-paid and low-skill work is requiring humans to behave more like robots. Frederick Taylor's 'scientific management', now over 100 years old, tended to see humans as functioning (and with any luck) efficient machines, repeating simple tasks again and again (Taylor, 1911). Today, some retail, warehouse and delivery jobs can evoke a kind of 21st-century Taylorism, with work monitored and managed by computers.

Fitbits and other gadgets can check up on how far and fast you are moving, what you are doing on your PC screen, when and where deliveries are being made, and so on. The human factor is menaced and can even get driven out by this sense of constant surveillance. Humans – managers – will have to intervene to make sure that machines do not destroy the dignity of labour. Who wants to be managed by a machine or a 'platform', really?

And, by the way, did you know that the term 'robot' is derived from a Czech word, *robota*, which means 'forced labour'?

It takes two to tango

In truth, it is in the complementarity of human beings and technology where the future will be built and where real value will lie. Tom Davenport and Julia Kirby, in their book *Only Humans Need Apply: Winners and losers in the age of smart machines* (2017), have said we should think of this as 'augmentation' rather than automation.

We should not exaggerate what 'virtual colleagues' and talking boxes can really do for us. The philosopher Daniel Dennett told the *FT* (2017): 'All we're going to see in our own lifetimes are intelligent tools, not colleagues. Don't think of them as colleagues, don't try to make them colleagues and, above all, don't kid yourself that they're colleagues.'

The chief executive of Microsoft, Satya Nadella, has spoken in similar terms (Murgia, 2017). 'It is going to be about people working with machines', he has said. 'So that means you have got to be able to understand machines and how they work.' If even the boss of Microsoft does not see technology replacing humans, there has got to be hope. In Amazon 'fulfilment centres', humans and robots work side by side – the machines doing some of the more arduous fetching and carrying, while humans finish off the job of making sure the right package is dispatched to the right customer. It's a complementary process.

The biggest questions are perhaps economic and political rather technological. If jobs are destroyed by automation, what will the workers who had those jobs do instead? How will they earn a living? Drones and self-driving vehicles alone could eliminate millions of jobs in due course. Will enough new jobs emerge to replace the old ones? And does this mean that some form of basic income (or 'citizen's income') will have to be offered to all, in lieu of the paid employment that can no longer be guaranteed?

And then there is the question of care. The growing ageing population will require a lot of skilful looking after. Robots might help with some of this task, but seriously, would you rather be 'looked after' by a machine or by a fellow human being? The care sector alone will demand the maintenance (and creation) of millions of jobs that will be best done by actual people, as long as we are prepared to pay properly for it. As far as the dreaded 'march of the machines' is concerned, we ought to get our thinking and our priorities straight. As Sarah O'Connor wrote in the *Financial Times* (2017): 'We should worry less about the jobs that might be going, and more about the jobs we know are staying.'

These questions all require books of their own, which are, happily, being written. Our task here is to stick up for people and the people who manage them.

Give humans a chance

'What a piece of work is a man!' declares Hamlet. 'How noble in reason, how infinite in faculty! In form and moving how express and admirable! In action how like an angel, in apprehension how like a god!' OK, so this may not sound like anyone you work with. But the point stands: humans are pretty amazing, and should not be underestimated. The human hand, for example, cannot yet be matched by any robotic technology for sensitivity and versatility. And perhaps never will be. Has a computer ever told you a good joke? Exactly.

For all the joys and excitement of new technology, this too remains essentially a human achievement. We made that. The internet, the writer Howard Jacobson has said, is really 'an encyclopedia with adverts'. It is up to us what we choose to do with it.

And we should be realistic about what technology can do for us, Jacobson said in a talk for the BBC (2017). 'The idea that if we feed enough lines of literature into a computer it will eventually be able to write its own *Iliad* is as preposterous as the old fancy that if a sufficient number of monkeys were given a sufficient number of Olivettis they would eventually hammer out a monkey *Macbeth*.'

When artificial intelligence and machine learning can produce work as good as Shakespeare's it will be time for us to worry. Until then, humans remain superior and rightly in charge.

After all, a robot couldn't even write this little book, could it?

Or could it?

– MYTH 24 –

LEADERSHIP MUST BE TRANSFORMATIONAL

Change doesn't have to be big, or clever. It can be small but necessary.
Lots of successful small changes can add up to something bigger.

Beware the seductive allure of grand-sounding polysyllabic terms. 'Business process re-engineering' was not as clinical or uncontroversial as it may at first have appeared (see Myth 37). 'Virtualization' could be good news, or not, but it is hard to be sure. And when someone tells you that what the business needs now is 'transformational leadership', pause for a moment.

Some new bosses like to declare right at the outset that they plan to transform the organization. It's a big claim. What, all of it? And every person who works there? You're ether transformative or you're not, surely. You can't be a semi-transformational leader. It is all or nothing. Guess which outcome you are likely to get.

Incremental change gets a bad press. It does not feature in many corporate mission statements. It's not what investment analysts, impatient investors or journalists want to hear. It does not usually stir great passions. Nobody ever went on a protest march with the following battle cry: 'What do we want? Incremental change! When do we want it? Phased in gradually over a number of years…'

The arrogance of 'transformation'

Thus the appeal of transformation. It is a nice story for self-aggrandizing chief executives to tell. It puts them at the heart of the story, and makes it all (or largely) about them. 'What a mess I inherited here,' this story goes, 'how lost they all were. But look how I transformed them.'

The problem with these stories is that they are rarely true, and contain within them dangerous delusions and the seeds of future disasters. Take three famous British examples.

Today's Tesco – check it out!

Tesco had long been seen as a cheap and not terribly cheerful supermarket, still adhering to its founder, Jack Cohen's, mantra of 'pile it high and sell it cheap'. Gradually, over a period of decades (1970s–1990s), the business changed, casting off much of its scruffier former image and becoming the leading British supermarket chain. This took time. It was a bumpy ride. Much of the hard work had been done by the leadership team which had worked under Ian (now Lord) MacLaurin. But by the time the outside world had really noticed how much Tesco had changed, another boss, Sir Terry Leahy, was in charge. And while Leahy was undoubtedly a strong and determined leader, who helped steer the business to continued success (while its competitors, most notably Sainsbury's, struggled), it was wrong to regard him as a transformational leader. The changes at Tesco had taken 30 years to come to fruition.

But the mythology surrounding Tesco's transformation grew. It proved too tempting for the company to believe its own hype. Having declared that they would never launch a business in the United States, Tesco… launched a business in the United States – called Fresh'n'Easy – which flopped. Then came scandals over the supply chain (some horse meat in your lasagne, anyone?) and accounting, where suppliers' pay-to-play fees were being booked in advance, and overstated.

It was Leahy's successor, Philip Clarke, who was CEO when the scandals emerged, who took the rap. But it was the myth of transformation that had done for them. Recovery has now begun, but Tesco's former swagger has gone, for now.

BP – be part of it

Another tale of transformational leadership gone wrong is that of BP, the oil major. Privatized in the 1980s, BP grew steadily until a series of opportunistic acquisitions saw it become one the world's largest oil companies. And at its head was John (now Lord) Browne. He too was acclaimed as a transformational leader. And under him the business certainly grew. A mythology grew up around him too. The *Financial Times* called him the 'Sun King', and wrote lengthy, largely positive pieces about him.

But again the story turned. In 2005, an explosion at BP's Texas City refinery killed 15 people and injured another 180. The following year, two leaks at the company's Prudhoe Bay oilfield in Alaska did vast damage. In 2007, Browne resigned after details of his private life appeared in the newspapers and he was found to have lied in court. He was succeeded by Tony Hayward. And then, in 2010, the Deepwater Horizon disaster killed 11 rig workers and caused the biggest offshore oil spill in US history. The bill for the clean-up and compensation, still unsettled, has run into many billions of dollars. The transformation of BP was not as soundly based as had been believed.

Fred the Shred

Our final transformational leader is Fred Goodwin, formerly Sir Fred, also known as Fred the Shred. He had helped to take the Royal Bank of Scotland from the middle tier of banking to the top table, in particular with the bold acquisition of National Westminster Bank in 2000 (he was still deputy CEO at the time, but was a driving force in the deal and became CEO the year after).

The deal too far came with the acquisition of ABN-Amro in 2007, on the eve of the global financial crisis. A year later, the then Sir Fred and colleagues had to call on the mercy of the government to prop up the bank and prevent them from having to turn the cash machines off. It was an utter humiliation.

Slow and steady wins the race

Small change is good. Bit by bit you can make things better. This is incremental rather than 'transformational' change. The Japanese call it *kaizen* – continuous improvement. It is a worthwhile and achievable aim. Look at where products 'made in Japan' were in the 1950s and where they are today. Japanese cars were a joke, once, certainly as far as US car-makers were concerned. (Ford, GM and Chrysler stopped laughing eventually.) That was a meaningful transformation, but it took decades and was not based on one individual leader, rather the work of millions.

The time to worry is when the board announces that it wants to achieve a transformation, and a new boss arrives promising to deliver one, quickly. It cannot be done, and should not be attempted. Real, lasting change takes ages, and does not depend on one heroic figure. And that is why this familiar quotation from Lao Tzu rightly remains popular, as an antidote to self-identified 'transformational leaders': 'With the best leaders, when the work is done, the task accomplished, the people will say: "We have done this ourselves."'

– MYTH 25 –

CONFORMITY LEADS TO SUCCESS

Playing it safe could be the riskiest thing you could do. There is more security, paradoxically, in daring to be different.

By their suits shall ye know them. Sensible, suited figures carefully keeping their mouths shut and trying to avoid offering an opinion on anything. It has long been a dependable career option: keep your head down, stay out of trouble, deliver steady but unspectacular results, hope to be allowed to stay. It is an entirely understandable and perhaps even respectable choice. But the days when simply conforming to the generally accepted standards of the bland middle ground guaranteed job security are coming to an end.

While the threat of automation has probably been somewhat overdone (see Myth 23), it is true that solid, average performance will not preserve your job at a time when an algorithm can be written to achieve the same result at vastly smaller cost. Humans, and the organizations they work for, have to prove their worth. If businesses copy each other too closely, they will be vulnerable either to low-cost new entrants or to radically different alternatives. The steady, safe middle is now a dangerous place to be. It is time to be brave.

Change to strange

Dan Cable, professor of organizational behaviour at London Business School, latched onto this idea in 2007 with his book *Change to Strange: Create a great organization by building a strange workforce*. If you develop a unique and special – even strange – culture, Professor Cable argued, you will be hard to copy and hard to beat.

Ikea, the Swedish furniture company, has grown to become the world's dominant player in its market, but without really compromising on its essential strangeness. It has always been quite a challenge to go shopping there. You get lost, pick up far more items than you meant to, and then have to assemble the furniture yourself, risking both physical injury and marital break-up. But still people go back for more. You couldn't mistake an Ikea store for anywhere else. Ikea is another country – they do things differently there.

How can others try to develop a similar kind of profitable strangeness? In his book, Professor Cable summoned up the slightly bizarre example of a hot-dog eating contest. It is not the greediest or the fattest person who wins. Rather, it is someone who 'executes a process like a machine', he says. 'The devotion to the craft is sort of unparalleled… it inspires awe. "That dude is strange", you say, but you also find yourself impressed and intrigued. And sure as hell unwilling to imitate it.'

Managers need to find their organization's equivalent of a hot-dog eating contest, Professor Cable suggests. Perfect that and you will be unbeatable. 'What strange activity is it that you and your workforce have mastered better than anybody else? What can you create in your market that inspires incredulity in both your customers and your competitors?', he writes. Don't just conform. Dare to be obsessively different.

Signature practices

Professor Lynda Gratton (see our interview with her in Appendix 6), also at London Business School, has written in the past about companies' 'signature practices' – those processes or capabilities which are unique to them, which they are very good at, and which set them apart. While a so-called 'best practice' might be an industry standard, widely known and therefore capable of being copied, a signature practice, like a written signature, should be one of a kind. The adoption of best practice is an 'outside in' move, whereas signature practices come from within.

Professor Gratton's colleague, Tammy Erickson, goes a little further, echoing the idea that apparent strangeness, or weirdness, can help you surpass mere best practice. 'Weird' in this context means bespoke and perhaps idiosyncratic. 'Companies with the most engaged people are the weirdest', Dr Erickson says. And, as she told *HR* magazine in 2017: 'Stop adopting best practice and start thinking about creating a unique experience. Don't try to be all things to all people; think about what makes your firm special. Be unique, be special and tap into discretionary effort.'

This may be hard to achieve. But it makes sense. In a world of reliably dismal customer service, for example, those employees who believe there is something positive and different about where they work will offer something better. That bigger sense of purpose and meaning can inspire. This can be self-reinforcing: as you start to do better and perhaps pull away from the competition, there is more reason to push the points of difference. True, at this point you may cross the line that separates 'culture' from 'cult'. Your company may not have to become as strange or cult-like as Ikea. But having a unique and strange culture will set you apart.

Dare to be a Daniel

The words of an old hymn run as follows:

Dare to be a Daniel!

Dare to stand alone!

Dare to have a purpose firm!

Dare to make it known!

It is easy, from the outside, to preach boldness and daring to those working inside a business or organization. Internally there may be a limited appetite for courageous decisions. (In *Yes, Minister*, the popular BBC comedy, the minister concerned, Jim Hacker, knew he was probably running a risk too far when his civil service colleagues observed that he was in danger of making a 'brave' decision.)

But without courage nothing will change for the better in business, and without courage organizations will fail. So the leaders who, explicitly or implicitly, instruct their people to conform to standards and play it safe are in fact being reckless. Business as usual may appear to work for them in the short to medium term, and help them avoid getting the sack. But the long-term interests of the business will not be served by such caution.

'Me-tooism' is not a winning strategy. Whatever people may have told you in the past about toeing the line and not drawing too much attention to yourself – forget it. Try being different. Conformity is the slow track to disaster.

– MYTH 26 –

FEELINGS ARE SOFT AND FOR LOSERS

Numbers may be a hard fact in business but they are driven by softer things – humans. It is not weak to acknowledge this.

Hug Me While I Weep, for I Weep for the World was the title of a book by Bel Littlejohn, the fictitious *Guardian* newspaper columnist created by the writer Craig Brown. His target was the overly sentimental, emotionally incontinent and self-obsessed type who sees and feels everything deeply, and emotionally. It was a good joke, a reaction perhaps to excessive talk of 'emotional intelligence', a concept which had become popular in the 1990s thanks in particular to the work of Daniel Goleman (see Myth 4).

Many bosses would be only too happy never to discuss feelings at all. Displays of emotion at work have traditionally been regarded with suspicion, and seen as being unprofessional or unbusinesslike. Balance sheets, numbers, cash flow and profitability: these are 'hard', emotionless things which have to be dealt with unflinchingly. In a male-dominated environment, manliness meant not admitting to finer feelings. One of the factors that made it more difficult for women to break through at work was the suggestion – accusation – that women would be less hardened and more emotional about business. (Confident or assertive women, on the other hand, could be dismissed as 'bossy'.) Result? Too few women at the top.

While money could (usually) be measured and viewed as a tangible item, feelings – morale, motivation, culture, engagement – remained intangible and harder to be precise about. This was not the language of finance, nor how business leaders saw the world. Even if many now agree that 'culture eats strategy for breakfast' (a remark often attributed, without documentary evidence, to Peter Drucker), there has been a lag between the acknowledgement of the importance of the emotional side of work and action to do anything about it.

Empathy deficit

In June 2006, at the graduation ceremony for students at Northwestern University, Chicago, the young senator from Illinois, Barack Obama, gave the commencement address. He had several lessons for the young graduates that day, but the most striking one had to do with what he called 'empathy'.

'There's a lot of talk in this country about the federal deficit', Obama said. 'But I think we should talk more about our empathy deficit – the ability to put ourselves in someone else's shoes; to see the world through [the eyes of] those who are different from us.'

He went on to denounce the culture in which we live as discouraging of empathy while promoting the values of wealth, physical perfection and celebrity status. He ended his speech by encouraging the young graduates to broaden their horizons and their capacity for concern for others, arguing that by concerning themselves with others they will also personally grow and develop for the better.

This was pretty grand stuff – at times, perhaps, almost worthy of Bel Littlejohn herself. But the concept of empathy had been championed by an orator who was about to go on and win the most powerful elected office in the world. It was no longer possible to deny its existence or fail to acknowledge that empathy had a role to play in the workplace as well as everywhere else.

Empathize, don't gush

You can overdo the tough talk, but you can overdo empathy as well. Work means deadlines and disciplines. It is not therapy. Managers need to be able to show empathy, but they need to be firm and even severe when necessary, too.

Paul Bloom, a professor of psychology at Yale University, has helped clarify this point with his book *Against Empathy: The case for rational compassion*. He rightly points to the danger of, for example, a doctor over-empathizing with a suffering patient and failing to choose a harsh but necessary course of action. The parallels for management are obvious. The workplace is rarely a collective where all decisions have to be agreed unanimously. Sometimes we will get told to do things we don't want to do, and will possibly feel bad about it. A boss can recognize that without indulging it. Intelligent empathy will help to civilize the workplace. Limitless empathy will hold it back.

Research carried out by academics at Norwich Business School at the University of East Anglia confirms that a manager's support can be a 'double-edged sword: on the one hand preventing the emergence of emotional exhaustion, but on the other hand diminishing the likelihood that employees will engage in planning to deal with the emotional exhaustion they are experiencing', Carlos Ferreira Peralta, one of the researchers, explains.

See the world feelingly

The sensible backlash against excessive, gushing empathy should not lead us to conclude that feelings have no place at work. One of the reasons people instinctively reject the idea of robots taking over the workplace – apart from the instinct for self-preservation – is that we want living, breathing (and feeling) human beings in charge, not machines (see Myth 23).

Intangible assets – ideas, brands, 'human capital', culture – are increasingly what distinguish successful businesses and organizations from their weaker competitors. The finance director may not always know how to measure these things, or prove what the return on capital is for investing in them. A lot of managers can keep machines running. But not all of them know how to deal with people.

Sensible leaders will want their managers to be able to display emotional intelligence, and show empathy, as well as having high standards and making sure that good levels of performance are maintained. Management remains a balancing act of heart and head. We should all feel OK about that.

- MYTH 27 -

KEEP YOUR DISTANCE
IF YOU WANT RESPECT

You have to show a bit more of yourself, and get up close and personal,
if you want your people to know and respect you.

'Don't smile before Christmas' was the old advice supposedly offered up to newly qualified teachers. The idea was that you needed to preserve an element of mystery, and menace, before relenting and revealing your more human side once the spring term had started.

This may have been a sensible approach in the classroom during Tom Brown's schooldays. But it seems unlikely that a new teacher would get very far today by appearing closed and withdrawn. It is hard enough to hold the attention of youngsters without manifesting some sort of personality, even if it is an unattractive one.

Some managers have not yet caught up with the more streetwise members of the teaching profession. They still hope to sustain a degree of mystique and unpredictability about their true identity. They believe that knowledge is power, and that by withholding information about themselves – by remaining closed, secretive and forever distant – they can maintain some sort of advantage over their colleagues.

While mood swings in a boss, indeed any kind of over-the-top reaction, might be undesirable, signs of life are also necessary. And if you want some commitment and engagement from your people, you have to give them something they can engage with. At some point you will have to reveal your personality, warts and all.

Don't stand so close to me

But managers need to know when to step in and when to withdraw; when to be at arm's length, or in somebody's face. The German sociologist Georg Simmel (1858–1918; Sociology in Switzerland) developed the idea of 'social distance', which is relevant here. One of his works looked at the concept of 'the stranger' in society. The stranger can be simultaneously near and distant, familiar yet ultimately unknowable. The parallels with the judgements managers have to make are clear. The slightly distant manager might come across as someone with an objective and detached view of your work, which could be healthy, in terms of assessing performance, for example (see Feedback below). And yet that very detachment might mean that we value their opinion precisely because the social distance between us and them prevents them from being too personally damning or critical.

There is an echo here of those two central management tasks – direction and support – discussed in the opening myth. When to step in and when to withdraw: that is the question. Rob Goffee and Gareth Jones – who cite Simmel as an important influence in their book *Why Should Anyone Be Led by You?* (2006) – talk about the need for 'tough empathy': being close enough to show you understand your colleague's point of view, but firm enough to provide direction if necessary. This is not easy. It is one of the reasons why it is hard to be a good manager.

Indeed, as Jones and Goffee explain in our interview with them (see Appendix 8), the demands of life in the big corporation can work against managers ever getting up close and finding out what is really going on. 'An Americanism I really like', Jones tells us, 'is be where the rubber hits the road. If you think about head-office-type jobs, if you don't deliberately go to where the rubber hits the road all you get is a kind of phantom version of the world. You get this sanitized, often quantitative, numerical account of what's happening.' And Goffee adds: 'The difficulty is that managers don't always feel they have the time to get out and see what is really going on. They misguidedly think they can do it all from their computer.'

You scratch my back...

You might not expect intimacy from an algorithm. But human beings should be able to do better than that. Teamwork requires reciprocity. It means looking out for each other – and that goes for managers too. So while it will be necessary at times to withdraw, to maintain a proper distance, and not pretend to enjoy a wholly informal 'mateyness' with your people, so at other times you will have to be fully engaged, up close and personal.

Levels of intimacy will vary from workplace to workplace. But it is interesting to hear the views of the chef and writer Anthony Bourdain, the author of *Kitchen Confidential*, once a notorious tyrant of the 'pass', now a more mellow and reflective observer of his trade: 'These are your co-workers, your friends, the people you will be counting on, leaning on for much of your career, and they in turn will be looking to you to hold up your end', he says in his book. 'Show them some respect by bothering to know them. Learn their language.'

Small is beautiful

This echoes something Charles Handy says in his interview with us in Appendix 1. Some business units are just too big. There is no chance of intimacy developing, or of rich and productive relationships growing between the manager and the team. We should always watch out when managers have too many people supposedly 'reporting' to them. The Chinese business Haier, which is the world's biggest manufacturer of fridges and washing machines, has broken itself down into 2,000 business units, run almost like family businesses with plenty of autonomy. Haier is deliberately trying to keep the distance between managers and the managed to a minimum.

Feedback

Managers worry about giving feedback, rightly. The whole conversation can be difficult for both parties to it. But remembering the importance of managing distance might help before the next 'difficult' conversation.

Kim Scott, author of the book *Radical Candor* (2017), makes several good points about this. Why not start the conversation by asking for some feedback first? This shows you can take it as well as give it. Admitting that you might be wrong in your perceptions – criticisms – may make any tough comments more palatable.

Saving up observations for one substantial download is a bad idea. Keep the conversation going by offering your view at the time something comes up. And, of course, feedback should be given in person whenever possible. If you are just at the receiving end of an unpleasant e-mail or voicemail, well, you might as well be being managed by a robot already.

Don't be a stranger (not all the time, anyway)

On the motorway you need to maintain a sensible distance between you and the car in front. Managers need to manage the distance between them and their people carefully. But 'keep your distance' is not the right advice. Sometimes you have to move in a lot closer than that.

– MYTH 28 –

BE YOURSELF – IT'S ALL ABOUT AUTHENTICITY

Management takes skill, so just turning up and 'being yourself' isn't enough. Don't be a phony. But don't be lazy either.

What could be simpler than being yourself? You know who you are, don't you? OK, so just be that person. Go back in on Monday and… be yourself.

The life of a manager is a bit more complicated than that. Circumstances change, as do the demands that are made on you. People, outrageously, are different. They can't all be treated in exactly the same way. So managers need versatility. One management style will not fit all teams and all situations.

As Herminia Ibarra explains in our interview with her (see Appendix 4), 'be yourself' is in fact 'terrible advice'. Why? It is not 'because it's not good to be yourself, but… what self are we talking about? We are as many different selves as the roles that we play, in a situation in which we have to perform', she says.

Nor is simply being 'authentic' an adequate game-plan either. What if you are, authentically, a horrible person? Your team will not thank you for your authenticity if the experience of being managed by you is unpleasant. And, as argued above, your authenticity may vary from situation to situation. Does that make it less authentic? In any case, 'authenticity' is a word that has become devalued somewhat through overuse. It should be handled with care.

It ain't what you do it's the way that you do it

In their important book *Why Should Anyone Be Led by You?* (2006), Rob Goffee and Gareth Jones go beneath the surface of the word 'authenticity' to develop a far more useful formulation and piece of management advice. They, too, recognize that 'be yourself' is too simple and too limited as a personal mission statement. Managers need to 'know and show themselves', they say. Disclose who you are and what you care about, where your strengths but also where your weaknesses lie. This will build a richer, more flexible and attractive kind of authenticity. You will show up as someone who is worth listening to.

They sum up their advice as: 'Be yourself, more, with skill.' What this means is: draw on and demonstrate your qualities ('more'), but use them intelligently and sensitively ('with skill'). Judging how to behave, when – 'situation sensing' – is a vital management task. Just 'being yourself' will not do.

Act like a leader, think like a leader

Career progression also raises questions about a kind of authenticity which is fixed and never develops. There was a reason why the coach Marshall Goldsmith used the title *What Got You Here Won't Get You There* for one of his books. We have to move on and change as the challenges that face us change. It is not phony to adapt and build your repertoire of skills as the situation requires.

It is also often said, rightly, that it is not possible to think your way into a new way of behaving. You may have to start trying to behave differently first. And this is why the words in the title of Herminia Ibarra's latest book, *Act Like a Leader, Think Like a Leader* (2015), come in that order. Not because you have to 'fake it until you can make it', but rather that experience shows you will have to try new things out before finding the right style for the context you are in.

We would urge you to read our interview with her in full, but what follows are a couple of highlights from it if you don't have time to read all of it.

Professor Ibarra's particular focus is on those moments of career transition and the 'dilemma of authenticity' such moments present.

One way of dealing with these transitions, she says, is to 'overplay your strengths'. 'That feels hugely authentic', she says. 'It's like saying "This is me!"... [This approach] becomes an anchor in the good sense in that it's our mooring, it helps us make choices; but it becomes an anchor also in the negative sense of keeping us from exploring other strengths and learning to do new things.'

Another problem with stepping up the career ladder, Professor Ibarra argues, is that you may feel obliged to try to copy bosses whose style you have not admired at all. 'It's not attractive,' she says, 'they think those people are political, they think they're manipulative, they think they're not transparent. They don't want to be that way, and they think maybe you have to be that way to be successful... So the transitions are quite fraught with a lot of ambivalence – "I don't know if I want to be that person".'

We shouldn't, Professor Ibarra says, have to spend so much money on books and courses on 'how to be yourself'. And yet: 'If you take a more reflective approach – "who am I, what are my strengths?" – that's only going to anchor you in the past', she says. 'And that's not going to help you figure out how to move forward to a future version of yourself that has a core but that also has learned new things and grown and maybe been surprised, even pleasantly surprised. It's not a case of "fake it till you make it", but it's "experiment until you learn".'

It's not just about you

Lastly, Professor Ibarra helps us raise our gaze a little and avoid complete self-absorption, which is damaging and does little to help us become better managers. Yes, we need to think about how we behave, but fundamentally we also need to think about how our relationships with other people work.

'Authenticity has been so much in the public discourse, people use it as an excuse for anything', she says. '"I don't have to change, I don't have to be a better listener, I don't have to worry about my rough side, I'm just being me" – with the idea that people are happy just to get full transparency... no, people are not happy to get full transparency! They want you to behave like there's some kind of interdependence, and that you have to work with people. It's not just about being yourself, it's about creating productive working relationships, and a culture and climate in which other people can be themselves and say what's on their mind. It's not just about you.'

– MYTH 29 –

DATE OF BIRTH IS DESTINY

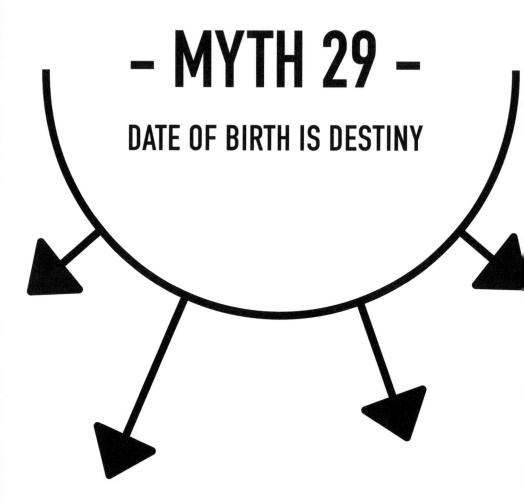

*Managers should make as few assumptions as possible about
their people on the basis of their date of birth.*

Everyone loves a label, don't they? Makes things so much easier to manage.
Put them away in a clearly marked box. It's tidier that way.

It is tempting for employers to do that with staff. How much more efficient to categorize people briskly in certain narrow ways. It saves time. 'Who
are you? Oh, you're Type A/Type B, I see. Well, in that case…'

It sounds a bit crude when you put it like that. And yet this is more or less
what some businesses and organizations have done when it comes to thinking about their people. They make a note of their employees' dates of birth.
And then they put them in a box marked 'Baby-boomer' or 'Generation
X/Y' or 'Millennial'. Job done. Next question.

There is an attractive neatness about generational cohorts, bracketing people off into groups according to when they were born. But it is a mistake to believe that everyone born in a certain timeframe is going to have similar goals, attitudes or aspirations. Thankfully life is more interesting than that.

People mature at different rates and at different times. They reach certain important stages in their life at different times too, regardless of age. So a single 40-something colleague might have more in common with a 25-year-old than another 40-something team member who is married with three children. It would be wrong to say that our 40-something singleton is a classic Gen X person. What is a 'classic Gen X person', anyway? People born at roughly the same time may share some memories and recognize similar cultural references, but that could be where the similarities end.

The neat bracketing off of age cohorts does not allow for what Andrew Hill in the *Financial Times* (2015) has called 'Generation Cusp' – those who were born at the overlapping edges of supposed generational eras. It also does not acknowledge that the age and attitude of parents have a big impact on people's upbringing and the formation of their character. Younger mums and dads are different from older mums and dads. It could be that Napoleon made a more useful observation about date of birth when he said that, to understand someone properly, you have to know what the world was like when they were 20. But even that only goes part of the way to grasping where someone is 'coming from'.

Of course, baby-boomers may share certain characteristics, some attractive, others perhaps less so. Things have gone pretty well for them, by and large. They were born at a good time. Boomers enjoyed some of the advantages of the post-war era of growth, which are not so readily available to subsequent generations. That much is known. More interesting, though, than the clichés about the age groups are the connections that people of different ages make (or fail to make) at work. This is where something dynamic and creative can emerge.

Generation game

Younger people today benefit from the freedoms that earlier generations (boomers especially) marched or protested for. That should be a source of pride and pleasure for the over-50s. The multi-generational workplace – rather like the multi-generational home – is here to stay. We are all going to have to get along together.

As Lynda Gratton and Andrew Scott argue in their book *The 100-Year Life: Living and working in an age of longevity* (2016), the familiar, rigid demarcations of life stages established in the past do not fit with the new world of longer life expectancy and multi-stage working lives. Many people will work until they are 70, or older, and will perhaps have several 'careers' in one extended working life.

'It's a myth that people are finished at 60', Professor Gratton tells us in our interview with her (Appendix 6). 'It's a terrible piece of stereotyping. It's terrible for a couple of reasons. One is that as we live longer we have to work longer. We're going to be working into our 70s and beyond, we can't really be tossed out at 55, it's wrong for the individual. We also know that when people stop working their health deteriorates.

'When I teach I say, "I'm 62 but it's the new 40", and somebody stopped me and said, "Lynda, it's the new 40, plus 20 years of experience." That's the point – as people age, if they've learned anything on the way, they have more to offer.

'That leads on to this myth about the generations. Gen X, Gen Y, boomers – there's very little evidence to support the claims that are made about them. People say, "Oh Gen Y, they love meaningful work." For God's sake, I was a hippy, do you think we didn't want meaningful work?! Or they say, "Gen Y, they're great at technology." We're all perfectly adept at technology. It's really bad because it stereotypes age. Andrew [Scott] and I in the book say, for goodness, sake, look at people for who they are. Stop being myopic about age. Some of the big accounting firms get rid of people at 55 – that's just ridiculous.'

As Charles Handy shows in his book *The Second Curve: Thoughts on reinventing society* (2015), date of birth or the expectations of careers advisers are of little consequence to those who wish to start again, doing something new while they still have the energy and desire to do so.

Age of possibility

Managers should make as few assumptions as possible about their people on the basis of their date of birth. Teams should have a mix of age and outlook. Research by Paul Sparrow at Lancaster University Management School into mixed-age teams at McDonald's showed that the restaurants where old and young worked side by side produced better results (Woods, 2009). It would have been wrong to suppose that this was only a young person's business.

A similar danger exists in the fast-moving world of high-tech, as described by Catherine Turco in her book *The Conversational Firm* (2016). At a so-called 'hack night' in the firm she calls 'TechCo', something very much like the dreaded 'mandatory fun' is arranged, when everyone is forced to talk to each other about their brilliant ideas. OK for informal, laid-back types who are comfortable in an unstructured conversation, a misery for those brought up to behave differently. Exclude mature colleagues and bad things will happen.

How many mistakes could be avoided by asking older workers for their view on some supposed 'innovation' that excited younger managers are trying to introduce? The first internet boom, Web 1.0, was characterized by the extravagant claims being made by wannabe gurus about the power and sheer novelty of the web. Some of it was true. But it took older heads to observe that the frenzy over the potential of internet shopping was slightly misplaced. After all, a hundred years ago people were able to call their butcher and get the boy to cycle round with a joint of beef for the weekend.

Creativity lies in the mix, the cross-fertilization of ideas from people of different ages and backgrounds. Beware the neat myth which claims the young are always better than the old at certain types of activity, or that sometimes only an older head will do.

In particular, today's hype over, and obsession with, millennials is over-done. Millennials do bring valuable skills into the workplace, not least the fact that they are 'digital natives'. But the idea that they are fundamentally different from young people from previous generations is wrong. A large survey of 19,000 21–36-year-olds in 25 countries carried out by the Manpower Group (2016) revealed that young people seek job security at least as much as any other generational cohort. They are not the footloose, fickle lot that some older managers might believe they are.

Young people have always challenged the old, rejected authority, been impatient. And yes, they have always irritated, and occasionally delighted, their elders.

Some of the descriptions offered today about millennials are breathless and absurd. Some are just plain insulting. Not everything has changed, including human nature. And date of birth is not destiny.

- MYTH 30 -

PEOPLE ARE MOTIVATED BY MONEY

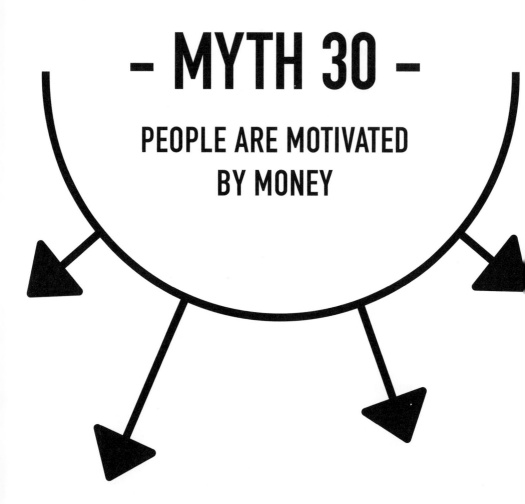

Amazing but true – people want to do a good job. More money won't make them do it but a better (fairer) working environment might.

Carrots and sticks. Or, as the Germans call it, sugar-bread and the whip (*Zuckerbrot und Peitsche*). This is how incentives, and deterrents, have traditionally been thought of at work. Dangle something juicy in front of our noses and on we'll go. But, in case we are tempted to slacken, there is the ever-present knowledge that corporal punishment is just a swish away.

This approach may make sense if you are working with quadrupeds and beasts of burden. But it is a highly reductive view to take of *Homo sapiens*. In fact, it is not merely reductive, but wrong-headed too. After all, *Homo sapiens* wouldn't be very *sapiens* if he or she couldn't work out how to game a so-called incentive scheme. If you give people targets they will try to hit them – as they did at Wells Fargo bank, with disastrous effect. So incentives per se may not do you or your business any good at all. You have to think hard about what sort of behaviour you are trying to promote. In terms of incentives, what you give is what you'll get.

Deep down a lot of us know this. And yet bundles of cash are still dangled, carrot-like, in front of our noses by employers who think – or rather hope – that this will help generate better performance. It is the thinking behind so-called 'performance-related pay', which has turned out to be a dead end and almost complete failure as a management technique, but one which, myth-like, retains some of its illusory power to dazzle the unwary. Excessive executive pay has come about to a large extent because of this basic misconception about motivation, pay and performance. And it hasn't worked: a 10-year study led by Professor Steven Young at Lancaster University Management School found no link between ever-rising pay at the top and the mediocre performance of businesses (Young and Li, 2016).

Competitive chief executives may feel motivated to try to get paid more than their peers. But this ratchet effect does not in itself provide motivation, which would lead to better leadership being displayed or better work being done. Mega pay at the top is about retaining people – dissuading them from leaving – not motivating them. But you can see the flaws in this at once, can't you? The next person to offer more has a chance of dragging a valued chief executive away. And so the upward pay spiral continues in the way that it has done for over 20 years.

It's the taking part that counts. And the winning

Some have likened life inside the organization to a tournament. The concept was popularized by the economists Edward Lazear and Sherwin Rosen, who first wrote about it in the early 1980s. In this way pay could be said to motivate people, but at one remove: you are motivated to try to attain the levels of pay above you in the corporate hierarchy. We used to call that process 'ascending the career ladder'.

But do you really want people trying to rise higher in the business essentially because they just want to earn more money? In an investment bank or a sales team you might understand such an uncomplicated approach. But work that is rewarding in the broadest sense offers people a lot more than just money. Meaningful career progression involves getting better at your job, not just being paid more for it. It means providing a valuable service for people, and also, of course, leading and managing others. Not all rewards are financial. And the most powerful form of motivation, intrinsic as opposed to extrinsic motivation, comes from within, as Fred Herzberg showed (discussed in Myth 22).

Who's gonna drive you home?

A solid blow was struck against the crude use of cash as a motivator with the publication of Daniel Pink's book *Drive* in 2010. Drawing on extensive psychological research, he pointed out that there was plenty of evidence which pointed to other factors as being more important in promoting intrinsic motivation.

While fair pay, and a sense of being fairly paid, matters, Pink suggested that three other aspects of work are more important: a sense of autonomy, the chance to develop mastery, and working with purpose.

Autonomy is what, in part, distinguishes a real live human worker from a robot (see Myth 23). It means having the freedom to exercise choice, and not feeling unduly constrained by rules or management. When work becomes repetitive and heavily regulated, intrinsic motivation subsides. So good managers try to offer as much freedom as they reasonably can.

Building mastery matters because it reinforces a sense of career progression and professional skills development. In short, mastery feels like progress and continuity. Mastery may also be transferable in a world where employers are reluctant to make long-term promises to their people. Mastery you can take with you if you have to move on. An employer that encourages employees to develop their skills and capabilities will win more trust from staff. The psychological contract will be maintained. There will be reciprocity in the employer–employee relationship. This too will motivate.

Lastly, it helps to have a true and proper purpose at work. (Rob Goffee and Gareth Jones talk about work having 'significance'.) When you have purpose you don't need such a big rule book. You don't need such extensive team briefings. You don't even need so much supervisory management. People know what they are supposed to be getting on with, and how, because they share and understand a common purpose. We all know what it's like to be served by a business that knows what it is about. (Sadly it is a pretty rare experience.) It follows that having a strong purpose can give you an advantage. A sense of purpose is also profoundly motivating.

It's a rich man's world

We should manage people, Peter Drucker once suggested, as if they were volunteers. This is a different way of saying that we can place too much importance on the role of money as an incentive or a motivating factor. Of course people should be fairly paid, and generously paid where possible and merited. Bad or unfair pay clearly demotivates, as research from the CIPD (2015) has shown. Life is expensive, and most of us have to work to earn a living.

But when money is the chief target, the main goal, the ultimate carrot, things can go wrong. We saw that most clearly in the financial crisis which built up over the last decade. This insatiable desire for more... it does us no good. Comparing ourselves with others, and trying to match the lifestyles of those richer than us, is no good either. With longer working lives ahead of us, the risk of getting trapped in a job you hate because of your need for a large monthly pay cheque will grow. But 30 or 40 years is a long time to spend doing something you don't enjoy, and a waste of 'your one wild and precious life', as the poet Mary Oliver called it.

Purpose, mastery and autonomy make better goals for working life than money. Deep down you know this is true.

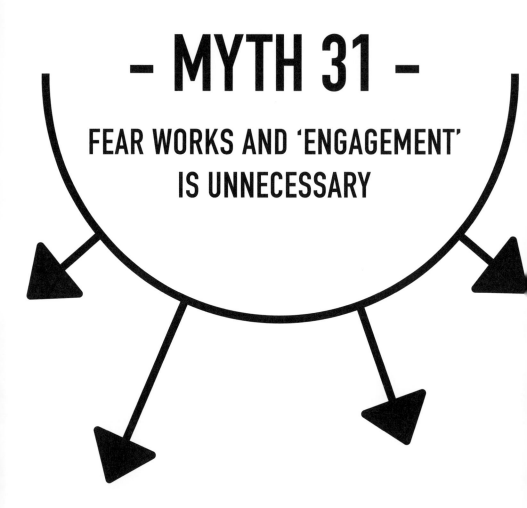

– MYTH 31 –

FEAR WORKS AND 'ENGAGEMENT' IS UNNECESSARY

We don't need mill-owner bosses anymore. Bullies always lose out in the end. You need to engage with engagement.

The film director Alfred Hitchcock could be intolerant of needy actors. When one, struggling to get into character to perform a scene, asked him what his 'motivation' was, Hitchcock replied: 'Your salary.' There have always been (and always will be) bosses who take a similarly uncomplicated view of managing people. According to them, workers should just get on with it and do as they're told.

Such bosses are followers – even if they don't know it – of what the American psychologist Douglas McGregor called 'Theory X'. Theory X managers have pretty low expectations of their staff. They presume that people will try to get away with doing as little work as possible, and therefore need constant supervision. Since early industrialization there has been a need for management, which ensures that production targets are hit and deadlines are met. And where work mainly involves the repetition of fairly simple tasks, there is a case for the Theory X approach. More complicated and less predictable work probably requires a different sort of approach.

This alternative, McGregor said, could be labelled 'Theory Y'. A Theory Y boss believes that people want to work and will commit energy to it, as long as they feel involved in the process and not merely dictated to. A Theory Y boss will ask and discuss, not tell. It is a more participative style. These ideas were set out in McGregor's *The Human Side of Enterprise* (1960).

Floggings will continue until morale improves

For two decades now, one of the most elusive but fashionable management concepts has been 'employee engagement'. Survey data appear to tell a worrying story. The Gallup organization, which has been tracking employee attitudes for many years, says that in the United States only a third of employees feel truly engaged in their work, and worldwide the figure is even lower – as few as 15 per cent are engaged (Clifton, 2017). That is a hell of a lot of people turning up to work who apparently don't really care about what they are doing. Such people cannot usually be scared, Theory X style, into raising their performance, at least over the medium to long term. Some parts of the service economy can survive almost indefinitely with a disengaged, lowly paid workforce. But in jobs of any greater complexity this would be bad news. If engagement levels are really as low as this, no wonder the developed world has a chronic low-productivity problem.

A sceptic asks: what is this thing called engagement?

Employee engagement, being essentially an abstract and quite hard-to-measure concept, has provoked some healthy scepticism, most notably from Rob Briner, professor of organizational psychology at Queen Mary, University of London (profile, Queen Mary University of London). Professor Briner has posed two fundamental questions to the advocates of employee engagement:

1 Do increases in engagement actually cause any increases in performance?

2 Do engagement interventions increase engagement levels and subsequently increase performance?

He argues that we cannot answer 'yes' to these questions with great confidence as, in his opinion, robust evidence has not been established to support these claims. A research firm like Gallup would doubtless contest that. Gallup offers results from large surveys into employee attitudes and performance, arguing that, for example, in business units where there are high levels of engagement, absenteeism can be around 40 per cent lower and productivity 17 per cent higher. Earnings per share can be four times higher at businesses with high engagement levels, and so on.

Perhaps in the end this feels a bit like a leap of faith. For the truly, deeply sceptical no data will ever confirm that something called 'engagement' can make a measurable or sustainable difference to business performance. Others will be happy to pursue employee engagement as a worthwhile management goal. It's a bit like the Theory X and Theory Y contrast. But are we really saying that, if we don't believe in engagement, we may as well believe in management by fear?

If it looks like a duck, walks like a duck and quacks...

What is the opposite of employee engagement? It is dejection, inertia, cynicism and despair. Is that what we want from our workforces? A survey by YouGov in 2015 found that 37 per cent of UK workers felt their job was making no meaningful contribution to the world (Dahlgreen, 2015). What a miserable thought to have in your mind when you start your shift. Just as the French philosopher Pascal said it was worth having a bet on faith, so giving employee engagement a try seems like a wise course of action.

OK, so it is hard to pin down or quantify precisely. But surely, as the American judge Potter Stewart said about pornography, you know it when you see it. Some workplaces buzz with energy, some don't. Some colleagues come up with ideas, make creative suggestions, suggest improvements, and some don't. Some people enjoy their work, are committed to it and 'go the extra mile', and some don't. The former are engaged, and the latter are not.

Engagement beats fear

Machiavelli may have said that it was better to be feared than loved, if you cannot be both, but today's workplace is not a scene of murderous Florentine intrigue… at least, it shouldn't be. Being feared may help your team hit a short-term deadline. There are some work environments – the newsrooms of certain newspapers, for example – where fear is still regularly used as a management weapon. But these are the exception.

In the emerging world of 'knowledge work', and with the growing need to work collaboratively with technology (see Myth 23), the idea that fear is a healthy or constructive emotion to go through at work is primitive and misguided. Rather, we need engaged workers who draw on all their talents and ideas, who feel enabled rather than inhibited.

Some bosses will be too frightened themselves to give engagement a chance. But natural selection will deal with them. Their best people will leave in search of others who let them perform to their best.

It is those bosses who manage by fear who should be really frightened.

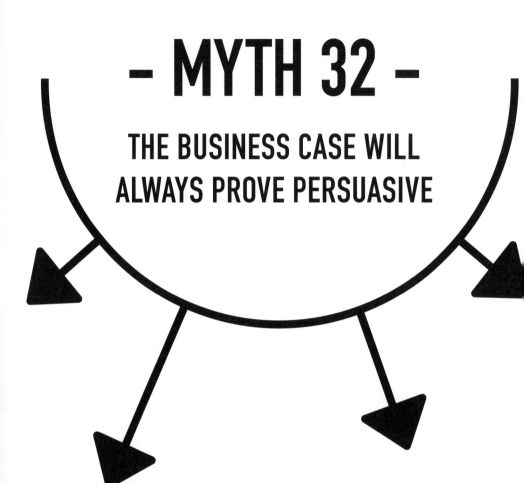

- MYTH 32 -

THE BUSINESS CASE WILL ALWAYS PROVE PERSUASIVE

People are not rational. Don't appeal to logic. Appeal to emotion.
And if that fails, change the rules. Or just behave better.

Hard-headed rationality: that's what business is about, right? Facts and figures. Percentages. Evidence. To be 'business-like' is to be unsentimental and efficient, rejecting superstition in favour of data. If you want to persuade a business leader to do something, then appeal to his or her reason and preference for empiricism. Show how the bottom line will benefit and you will be away.

This is what we might want to believe. Unfortunately it is not true. 'We are not rational, we are rationalizing', says Keith Grint, a professor at Warwick Business School. Or, as others have put, it: we feel before we think. Gut feel or emotion comes first, and only subsequently do we find the post-hoc arguments to justify those feelings.

Drawing on Daniel Kahneman and Amos Tversky's work on 'system one and two' thinking, some have compared the 'rational', more contemplative mind (system two) to a rider who is sitting on top of an elephant (system one, the quicker, more instinctive mind). When the elephant really wants to move somewhere, there is little the rider can do about it.

Rationality, in business at any rate, is probably much less common than we think it is. Or, at least, we tend to hold out too much hope for it. This partly explains why the so-called 'business case' for something is harder to make successfully than it should be. Facts may just not cut it.

I can't believe you are even asking that

Even that phrase, the 'business case', can make the heart sink a little. It feels like someone is trying too hard to convince us of something that should be self-evident. There is a glaring paradox here. If business people were even half as rational as they claim to be, why has it proved so difficult to make a successful business case for greater diversity, or for more humane management practices, or for more flexibility at work? You can list all the potential advantages of changing the way you work. You can point to the disappearance from the workplace of women in their 30s, or their decision not to return to work after having children. You can highlight the findings of audits which reveal how lacking in ethnic diversity you might be, and what consequences this could have for attracting and retaining more interesting candidates, or for thinking and acting more creatively, or for satisfying customers.

But what actually changes? How persuasive is this 'business case'? Are there lots more women at the top? Are the over 50 per cent of graduate recruits who are female still in the business 10 years later? Is your organization still 'hideously white'? Can everyone work flexibly if they want to? Executives nod during the meeting when the 'business case' presentation is being made, but then... inertia at best, active resistance at worst. These serious, rational, business-like businesspeople find the business case utterly resistible.

Rationality crumbles when it is up against prejudice and the selfish instinct to preserve a status quo that has served some people very well until now.

When an experienced headhunter was asked recently why practical businesspeople did not act in response to business cases, his startled reaction was striking. 'I can't believe you are even asking that', he said. To him it was self-evident that, whatever they might sign up to in public, business leaders were never going to let a mere business case persuade them to do anything they didn't like the sound of. (The one possible exception to this is in the area of the efficient use of natural resources, where a straight cost-saving argument can actually lead to better behaviour. But even here this is more about cash than a conscious conversion to 'the business case for sustainability'.)

Get real

Is it all over, then, for the 'business case'? Not necessarily. It turns out that using a business case can, if nothing else, serve as useful cover for more delicate or sensitive conversations that executives might be uncomfortable having.

On matters of diversity or equal opportunities, for example, some leaders might feel a moral pressure to behave better and 'do the right thing'. But they may be working in an environment in which admitting to moral feelings might not look good. It may not sound tough or ruthless enough, for example, or sufficiently financially driven.

Dr Louise Ashley of Royal Holloway, University of London (profile, Royal Holloway University of London), has argued that in such circumstances describing a business case can help executives avoid having the more explicitly moral (and therefore awkward) conversation. It is almost as if everyone knows that they don't really believe the business case, but it sounds more purposeful and commercial than simply arguing for more ethical practices.

Head versus a brick wall: who will win?

Campaigners who keep working and never give up are to be admired. Sometimes you need unreasonable people to make things change. However, it is time, after three decades, to find a cleverer and more effective way of campaigning than simply churning out 'the business case' for this or for that.

Business is not listening to the business case. It switches off. It has heard it all before. And it is not buying.

Sometimes the right thing to do is the right thing to do. If business is to win back trust and some of its lost reputation, it is simply going to have to behave better, and be seen to be behaving better. Not because of legislation, or the threat of legislation. But because it is the right thing to do.

As a manager, you should worry less about trying to persuade bosses with the business case for something. Instead, tell them that you just want to do the right thing. You may be pleasantly surprised by their reaction. And if not, you'll know that it is probably time to find somewhere better to work.

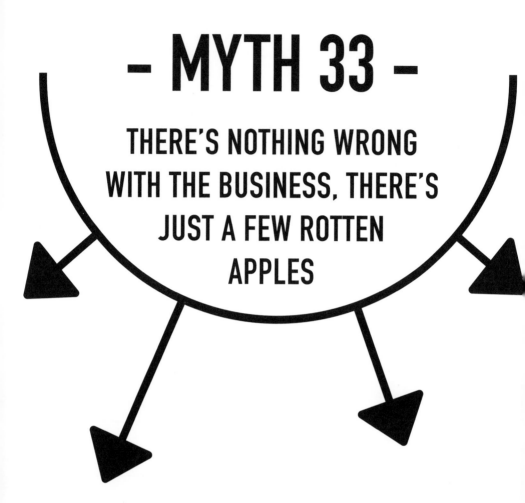

– MYTH 33 –

THERE'S NOTHING WRONG WITH THE BUSINESS, THERE'S JUST A FEW ROTTEN APPLES

Systems make people behave badly. When things go wrong you need to look at the whole system, not just scapegoat those who get caught.

It is hard to see the whole business from the top. 'The top is the worst place to manage an organization: looking down on everybody else', Henry Mintzberg says. 'Try the ground instead.' At the top, not all the real news gets through to you. Managerial filters and self-censorship come between you and the truth. Advisers may tell you what they think you want to hear – that is certainly one way a professional adviser can hold on to a client. But as with the phony tailors telling the emperor that his non-existent finery was a stupendous new outfit, such advice can leave you embarrassingly exposed.

Formal structures and organization charts can create the illusion of order. When things go wrong, it is easy to pick up the chart and draw an arrow pointing to the defective part. This is the reassuring story senior managers can tell themselves. It wasn't us, it was them. There was nothing wrong with the organization. It was just those few 'rotten apples' in the barrel who spoiled it for the rest of us.

But this is too convenient and self-serving. It ducks the real issue. At Halifax Bank of Scotland (HBOS), in the run-up to the financial crisis, the bank's head of group regulatory risk, Paul Moore, reported that badly designed sales targets and weak risk controls were putting the health of the business in danger (Moore, 2015). The reward for bringing this important information to light was... the sack. This was in 2004, almost four years before the bank was to require an emergency rescue (by Lloyds TSB) and an eventual vast government bail-out.

It was easy for top management to discount Moore's warnings as the crazed mutterings of an awkward colleague. (Moore was, by his own admission, an awkward colleague.) But by failing to see the problem as the structurally flawed system of the bank, and limiting their focus to one irksome co-worker, management fell down on the job.

In the *Evening Standard* Anthony Hilton (2016) summarized the issue well. Companies the size of HBOS can grow to such an extent that they lose coherence and are hard to manage, he wrote – which is why targets and 'incentives' are used to try to hold the thing together.

But: 'These are normally so badly designed that they bring out the worst in people, destroy culture, reward bad behaviour and reinforce those tendencies which make employees tribal and self-serving', Hilton added. There may be some rotten apples in the system. But it is the system that has made them rotten.

Systems thinking

We need to consider businesses and organizations as systems. The system provides the context, the territory on which people will operate and in which work will get done, or not. It is the flow of work and output through the system that counts. This was the approach that lay behind the growth and dominance of Toyota – inspired by the thinking of Taiichi Ohno – until it became too big and chased growth in a manner that militated against its own ethos.

The late Russ Ackoff, formerly a professor at the Wharton School at the University of Pennsylvania, was arguably the greatest popularizer of systems thinking in the Western world. He too would have rejected the 'rotten apples' diagnosis – excuse – deployed by complacent leaders of failing organizations. What are people set up to do? How does the work flow? Can people make mistakes and learn from them? These are some of the questions a systems thinker asks.

Too much management involves 'doing the wrong thing righter', Ackoff used to say. Far better to do the right thing wrong, and learn how to improve. And above all, recognize that you are in a system. You cannot solve a problem by tweaking part of a system, he said. That would be like putting a too powerful engine in a car that cannot handle it. You have to consider the car as a whole.

This has implications for managers in how they work together. Ackoff used to tell a story about how he had visited one of the great US car-makers, and that as he made his way up the management hierarchy, each level told him he had to go higher to where the power and influence were. And when he finally met the CEO, he told Ackoff: 'You should be speaking with my subordinates – I need their support to make all this happen' (Stern, 2007). They were all in a system, and yet they didn't appear to know it.

Your call is unimportant to us

If you've ever had a frustrating experience dealing with a call centre – that would probably be roughly 99.8 per cent of everyone reading this book – your first instinct may have been to blame the poor operative who was struggling to answer your questions. But it was not their fault, of course. Bad design of work flow, and the disempowerment of frontline staff, guarantees disappointment. The people at the end of the line are unable to help. Indeed, they may well have been given a perverse incentive to get you off the line and on to another colleague as quickly as possible. This all leads to what the noted systems thinker John Seddon calls 'failure demand': customers become trapped in a system that cannot solve their problems (Seddon). A lot of futile work is created. But nothing valuable gets done. It's not the workers who are bad. The system is.

Fantasy island

In his award-winning book *Swimming with Sharks: My journey into the alarming world of the bankers*, the Dutch writer and anthropologist Joris Luyendijk (2015) described the amoral system in which financial professionals are trapped. He spent two years interviewing over 200 people for the *Guardian*'s 'Bankers blog', which he later turned into the book.

He imagined at one point what would happen if you removed everybody currently employed in the system and replaced them with a new cohort of ethically sound people: 'I am convinced that were we to pack off the entire City [of London] to a desert island and replace them with a quarter of a million new people, we would see in no time the same kind of abuse and dysfunctionality', he wrote. 'The problem is the system, and rather than angrily blaming individual bankers for acting on their perverse incentives we should put our energy into removing those incentives.'

But almost a decade on from the financial crisis the system, fundamentally, has not changed. People still 'chase yield' and 'pick up pennies in front of the steamroller'. And that means that the next crash cannot be far away.

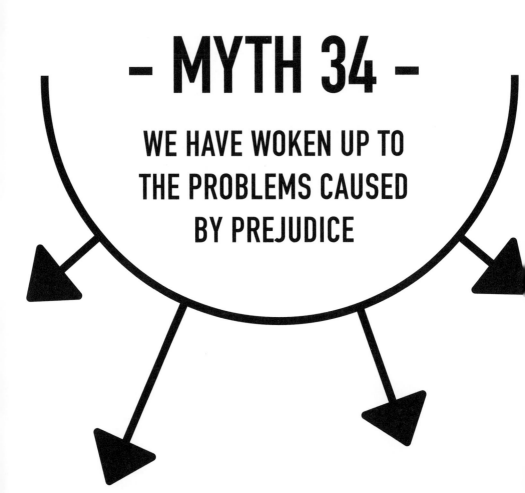

- MYTH 34 -

WE HAVE WOKEN UP TO THE PROBLEMS CAUSED BY PREJUDICE

It's still far too white and male at the top. Some may claim prejudice has been driven out. They are badly wrong.

A startling statistic: in the United States, 62 per cent of LGBT (lesbian, gay, bisexual, transgender) graduates say that, having been open about their identity at college, they felt they had to conceal it again on starting their careers, according to the Human Rights Campaign. Just reflect on that for a moment. Young people, as they begin their working lives, and having experienced some freedom and equality while studying, feel forced to hide their true identity when going to work.

First jobs can be challenging enough. There is so much to learn and so many new ways of doing things to get used to. The idea that, in a daunting setting, you have to put up a façade about your true identity sounds dreadful. This can only heighten the stress of an already stressful situation (Sandhu, 2014).

Consider too the experience of BME (black and minority ethnic) employees in workplaces that remain overwhelmingly white. Where are the signs that they will have a fair chance to get on? Who are the role models at the top? There are only two non-white FTSE 100 chief executives, fewer even than the number of female ones (seven). In the public sector, too, there are some horrendous gaps. In the UK, only 2 per cent of NHS Trusts are chaired by people from a BME background, a tiny fraction of the UK population (and the NHS workforce) that has BME origins. The experience of too many talented employees is to look around the office and be confronted with a sea of white faces, particularly in senior roles.

A change is gonna come...?

We have already considered the damaging lack of women at the top (Myth 14). And this after decades of debate, campaigning, protesting and limited legislative reform. The old guard, and old prejudices, cling on. Economic inequality, manifested in the high cost of housing in cities, is making inheritance an even more important factor for people's life chances, further entrenching that inequality.

Progressive types may have laughed as reactionaries denounced 'political correctness' over the past two decades. But those sneers should have been combated much more aggressively. Donald Trump rose to power after an extended demolition job on what he called politically correct talk. But fairness, justice, respect, equality of opportunity, decency and basic human courtesy are not matters of political correctness. They are the building blocks of a good society – and a good workplace.

We may not like quotas but, in the phrase often attributed to the former EU Commissioner Viviane Reding, 'we'd like what they'd do'. The powerful have chosen to resist moves to create greater equality and fairness at work or, at least, have done too little about it. People at the top may or may not be aware of their prejudices and blind spots. But even where they know there is a problem there is a lack of will to do enough about it.

It is, sadly, a huge myth that any of the battles on equal opportunities have been won. In our harsh political climate, where some unacceptable and long-suppressed views are being given voice once again, further legislative action is required to even up the chances facing talented but overlooked minorities. That is not PC bullsh*t. It is hard economic necessity.

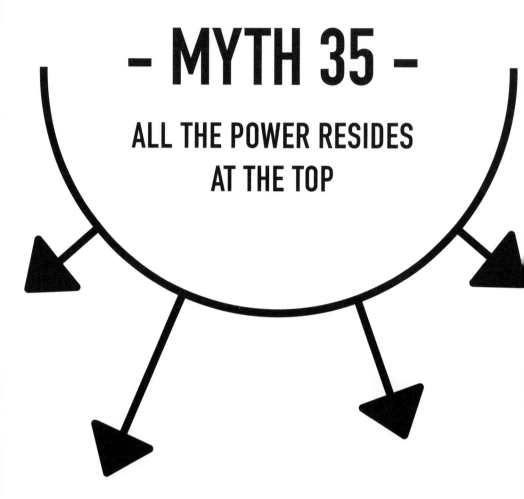

– MYTH 35 –

ALL THE POWER RESIDES AT THE TOP

*We worry too much about a few bosses high up. The real action,
and power, often lies below. Worry about that!*

Leaders matter, and bosses can be powerful. This much is true. They may
have the final say in meetings, or on big decisions. The buck will stop with
them. But this sense or impression of power is misleading. The job title may
sound good, and the pay package may be vast. But how much power does
the boss really have?

'In management we have tended to make everything so hierarchical',
Professor Lynda Gratton tells us in our interview with her (Appendix 6).
'A manager is the most senior person. But actually the manager may be
simply the person who is responsible for a task... the role of the manager
is to have protocols... and the job of the manager is to take people through
those protocols.'

In fact we risk being distracted by the trappings of power, and pay insufficient attention to where the action really is, out there in the business, on the 'shop floor', where customers meet sales staff, where reality bites. Selling more stuff, or providing a necessary public service promptly and efficiently? That's powerful.

As levels of education have risen, and the complexity of work has increased, greater demands have been made on employees. This makes them powerful, if only their managers could see it. Instead of nervously looking up the management chain in anticipation of the next command, or to anticipate and avoid senior executive displeasure, middle managers and supervisors should worry about the people they are working with. The frontline staff have the power to make or break the business. So attention must be paid.

It was Vineet Nayar, the former boss of the Indian IT and outsourcing company HCL, who devised and popularized the notion of the 'employees first, customers second' enterprise (Nayar, 2010). At the heart of this simple approach lies a recognition of where the power – and value – in a business truly lies. You make money by selling things, by completing transactions. And this will happen if the staff dealing with customers are confident and comfortable, ready to do their job. (Online shopping has altered the nature of many transactions. But by no means all of them. And the essential focus on employees' needs still holds.)

Recognizing the centrality of your staff to the success of the organization means recognizing the power they have, either to do good work or to harm the enterprise with poor performance or, worse, sabotage. Employees have a power that should be respected, if not actually feared.

The people are revolting

The electoral earthquakes which hit both the UK and the United States in 2016 – the vote for Brexit and the election of President Trump – also served to show that, in the words of the dean of Bath University's school of management, Veronica Hope Hailey, 'the powerless can be powerful'. Both these unexpected outcomes – unexpected by most of the 'elites', that is – felt rather like a protest coming up from the shop floor to let the boss class know that the workers had had enough. It was not good enough for those at the top to tell others that everything was getting better and would be fine, that they should trust those in authority and let them carry on in charge. That line did not hold on either side of the Atlantic.

As Joan Williams, a professor at the University of California, Hastings College of the Law, wrote in a celebrated *Harvard Business Review* article (2016) just after the US Presidential election, to many voters Hillary Clinton seemed to epitomize 'the dorky arrogance and smugness of the professional elite'. By contrast, she wrote, 'Trump promises a world free of political correctness and a return to an earlier era, when men were men and women knew their place.' His supporters were powerless, but became powerful: 'Today they feel like losers – or did until they met Trump.'

In the UK, 3 million voters who had not made it to the polls in the general election a year earlier turned out and voted to leave the European Union. The opinion pollsters never saw them coming. It was a display of power. The powerless had grabbed the attention of the apparently powerful. It cost the prime minister, David Cameron, his job. And opened up that top position to a new candidate, Theresa May, who had not supported the Leave campaign but found herself in 10 Downing Street complying with the views of the majority of those who had voted. It was a classic case of 'I must follow them, for I am their leader'. So who really exercised power here, senior ministers or ordinary people?

Power to the people

Many managers still instinctively look up the career ladder and wonder how they might climb higher. There are bigger cash prizes for those who rise, but also bigger responsibilities, more pressure, probably more time away from home… and further to fall. It's a long way down.

Some of these top management jobs are stretching beyond belief, with a permanently full inbox and a working day that starts too early and ends too late. And somewhere in that schedule you are supposed to be able to think, too. Perhaps this pursuit of power is misguided, or simply a bad choice for many people who may not realize it, or like to admit it.

There is, or should be, dignity in labour, at all levels. And recognizing the power and importance of even apparently mundane tasks might offer a more satisfying career path for a lot of managers. Why not just keep getting a few simple but important jobs done? Why not keep frontline staff and customers happy? That's a pretty powerful idea.

We have traditionally seen organizations as pyramids of power, with most of the excitement and glamour residing at the top. But while there may seem to be executive power at the sharp, or pointy, end, there is more power lower down than is obvious at first sight. The power to do a good job. The power to do good. It's down at the base of the pyramid where people keep their feet on the ground.

So let others pursue their dreams of power if they want to, as they struggle to rise above their colleagues, whom they see more as competitors than collaborators. Some managers, possibly wiser ones, will choose not to take the express elevator to the 47th floor, but rather will stay close to the action nearer to sea level. They will experience the satisfaction and power of getting the job done with and through people, which is really what good management is all about.

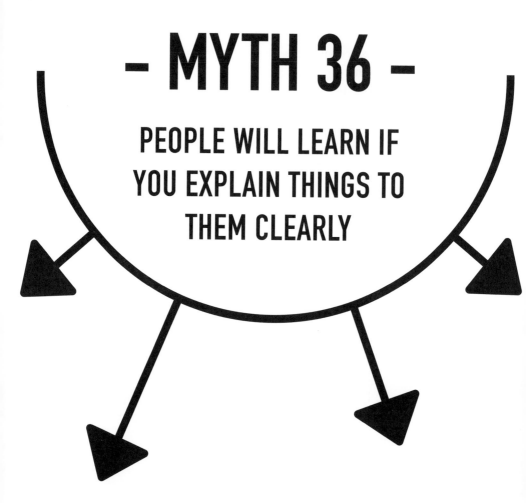

− MYTH 36 −

PEOPLE WILL LEARN IF YOU EXPLAIN THINGS TO THEM CLEARLY

We're only human – all of us. People will make mistakes and not get things right first time. That's OK. Be firm, but be patient.

Staff attitude surveys can be dangerous. Managers, like the rest of human-kind, cannot bear too much reality. Little makes leaders' hearts sink faster than the feedback which reveals that, in spite of extensive and repeated efforts, colleagues out there do not understand (or perhaps do not believe in) the 'vision' they have been offered. 'But we've communicated this!', the exasperated boss will cry. 'We spent all that money on the brochure, we had the off-site event, and I send out a regular e-mail to all staff telling them what we're up to and why…'

People are busy, distracted, stressed and sceptical. They have been through 'initiatives' before. They might actually quite like their work, when they are allowed to get on with it. For the most part, though, the message coming down from the top will be regarded as being 'dubious until proved useful'. The brochures and the e-mails will go unread.

Myles Downey, the executive coach, suggests that 'communication is a result, not an intention' (conversation with authors). This is a good point. Just communicating at people – making noise – is not enough. Communication has not taken place until people have heard, understood and believed what you have said. There has to be a credible message which can be easily grasped. A G Lafley, the long-time chief executive at Procter and Gamble, says that when he is trying to communicate with staff the message should be 'Sesame Street simple' (Sutton, 2008). He is not being patronizing. He is simply recognizing how busy people are and how little mental energy they may have to engage with new information. This is tactful, not condescending.

Dave Ulrich, the HR guru, advises that leadership teams should 'expect to share a message ten times for every one time that it will be heard and understood' (Stern, 2009). That is not an encouraging ratio. But it may be a realistic one.

Frailty, thy name is... us

At an event at Cass Business School in London in 2016, the management guru Tom Peters spoke with characteristic energy and flair on, among other things, the difficulty of getting things right at work (see interview with Tom in Appendix 9). Towards the end of the evening one questioner asked why, since people like Peters had been thinking about management for such a long time, and since so many good managers and leaders had tried to make things better, did so many things still go wrong in businesses and organizations? Why were people apparently unable to learn lessons from their own and other people's mistakes?

Peters paused, thought for a moment, and then gave a heartfelt and resounding answer: 'I DON'T KNOW!'

The audience laughed, loudly. But – as is often the case – Peters had managed to convey an important point in an apparently light-hearted way. Unlike robots, people are... people. They are not perfect. They make mistakes. And organizations, designed by people, are flawed, too. Systems go wrong, repeatedly. When you add in management to this situation things do not necessarily get better. (Peters has been working on this for over four decades and still doesn't know for sure how to fix it!) Let us repeat that key Peter Drucker quote: 'So much of what we call management consists in making it difficult for people to work.'

This all suggests that we should not necessarily be too hard on colleagues when things go wrong. Repeating the same mistake, again and again, is intolerable. But making a mistake because you are in a new situation of which you have had no previous experience, well – that's life. And without experimentation, and failure, we cannot learn anything or build anything new.

Churchill may have despaired, in his 'wilderness years', of what he called the 'confirmed unteachability of mankind' and the 'features which constitute the endless repetition of history'. But we need not be so pessimistic, so condemnatory. A more realistic view is: yes, mistakes will be made, and things will go wrong. And that is when recovery and improvement can begin.

- MYTH 37 -

YOU MUST KEEP UP WITH ALL THE NEW MANAGEMENT IDEAS AND GIVE THEM A TRY

Relax about management fads. There will be another one along in a minute. Stick to first principles, not fashion.

It is natural, and probably healthy, to worry about what the competition is getting up to. Are they stealing ahead? Have they found a secret formula? Food companies have long enjoyed building and maintaining a mystique about their magic ingredients, whether it is Coca-Cola's '7X', Colonel Sanders' '11 herbs and spices' or McDonald's 'Big Mac sauce'. (Healthier secret sauces are doubtless available.)

In business, when competition is fierce, the idea that a rival may have latched onto a genius management formula can provoke both envy and paranoia in equal measure. 'What do they know that we don't?', runs the question. 'Are they getting away from us?'

Such nervousness partly explains managers' vulnerability to the illusory power of fads, 'new ideas' that appear quite suddenly, almost from nowhere, but which rapidly acquire adherents and true believers, a bit like members of a cult. Soon the magazine articles are being written, conferences are being held, and management consultancies are producing marketing material which suggests that they have been long-time believers in this great new thing. You will be familiar with those fad-surfing bosses who, like the dedicated follower of fashion in the song by The Kinks, is in polka dots one week and stripes the next.

Fads are the unfortunate if inevitable result of a serious desire: to get better at running things. For over a hundred years, since F W Taylor first codified his ideas about 'scientific management', there has been an outpouring of books and theories. The management consulting industry has benefited enormously from this: if we had never moved beyond simple 'time and motion' studies, the big consultancies would have had much less to talk about, and sell.

Pilgrims on the conference circuit

Professor Eric Abrahamson of Columbia Business School in New York has charted the growth and spread of management fads more thoroughly than most (Abrahamson, 1991). He has described them as 'transitory collective beliefs' that a new (or reinvented) management practice will lead to better results. This is not to say that all fads are rubbish. Only a few are utterly ridiculous. Most have something to recommend them. The problem comes when people sign up to them in full, like converts to a religion. This is a faith-based rather than evidence-based approach to management. Complicated problems, like running businesses and organizations, do not have simple solutions. But a time-pressed and hassled executive is bound to be tempted by the idea that there is a new and simple formula that greatly improves your chances of (or even guarantees) success.

A very brief history of management fads/ideas

Frederick William Taylor's *Principles of Scientific Management*, published in 1911, argued that greater efficiency was within everyone's reach, if you took a more mechanical view of the contribution made by employees. Its logic was harsh: people did not need to think, as such, but they did need to repeat tasks without fuss. The huge production lines of emerging industries, such as car manufacturing, were a monument to Taylorism. Look around even seemingly modern workplaces today. There is still more than a hint of Taylorism about.

As such, scientific management can hardly be called a here today, gone tomorrow fad. But it did help establish that there was a new professional discipline called management, one that was worthy of study and open to new ideas. It also opened the door to the new (and invented) industry of 'management consulting' – these new gurus were formerly simply known as 'cost accountants'. McKinsey rebranded in the 1930s: the 'certified public accountants' became 'accountants and engineers'.

Post-war reconstruction in Japan helped W Edwards Deming and colleagues develop the idea of Total Quality Management (TQM). Driving out waste, drawing on the skills of employees, searching for continuous improvement: these were ideas that struck a chord with Japanese businesses but which, paradoxically, proved harder to make work back in the West. The overblown but under-realized benefits of TQM in the 1980s did much to undermine employees' faith in the management fad industry. In fairness, however, and as is so often the case with fads, it is not so much the idea as the execution of it that is crucial to its success or failure.

Also popular for a time in the 1950s and '60s was the concept of 'Management By Objectives' (MBO – so many of these ideas come ready with their own Three Letter Acronym, or TLA). The apparently uncontroversial idea, popularized by the management writer Peter Drucker, was to maintain your team's aim on specific goals. Sensible enough. Except that different objectives within a business might clash and be incompatible. And teams would be tempted to game the system to pretend objectives were being met when in reality they were not.

Recessionary times in the 1980s and '90s created space for a tough and unflinching approach. The 'corporate killers' of the 1980s 'downsized' (or more euphemistically 'rightsized'), sacking hundreds of thousands of workers. By the early 1990s this technique had been semi-dignified by a new fad (and compulsory TLA label): Business Process Re-engineering (or BPR). This theory gave carte blanche to managers who wanted to carry out radical surgery on their businesses. But re-engineering was easier to speculate about than actually put successfully into practice.

The pendulum was to swing back, of course. The arrival of the internet and the so-called 'new economy' of the late 1990s prompted a return to a less abrasive style of management. The offices of 'Web 1.0' businesses were filled with pool tables, skateboards and beanbags (see Myth 43). Unfortunately, revenue was not seen quite so frequently. And once again, as the economy turned down, toughness was back: 'execution' was hot. 'Lean' became a much-vaunted approach, albeit frequently a too rigid and inflexible one. Today the talk is of 'agility' rather than leanness, and the need to 'pivot'. Some have dabbled with the so-called post-hierarchical mode of 'holocracy' (see Myth 7). Chuck in some 'mindfulness' while you are at it and your early-21st-century fad collection is more or less complete.

Keep calm and carry on

And breathe. As you can see, there is a never-ending, renewable supply of management fads and ideas. This is one sector of the economy where productivity – if not necessarily quality – never seems to be a problem.

New ideas are a good thing. They are worth thinking about, for a bit at least, and possibly worth trying out as an experiment or pilot. But beware the fashionable cool idea that is getting lots of hype before any positive long-term results are visible.

Look out in particular for the megatrend prediction of Big Changes To Come. The optimal period for forward projection, for any aspiring guru, seems to be about 20 years: close enough to matter and be almost imaginable, yet far enough off to be mysterious. And, crucially, when your 20-year-old prediction turns out to be wrong, hardly anyone will remember what you said. But there will always be money to be made making big claims about the future. 'Everyone seems to know the future even though no one has been there yet', says the writer Margaret Heffernan (see our interview with her in Appendix 7).

Remember: human nature has not changed, and the fundamental challenges of managing people have not changed either. Some timeless truths about people: showing them respect, listening to them, setting clear and achievable targets, providing constructive feedback at the right time – all these things matter more than any TLA or funky new idea.

The only fad this book wants to popularize is this: management is an important human activity or task, central to our economic and general well-being. It needs to be done thoughtfully and well. That is all. Crazy or what!

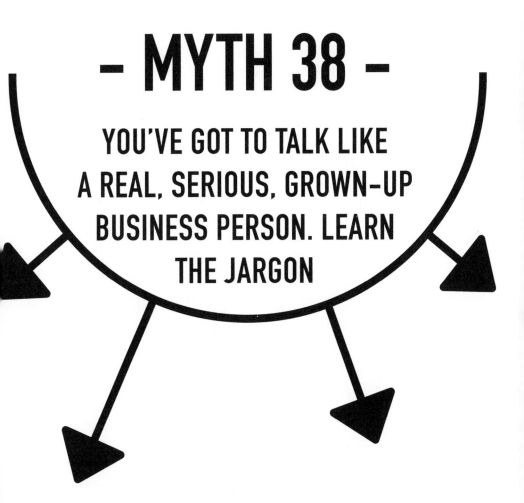

– MYTH 38 –

YOU'VE GOT TO TALK LIKE A REAL, SERIOUS, GROWN-UP BUSINESS PERSON. LEARN THE JARGON

Muddled thinking leads to muddled language.
Speak simply and clearly. Reject the jargon.

All professions, it is said, are conspiracies against the laity. When George Bernard Shaw first expressed that view over a hundred years ago, he had never met a management consultant. But GBS would not have been surprised that in the field of management an entire dictionary of jargon and spurious technical language has emerged. Many crimes are committed every day against the English language, but those perpetrated by managers are among the most heinous.

Why does this happen? Partly it is a question of speed. Who's got time to stop and think about a fresh way of expressing a view when there are a dozen or more clichés ready to deploy? But that is the problem with clichés, of course: using them is a sign that you have stopped thinking. A complete ban on clichés is probably unwise as well as unworkable. Sometimes they may express precisely what you want to say. But in such a rich language as English there should always be a few other words you could use as well.

Join the club

Lazily repeating the language you have heard other bosses use may reflect a certain insecurity on the part of the speaker. It is a way of saying: 'Yes, I'm just like all those other manager-types you have met before.' Using the apparently approved language is a bid to become a member of a perceived in-group, the managerial class. But you are your own person and are free to use your own words. Doing so might even mark you out as something superior.

Get on with it

When you have so little time to gain and hold the attention of colleagues, wasting it with flabby prose is a shame, and a mistake. Their e-mail inboxes are already full. Anything you send them should be concise and easy to read. It should be clear and unequivocal. There should be a point to it.

For those in need of tips on how to sharpen up their language, both written and spoken, it is well worth looking up an essay written by George Orwell in 1945, called 'Politics and the English language'. As the title implies, political rhetoric is one of its main topics. But the essay contains useful advice for anyone who ever has to send a memo or make a short presentation to the team or potential clients.

Orwell is clear: 'Modern English, especially written English, is full of bad habits which spread by imitation and which can be avoided if one is willing to take the necessary trouble. If one gets rid of these habits one can think more clearly', he writes.

He comes up with six sensible rules:

1 Never use a metaphor, simile or other figure of speech which you are used to seeing in print.

2 Never use a long word where a short one will do.

3 If it is possible to cut a word out, always cut it out.

4 Never use the passive where you can use the active.

5 Never use a foreign phrase, a scientific word or a jargon word if you can think of an everyday English equivalent.

6 Break any of these rules sooner than say anything outright barbarous.

Business meeting bingo

OK, since you've been good and read this far, let's consider some of the worst jargony words and phrases, and the bad habits, which pollute our conversations today:

- *Nouns used as verbs*: Something has an impact, it does not 'impact' you. Matters come to the surface – we should not try to 'surface' them. Nouns are nouns and verbs are verbs, and it is usually wise to respect the difference.

- *Drill down*: Do you work on an oil rig? If not, you probably won't be needing to drill down anywhere. Why not just investigate or research things instead?

- *Think outside the box*: Do you mean 'use your imagination'? Why not say so? (The writer James Woudhuysen points out, rightly, that people should continue to think inside their box if they want to come up with good ideas (conversation with authors). It is too tempting to move on before you have finished all the hard work.)

- *Blue-sky thinking*: Sounds unBritish. What do you do on all those grey days? Just call it an ideas session and be done with it.

- *Low-hanging fruit*: Do you work in an orchard? If not, what you are referring to here are some opportunities for short-term success.

- *Reach out*: Means 'to contact'.

- *Revert*: Means 'to reply'.

- *Bandwidth*: Fine if you work in IT/high-tech, not fine if you don't. You mean 'capacity' or 'attention span'.

- *Proactive*: Means 'active'. Please try to stop using this term.

- *Move the needle/dial*: Do you work in a laboratory? If not, you are probably trying to 'make a difference' or 'change' something.

- *Escalate*: This verb features on the scripts given to call centre staff. The call handler promises to 'escalate' your request, which usually means that nothing at all will happen. So, in this context, escalate means 'I will fail to make a note of what you have just told me and will do absolutely nothing about it.'

- *Behaviours*: This is an uncountable noun. People behave in a certain way. Or display certain types of behaviour. The noun should not appear as a plural.

- *Curate*: A grossly overused verb, which really belongs in a (living) museum or art gallery. Otherwise you need 'demonstrate' or 'guide you through'.

- *Going forward*: Spotted first by the great Lucy Kellaway of the *FT*. It means 'in the future'.

- *Leverage*: As a verb it means 'use'.

- *Sub-optimal*: Means 'not as good as it could/should be'.

Here endeth the lesson

You get the point. Have some respect for the people you talk to, and have some respect for yourself. English is a rich, subtle, beautiful language. It is capable of conveying an infinite range of thoughts and feelings. In the hands of great writers and speakers English can be used to powerful effect. There is no law that says our exchanges at work have to be drab, flat, cliché-ridden or vague.

Words matter. Use them carefully, with precision but also with feeling. And reject the tired jargon. You may be surprised how much more successful your dealings with colleagues will be once they recognize that you say what you mean, mean what you say, and never waste their time with empty or meaningless verbiage.

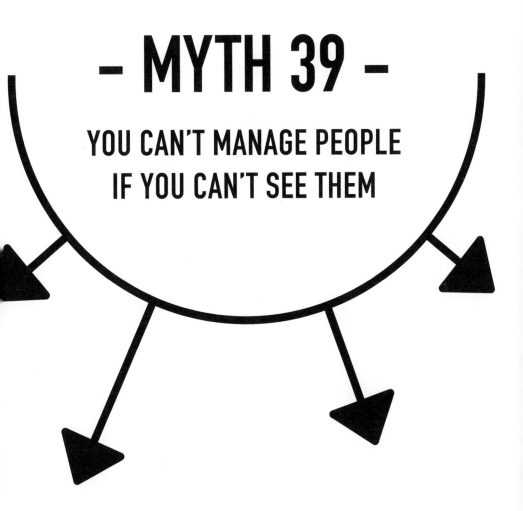

– MYTH 39 –

YOU CAN'T MANAGE PEOPLE IF YOU CAN'T SEE THEM

It's what people do that counts, not how many hours they stay at their desk where you can see them. Trust people to do their work.

Maybe Marissa Mayer's tenure at the web firm Yahoo was bound to end badly.* The company was struggling when she arrived in 2012, continued to struggle under her, and was finally sold to Verizon in 2017 for just under $5 billion, a tiny fraction of its former value. But if one moment signalled the mismatch between the high hopes extended to this Silicon Valley star and the bathetic reality of her performance, it was the memo sent out by the company's head of human resources, Jackie Reses, on Friday 22 February 2013.

'To become the absolute best place to work, communication and collaboration will be important, so we need to be working side-by-side', it ran.

'That is why it is critical that we are all present in our office. Speed and quality are often sacrificed when we work from home. We need to be one Yahoo, and that starts with physically being together' (Swisher, 2013).

Mouths dropped. Lattes were spilt. Here was one of the supposedly forward-looking, new-age mega corporations bringing back some old-economy concepts such as clocking in and, after a day's work, clocking out again. It was all the harder to take as Mayer was at that time a new mother returning to work – but having handily installed a nursery next to her office to allow her to work longer hours. (She once told Bloomberg News that she worked 130 hours a week… do the math, as they say.) Even employees who did only one or two days a week at work were told to start showing up if they wanted to keep their job.

Mayer found little support for this proposal. It went against the grain of modern working life, where mature bosses would trust people to get on with their work away from the office if necessary. Even Sir Richard Branson was moved to blog in criticism. 'This seems a backwards step in an age when remote working is easier and more effective than ever', he wrote (2013). The company was not entirely friendless, however. Someone called Donald Trump tweeted his support – it was 'right to expect Yahoo employees to come to the workplace vs working at home', he said. (Whatever happened to him?)

Out of sight but not out of mind

There is a reason why supervisory management is called supervisory management. You watch people. You look out for them, and at them. It is a traditional, even quaint-sounding term. But it has a long and distinguished history. Management means paying attention. Well-run restaurants and bars, for example, always have a good supervisory manager at their centre. One of the things that went wrong in the run-up to the great financial crisis was that people – bankers – were simply not being supervised well enough. (It is not fair to say that the banks were being run like casinos, by the way. As Chris Brady, professor at Salford Business School, likes to point out, casinos are usually very well-run places. That's why they stay in business. Their managers pay attention and manage risk intelligently.)

The task for managers today is to worry about what people actually do ('outputs'), not where they sit. It's still 'supervisory management'. It's just that you may not always be able to see every member of your team in front of you. New online teamwork technology, such as the 'Slack' system, can allow colleagues to communicate with each other and even re-create so-called 'water cooler moments', even when sitting hundreds or thousands of miles apart.

There will be those for whom the journey in to work is simply impractical, because of caring responsibilities, disability, or the sheer cost of travel. Managers need to remember that there are people who love work – they just hate going to work. If they can work where they are, why shouldn't they?

Proximity matters, and nothing – not even super high-tech video conferencing – can ever truly replace the face-to-face meeting. But technology, managed properly, can make working life both more productive and more agreeable.

In fact, marrying office work with remote working might create the best of all possible worlds, avoiding the perils of 'presenteeism' (simply staying in the office for show without achieving anything) while allowing productivity to rise. As Monideepa Tarafdar, professor at Lancaster University Management School, says: 'Flexible working and "always on" routines have made the traditional nine-to-five workday less meaningful... It may well be that the use of technology that enables a continuous flow of meaningful tasks – and they might be work-related or they might not – is more beneficial for managers' well-being and productivity than this kind of rigid divide' (Tarafdar, 2016).

Virgin on the ridiculous

Sir Richard Branson may not be everybody's cup of tea, nor everybody's idea of a management guru. But on this question of flexible working, and using new technology to get the best results, he talks a lot of sense. Here was how he summed up his view in the blog post he wrote about Yahoo's 'get back to the office!' memo:

> If you provide the right technology to keep in touch, maintain regular communication and get the right balance between remote and office working, people will be motivated to work responsibly, quickly and with high quality. Working life isn't 9–5 any more. The world is connected. Companies that do not embrace this are missing a trick. (Branson, 2013)

Well said, Sir Richard. And, by the way, two years after that Yahoo memo was sent out, many Yahoo employees were still working from home. The new rule never really stuck. People are cleverer than that.

Note

* Did we say Mayer's tenure was bound to end badly? She was paid $200 million in salary and bonuses over that five-year period, plus a final pay-off of $186 million in stock. So, not too badly when you think about it.

– MYTH 40 –

WHO NEEDS EMPLOYEES ANYWAY? GET WITH THE GIG ECONOMY

If you're going to be an employer, be an employer. Provide decent pay and benefits. Don't cheat or pretend workers are self-employed.

Accenture, the consultancy, calls it the 'liquid workforce'. They predict that 43 per cent of the US workforce will be freelancers by 2020. And in a series of breathless and hyperbolical claims they try to describe this exciting new employee-less future (Accenture, 2017): 'Within 10 years, we will see a new Global 2000 company with no full-time employees outside of the C-suite', Accenture say. 'The liquid workforce is rapidly becoming the new normal for how businesses organize themselves', they declare. 'Traditional methods cannot keep up with the pace of change in the digital age', they add. We need to 'optimize workforce responsiveness with insightful analytics that provide a real-time view of organizational capabilities.'

Gosh. So: no more employees, eh? Not so fast. The hype has gone too far. The labour market is changing, and the nature of some jobs is changing too. But not everything has been turned upside down in the way that certain management consultants touting for work might try to suggest.

Some things change, some stay the same

The media discussion is taken up with big claims about the so-called 'gig economy', the apparent rise in self-employment, the growth in 'zero-hours' contracts, and the end of permanent employment as a viable option. But, as the UK Labour Force Survey shows (Office for National Statistics), four in five people at work (whether full- or part-time) are employees with a permanent contract. Yes, at 4.7 million, there are a lot of self-employed people in the UK economy, but as a share of total employment this is in fact only 3 per cent higher than it was in 1986. Yes, zero-hours contracts have grown, but there are still under a million of them (in a workforce of 32 million), and according to survey data from the CIPD (2013) there is a reasonable level of satisfaction with them from both the employer and employee point of view.

This term 'gig economy' is also used and abused. It really all depends on what sort of gig you are talking about. Some are well paid and probably quite civilized – management consultants (them again), designers, writers, IT experts and so on. Others – delivery drivers, care workers, cycle couriers, taxi drivers and take-away food deliverers – will be on very different terms. Quantifying the size of this part of the economy is hard. The terminology and legal status of those doing the work in this category are contested and are changing. Many workers at the lower-paid end of this sector seem to have been classified, inaccurately, as self-employed, even when they are fully dependent on one business for their income, and have to wear a uniform and be told what to do by a web application owned by that business. The legal dodge to claim that these workers are sole traders may have saved those businesses a lot of money in tax and benefits, but it is unseemly. It is wrong. It is a nasty way to boost your profits.

For many years employers have claimed that their people are 'their biggest asset'. The truth has been that only some of their people have been seen as an asset. Some employers have made it pretty clear that they have 'people who matter' and 'people who do not matter', as the former HR director of the supermarket group Morrisons, Norman Pickavance, has put it. The coming of the 'gig economy' has made this sort of stratification in the labour market even more apparent. Hence the claims from Accenture about the inevitable coming of a global business with 'no full-time employees outside of the C-suite'.

Virtually if not virtuously an employer

Of course, the new-found flexibility, made possible by apps, is powerful, and an attractive option for some businesses, workers and customers. The problems come when employers try to duck out of the responsibility of being an employer. They are happy to keep their costs right down. But they shirk their duty to provide proper benefits: sick pay and holiday pay, maternity pay and so on. They also on occasion dodge paying even a minimum wage because of the costs they impose on workers, or (as in the case of the care sector, for example) paying only for a 15-minute slot of work which may nonetheless take 30 minutes or more to travel to and move on from. Thus to earn eight hours' pay it may be necessary to do a 12-hour day.

Labour is a big cost for any business. But if you are going to be an employer, why not do it decently and properly? The 'psychological contract' between employer and employee is under enough pressure as it is. But by withholding what is due to any worker, bad employers undermine trust further and create bad feeling. The quality of customer service is bound to suffer in those circumstances – which seems an odd goal for any business to aim for in a time of increased competition.

Keep it human

Companies and organizations, even very small ones, are not by and large virtual. They are real. They have brands, products and services, reputations and cultures. And, usually, they have (and will continue to have) employees too. That is one of the reasons why management remains important. You cannot outsource your responsibility to manage people well.

If you are trying to build a business, you are going to have to take on staff sooner or later. This is a profoundly good and moral thing to do. People need jobs, and creating employment is both positive and necessary.

Be as flexible as you have to be. Keep fixed costs down. But don't, for goodness' sake, fall for the myth which says that employees are no longer needed, and that the concept of the workforce can melt away into some wonderful 'liquid' future vision.

People are not liquids, they are people. Try hiring some. You'll be amazed at what they can do for you.

– MYTH 41 –

PEOPLE HATE CHANGE

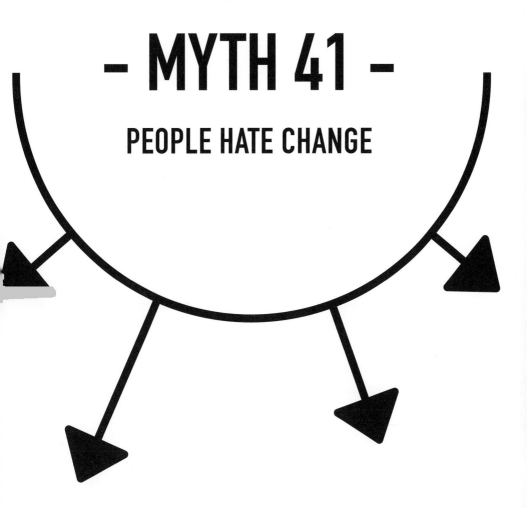

It's not true that 'people hate change'. Bought any new clothes recently?
Or even a new car? People hate stupid, unnecessary, imposed change.

Of all the myths and clichés about the difficulty of managing people, one possibly endures more than any other. It is usually uttered with a resigned or knowing shrug, in just a few words. And these words are: 'people hate change'.

Ah yes, people. They're so tricky, aren't they? Always objecting to stuff and being awkward. They should be grateful they've got a job here in the first place. And so on.

The bad change manager blames his or her people. But after all the experience organizations have had by now of trying to introduce change, the track record really ought to be a bit better than it is.

Deep freeze

Since the 1940s, when the psychologist Kurt Lewin (1947) explained how organizations had first to 'unfreeze', then change, and then freeze again into a new shape, managers have tried to understand how to bring about successful and lasting change. These ideas emerged in a world which arguably moved a little more slowly and steadily than it does today. Change was a formal, episodic process rather than a more rapid or (seemingly) almost continuous one. After all, we are always being told these days that 'the only constant is change'. (It's not true, but at first hearing it sounds clever. It's the sort of thing that highly paid speakers get highly paid to say.)

In more recent times the Harvard Business School professor John Kotter established a framework for change management which has proved hugely influential. His eight-step process, set out originally in his book *Leading Change* (1996), will be familiar to many (although different forms of the wording exist):

1 Create a sense of urgency.

2 Build a guiding coalition.

3 Form a strategic vision.

4 Communicate the change vision / enlist a volunteer army.

5 Remove barriers / empower employees.

6 Generate short-term wins.

7 Consolidate change and create more wins.

8 Anchor new approaches in the culture.

You see – simple. But not easy.

What about the workers?

So far, so logical. But of course logic forms only part of a successful change process. As Professor Dan Cable from London Business School (LBS) has pointed out (2012), change programme structures such as Kotter's are now so familiar that employees can see them coming. And they may not find the prospect of yet another 'change initiative' encouraging.

'It is a workforce that is more sceptical and questioning than ever before', he told the LBS magazine in 2012. 'It is more sophisticated, more cynical, more educated – a more tuned-in and plugged-in workforce, in large part because so many people now are enlightened by the internet and social media. These are workers who already know the old models of change, such as John Kotter's eight-step model, often better than their leaders do. Today's workforce has been through so many "change initiatives" that change is a bad word.'

There is another problem with the dry, bare bones of the eight-step programme. Unless it is deployed skilfully, it may allow little room for employees to speak up, take part and get engaged. There may not be enough time for emotional as well as intellectual 'buy-in'. To make it work at every stage there should be time, space and encouragement for discussion and participation.

People like change

The psychologist Rob Davies sometimes asks attendees at one of his training sessions if they like change or not. Many hands go up to indicate that they don't. And then he asks: how many of you have moved house recently, or redecorated, or bought a new car? And almost every hand goes up. So people can cope with change. They even seek it out. What they don't want is stupid change, change that is imposed on them without effective consultation, change that makes no sense or that makes things worse. Sure, there may sometimes be cries of 'Can I have my old computer back?' But, in time, most usually adapt quite happily to new technology, or new ways of working that work.

A sense of urgency

When John Kotter returned to the theme of change a decade after his best-selling book on the subject had appeared, he had a simpler story to tell (Kotter, 2008). It was that out of the eight steps he had described in his original programme, the most important one of all was the first: creating (and maintaining) a sense of urgency. Without that urgency change programmes would fail. And you had to get this right from the start.

But his argument had more layers to it than that. Urgency does not necessarily mean speed, or rushing around thoughtlessly. Rather, managers needed to cultivate 'urgent patience' – the ability to transmit a sense of purpose and drive without creating panic or wasteful, inefficient, frenetic activity.

Urgent patience, he wrote, means 'acting each day with a sense of urgency but having a realistic view of time. It means recognizing that five years may be needed to attain important and ambitious goals, and yet coming to work each day committed to finding every opportunity to make progress toward those goals.'

Only urgent patience can drive out the complacency which blocks useful and necessary change, Kotter says. And he supports the idea that emotional engagement is as important as rational argument. 'Complacency... is usually less a matter of conscious, rational analysis than unconscious emotion... This point is extremely important because people usually treat complacency as a state of mind that can be changed solely with "the cold, hard facts".'

We all have to see the need for change, Kotter says, and recognize the steps we have to take personally. 'Complacency is a feeling that a person has about his or her own behaviour, about what he or she needs to do or not do', he says. 'This point is also extremely important, because it is possible to see problems and yet be astonishingly complacent because you do not feel that the problems require changes in your own actions.'

All for one and one for all

Change has to be a team effort, not something that is imposed or led only from the top down. As LBS's Professor Cable says: 'Collective action has to be about more than the leader's yacht: it has to be about a common sense of purpose. And if the leader can't convince them of that, it's unlikely that lots and lots of people are going to make a sustained common change.'

Remember: people don't hate change. They can and will cope with it – even enjoy it – if you give them a chance... and a say in the process.

- MYTH 42 -

BIG DATA WILL FIX EVERYTHING

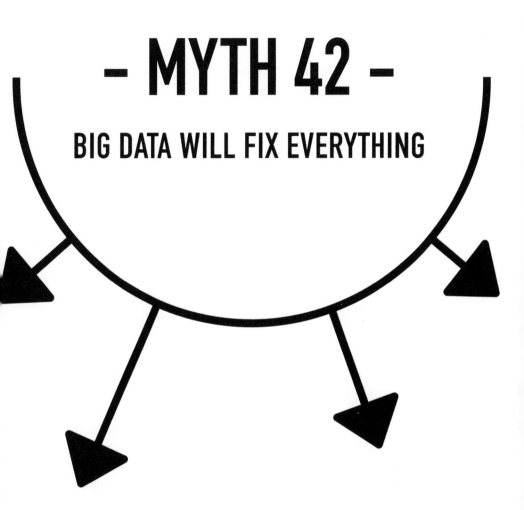

Beware the simple (tech) solution to all our problems. Better data can help, but it will not remove the need for judgement.

A popular management saying, often attributed to the guru of quality W Edwards Deming, runs: 'In God we trust – everyone else must bring data.' It makes a nice point. In an era of 'post-truth politics', 'fake news' and out-of-control social media frenzies, to insist on factually accurate information is to do one's bit for Enlightenment values. Hearsay and rumour are not data. Difficult and complicated decisions should be based on evidence and not mere whimsy or prejudice.

In fact, the only controversial thing about data, in one sense, is whether it should be taken as a singular or plural noun (this myth will probably try to blur that distinction a little). What do we want? Facts. When do we want them? Now.

Nothing in management remains that simple for very long, of course. Seemingly uncontroversial data has succumbed to the inevitable curse of management faddism (see Myth 37). That is why the 'big data' mythology grew up, and why the next few paragraphs had to be written.

OK, computer?

It is easy to make fun of Thomas Watson Snr, former head of IBM, for his supposed claim (said to have been made in 1943) that there was a world market 'for maybe five computers'. He may have understated popular demand for magnificent data machines, or perhaps overstated their potential processing power. But the (apocryphal) quotation is a reminder that some of the predictions made about IT, even those offered up by people at the heart of the industry, are not always borne out by reality.

So it is with data, or rather, 'big data' – the addition of the adjective 'big' being the clue that faddism has claimed another victim. Of course, increases in processing power have made it possible to assemble vast data sets. Regression analyses can find patterns and connections which the naked human eye may not. Bigness can be impressive. Quantity has a quality of all its own, some say.

But it is also true that 'if you torture the data for long enough it will confess to anything'. And when people place too much reliance on big data sets, and overlook the need for judgement, things can go wrong.

'I have sat in too many board meetings where we all pored over spreadsheets with masses of data', Margaret Heffernan says (see full interview in Appendix 7). 'I don't think anybody understood what the data was saying. And so what they did was ask for more... It's become this fantastic alibi. And we can now generate so much data we can all drown in it, and mostly do.'

Margin of error

The last couple of years of political uncertainty should have confirmed to even the biggest big data fans that sometimes the apparently solid numbers can let you down. In 2015, there was 'no way' the Conservative party could possibly win a majority in that year's British general election, according to the voting intention data. But they did so. A year later, with some trusted research companies declaring that the Remain camp in the UK's EU referendum was clearly ahead – some said by 10 percentage points – it was in fact the Leave side that came out on top, by a margin of four points. And then in November 2016, most dramatically of all, the 'unbeatable', 'inevitable' Hillary Clinton also lost out, contrary to what almost all expert opinion (sustained by expensively gathered data) was saying. True, the prediction that she would win most votes proved correct. But the big data sets failed to indicate that in the places where it mattered, Donald Trump was doing better. Finally, the UK's 2017 general election also saw most pollsters getting their predictions badly wrong.

Opinion polls, designed to discover people's voting intentions, may not be hard science. Voting is a highly personal matter, and it may not always be possible either to reveal true voting intentions or find hard-to-reach people who do not wish to say how they will vote. And of course people may change their mind after having been polled, and so on. Psephologists have long conceded that the figures in opinion polls contain a 'margin of error' of perhaps plus or minus three percentage points for each finding, so long as a big enough sample of voters has been used.

Is it unfair to pick on opinion polling as an example of why big data may not always be wholly reliable? Hardly. The firms that carry out these voting intention surveys are in truth market-research companies, who make most of their money doing consumer and product research. (Political polling is not very profitable: it is done for their own marketing reasons.) But it follows that managers should never place too much reliance on, or faith in, market-research data. Can you be sure that customers are really telling you what they think? Henry Ford's customers didn't know they might want to buy a car, and Sony's customers didn't know we might want a personal stereo cassette player.

What does this tell us about our growing dependency on big data? What are the health warnings we should bear in mind? For one thing, qualitative methods, used carefully, may be just as (or more) revealing than a big data set. But above all we need to remember that human judgement has to be applied. That means drawing on experience, intelligence, imagination and, yes, gut feel.

Big data and a big hunch

The anthropologist John Curran likes to say that, while big data can be important, a big hunch can be too. He practises what he calls 'deep hanging out' with customers on behalf of his commercial clients, studying their behaviour and asking questions. This does not generate a big data set. But it could reveal something truly valuable, which has not been seen before, and which would not get picked up in a standard mass survey.

It remains true: garbage in will give you garbage out. Big claims made for big data should be tested. Algorithms are not flawless. They do what programmers tell them to do, and programmers have their own biases (prejudices) and make mistakes. Numbers alone, presented without any human judgement being applied to them, do not necessarily mean anything. A famous remark (often attributed to Einstein, but in fact probably first used by the sociologist William Bruce Cameron) runs: 'Not everything that can be counted counts, and not everything that counts can be counted.'

In Norman Jewison's 1965 film *The Cincinnati Kid*, Edward G Robinson and Steve McQueen outclass all the other poker players round the table by using their judgement and daring. Another player, drawing on mathematical tables of probabilities, leaves (poorer) in disgust, appalled at the apparently irrational risks the two protagonists are taking. But McQueen ('the kid') and Edward G (Lancey, 'the Man') know what they are doing. They know the limits of big data. They know when you have to trust and use your own judgement.

– MYTH 43 –

A COOL OFFICE WILL MAKE EVERYBODY MORE CREATIVE

'Culture is one thing and varnish is another', as Ralph Waldo Emerson said. Beanbags cannot make up for a bad corporate culture.

Scooters. Pinball. Beanbags. Table football. These things were not enough to save dozens of start-ups during the 'Web 1.0' mini boom at the turn of the millennium. Sure, some pretty and fun-packed workplaces were set up. They were cool places to hang out. But the iron laws of business could not be denied. Without revenue – sales – you haven't got a business. Some Web 1.0 start-ups may have been creative, but they met with creative destruction. It was time to scoot off into the sunset and try to find another job.

Businesses succeed when they have robust, sustainable and adaptable business models, supported by a similarly robust and adaptable culture. It is important that the workforce is content and stimulated. But it will take more than soft furnishings to achieve this.

I'm h-a-p-p-y, I'm h-a-p-p-y

Some of the high hopes for 'open plan' offices have not been realized. The thinking behind the removal of partitions and the opening up of oppressive little office spaces was sound. Let air and light in. Challenge over-rigid hierarchy with more generous, equalizing work zones.

But noisier, busier offices can also be distracting. Having your computer screen on public view might inhibit rather than encourage creative work. Personal space may be invaded. And necessary privacy can be hard to achieve.

Well-meaning bosses may invest in improved furnishings, fabric and paintwork. And all these things can raise morale, if only temporarily. But while happiness at work may be attributed, wrongly, to the aesthetics of the office, this can overlook more important factors such as job security, fair pay, decent treatment and work satisfaction. Indeed, a Society for Human Resource Management (2016) study found just that: it's pay, prospects, trust and feeling respected that give the most happiness to employees. But you can't take a photo of job security and the like, so pretty designer offices sometimes get the credit.

At the same time there is little doubt that getting the environment right *should* help people give of their best. Dr Jim Goodnight, founder and chief executive of SAS, the US high-tech firm, understood long ago that providing a comfortable place to work would help his employees work better (Stern, 2005). He was one of the first employers to offer so-called concierge services (dry-cleaning, haircuts and so on) at work. Tech giants such as Facebook and Google have followed his example.

Do sit under the apple tree

The ultimate new high-tech workplace has been established, of course, by Apple, in Cupertino, California. In the *Financial Times* Lucy Kellaway (2017) hailed this new building as a grown-up achievement. Yes, it is modern, bright and beautiful, but it is also free from that Web 1.0 frivolity which proved to be both a red herring and a dead end. But then, at a cost of a reported $5 billion, it ought to be a half-decent building. It will stand for years as a final monument to the late Steve Jobs.

Relationships – it's simple, and complicated

People usually need to be quite close to each other to work well together. But too much proximity of the wrong kind becomes a barrier. So while social events at work can and should be encouraged, too many intrusions into colleagues' private lives (and downtime) should be avoided.

People also need to get out more. Mike Bloomberg, the billionaire founder of the eponymous news business, has said he wants his employees to get out of the office at lunchtime and spend time (and money) in the local community where they work, not remain 'trapped' in the golden cage of a plush office with nice food. Bloomberg's new £1.1 billion London HQ has 'pantries' providing snacks but has no staff canteen.

The success of a workplace depends ultimately on the quality of the relationships that exist there. Cleanliness and comfort are (literally and metaphorically) hygiene factors. But these aspects alone have little to do with the productivity you achieve. That is down to the skills of the people you employ, how well they are managed, and the work that they do.

Think inside the box

Workplaces should be safe and civilized. They should be as comfortable as possible. You should not dread going in. Natural daylight (and the clever use of artificial light) help. 'Free' (or subsidized) healthy food can improve morale. But these things do not build a rich culture, and nor do they make people more creative.

In the end it's the quality of management that counts. Are people being stretched and supported, guided and encouraged, developed and inspired? It's the management, stupid, not the beanbags, that you need to think about.

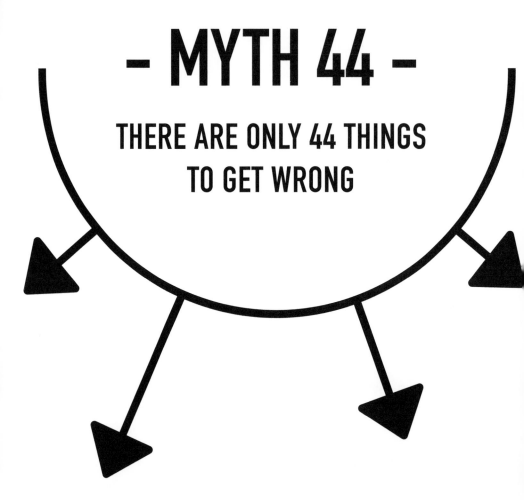

- MYTH 44 -

THERE ARE ONLY 44 THINGS TO GET WRONG

Frailty, thy name is… management. We are all flawed and will make mistakes. But we can get better, and do better.

Were you hoping for a happy ending? Did you turn to the final page expecting to find a list of bullet points, a few foolproof steps to success in management and career fulfilment? Sorry to disappoint. There are no simple solutions to the permanent challenge of managing people. There is only practice, experimentation, learning, developing, and carrying on.

That is what we have been trying to show in the preceding pages. Management is a human task and, as such, mistakes will be made. There are doubtless many as yet unimagined things that machines can and will do for us. But for the time being and for a considerable time to come, people will make the decisions that affect us at work. And while that is the case, management – that human activity, that liberal art – will matter very much indeed.

And finally...

Above all, we would urge managers to be brave, to challenge the myths we have tried to expose, to take chances, to try things out, and to civilize the world of work as far as is possible. We spend so much of our lives at work. The least managers could do is make this experience as productive, successful and rewarding as possible.

This means showing respect for each other, having high expectations for what people can achieve, and maintaining high standards. It means getting out of your office, putting the smartphone down and actually listening to people. It means being optimistic. It means keeping a sense of proportion.

It is not easy being a manager. Being a good manager is even harder. But we have to try to do the job as well as we can: deploying resources, encouraging people to grow, and raising the quality of what we do. Management, in the end, is our best hope for the future. We have to try to get better at it.

APPENDICES

FIRESIDE CHATS
WITH PROMINENT
MANAGEMENT
THINKERS

APPENDIX 1
Charles Handy

Charles Handy is the author of several bestselling books, including *The Age of Unreason*, *The Empty Raincoat*, *The Hungry Spirit* and most recently *The Second Curve*. He is Britain's most influential management commentator (although he is of course Irish by birth). In partnership with his wife Elizabeth (also an author and photographer) he continues to travel, speak and write, finding eager audiences around the world.

If I say the word 'management' to you, how do you react?
CH: I shudder. I don't like being managed. I don't think I'm different from anybody else. Mind you, I don't mind managing! So I think we've got it wrong. People don't like being managed... and perhaps they are right.

Management is actually about things, and not about people. It's about systems. If you go into a professional organization where people are the most important things – a lawyer's office or a medical practice – the only people called managers are people who look after things – the car service or the technology systems and so on. I think management should be applied to systems, the infrastructure of organizations, the way the thing works.

But the people... they need to be led, or cajoled, or involved, or other words that give you some form of independence, some choice. Whereas in management, if you start treating people as things, if you slot them into little holes where they have to do as they're told, they are part of the system then and that's why they don't like it.

So please don't use the word management in my presence with regard to people because I shudder.

So a good manager is creating space, worrying about the system, so the system doesn't get in the way?
CH: Absolutely. He's setting the conditions, he or she is setting the infrastructure, the rules as far as they are necessary, but please don't try to

manage the people. You should work with the people. Concentrate on the management of the things.

Because people don't understand that they think their job is to bring people into line, to manage the behaviour of people, and I just think that's counterproductive. By all means change the conditions in which they work. But please don't try to change them.

When I was working at Shell in a large central office there was a brass plate outside the door, which had the name of my section, which was 'Marketing co-ordination Europe, Mediterranean region', and that was stamped into the brass plate, and there was a little slot underneath it, for my name, which was written on card, so it could be replaced by any other name, and I was just part of that system. And I had a job description which was three pages long, of all the things I was expected to do, and how I was to do them, and at the end it said, 'Authority: to initiate expenditure on own account up to a maximum of ten pounds. That was my freedom of manoeuvre. So I was being managed as much as my job was being managed. So: manage the job but don't manage the people. Leave them free and for God's sake leave them room to do something interesting in that space which you have created for them.

There's no room for people to do good work?

CH: Which is why 75 per cent of people in organizations are not in any way committed to the work of that organization. They're not necessarily unhappy, but as one chief executive said to me in France: 'My people turn up to go home' – carrying their wage packet with them, but leaving nothing of themselves there.

I think that's very sad. That's why I say sometimes that organizations are prisons for the human soul. Because people are being managed rather than worked with. So manage the system, manage the infrastructure, manage the job, but not the person.

No one tells new managers that, do they?

CH: We've given to management this grand idea of power, and, as I say, people don't like being managed but when they become a manager... wow! Then we've got all these people to manage.

Words are much more important than people think. If you discipline yourself not to use the word 'manage' it's very interesting what is released.

If you go into organizations where people are precious you don't hear the word very much. You don't go into a doctor's surgery and say, 'Where are the managers here?' One of the problems with the National Health Service is that they've created this terrible job called 'manager'. Instead of working with the systems they start bossing people around. The consultants, the powerful people who do the work, don't like it.

Managers are counterproductive?

CH: If in the future you are managing robots or computer systems this may get better... maybe being managed by an algorithm will be better...! If the feedback comes from a machine it might feel easier somehow.

Is bigness in business part of the problem here?

CH: Yes. Professor Dunbar came up with this idea that 150 people were the maximum you could actually relate to in a community. He has another measure which I find interesting that goes up in threes. There are probably a maximum of five people you can call your greatest friends, who will lend you money without asking why you need it. And then there are 15 people that you love spending time with. Then there are 45 people who you'd be very happy to go to dinner with, and then maybe there are 135 people who are on your Christmas card list if you still send them, or your Facebook friends.

So I would say 135 people might be the maximum size of any unit in an organization because at least you can know their names. Probably 45 is the number of people you can trust when they're out of your sight to get on with the job because you know them well enough, and 15 people that you would really like to go into battle with – an army platoon – and then five people you might be married to or are very close to. So if organizations start having numbers above that for the operating groups, they have to systematize it, you become a number.

Delayering made this worse? Managers with hundreds or even thousands of 'reports'?

CH: Yes, it's nonsense. You can't possibly know them all. They become numbers. You will only really know 45 of them, or even fewer, so it becomes a clique, it's the only way you can cope. You see this happening in government. Those outside the clique get very cross.

So why not go with the grain? And say all units in this organization will be 45 people. We will then have a proliferation of units, which looks untidy, and the accountants will come along and say, 'Why don't we combine all these people?' and I'm saying, no, don't do that, the work has to be done in groups of 45. Natural leaders will develop, those who are skilled in certain key specific roles.

Riccardo Semler, of SemCo, said – you don't need job titles, we all know what role you perform. Print your own business cards, but don't use them in the office!

It follows from all this that what we call management education...
CH: ...is crap!

Well, it doesn't cover any of this ground at all
CH: Because it is so difficult to formulize. Basically, business schools are training institutions, they're not educational institutions. They don't challenge convention and so on. They're training people to turn them out for their ultimate customers, who are the organizations. And if you're training people you need a manual, you've got to write it all down, so there's a thing you can teach. They do it in quite imaginative ways with case studies, but it's infuriating if you're teaching a case study and the class doesn't come up with the right answers! And the students say, well, why didn't you just tell us what the answer was! It's a bit of a charade.

We tried to replicate the American business school (at London Business School), but we got it so wrong. But we ignored the British tradition of professional education. Doctors, lawyers, accountants – they all have a bit of classroom stuff and an awful lot of tutored experience. And that's what we need. There are things that you need to know, not about managing people, but about how business works, about accounting, marketing and so on, you learn those in the classroom. But the real human stuff – you can't learn in a classroom. You can only learn it out there in the thick of it, with a mentor around... so why the hell didn't we do that?

It's going slowly in that direction, with part-time courses and so on. The only business school I really approve of (and I've been involved in the launch of three) is the Open University, where the studies are more tied in to the real world.

Business schools... they tried to make management into a discipline, so it could be taught as a scientific kind of thing, all the research that has tried to find out what worked and what didn't work, as if it was a science, but it's a human science, it's more like history... what works here may not work there because it all depends... history is a very good preparation by the way for management, trying to work out why what worked here didn't work there.

The drive for efficiency?

CH: Yes, but they confuse efficiency and effectiveness. Set people free, on the whole it will be much more effective, but it looks messy. Accountants don't like mess, and managers don't like mess because they like systems.

But we aim for the wrong numbers?

CH: Yes. When I was at Shell I knew that we were there to sell as much of the stuff [oil] to as many people as possible – it was a market share number. Nobody mentioned shareholders! We had to pay a kind of rent [dividend] for the use of their money, but we kept it as low as possible.

I remember once hearing Peter Holmes, the former chairman of Shell, ask some other business leaders: 'Any of you ever worried about your share price?', and they all said: 'No, no.' And he said: 'I know, it's ridiculous isn't it, all this nonsense about share prices, I never bothered about it.'

We used to worry about market share, but after the Meckling and Jensen paper and the so-called alignment of managers with shareholders it was all quarterly profits and earnings per share... we never talked about earnings per share!

So numbers matter as much as words. And the idea that shareholders are owners... just not true. And so-called shareholder primacy is all part of that.

Ticking financial boxes instead of working for a purpose?

CH: Well, this gets back to growth. I think growth is a human concern. We all need to grow, but we don't want to grow fat. We want to grow to be different or better. So why do organizations always want to grow bigger? Well, we know why they do, because it gives them more money or power, or salaries, but it does mean that the people become ever-smaller cogs. It's fine for the people at the top but it's lousy for everybody underneath.

I was talking to someone the other day who had been a proud member of the top management at Alcan, and he said it was very sad. It became RTZ Alcan, then it became the Alcan division of RTZ, and then it became the aluminium division of RTZ, and now it's gone. The word has gone. Swallowed up. Very sad. Lots of people like that find the company they worked for has just gone.

So why can't we be better or different but keep the same size? You can make more money that way. But people think growth means bigger, but it doesn't have to.

I remember the owner of a vineyard in Napa Valley telling me he wanted to grow and grow, and I looked around said, 'Where?', and he said, no, not in size, I want to make the best wine. I want to grow better. His wines are very expensive!

Finally, what is there to hope for?

CH: If we're clever we can use the new technology to allow people a lot more freedom, without the intervention of managers. They can get their own feedback from the system.

In Borneo and Sarawak, when I worked for Shell, there was only mail, no telex or phones, so I could learn and make mistakes in private. At first it was daunting, but in the end, I benefited from it. The people in Singapore didn't know what I'd got wrong, because I didn't tell them.

The same thing could happen now: the technology could free you from intrusive supervision. I fear we may not use the technology in that way, however.

Another significant development is that talented young people may reject the big organization and set up their own independent entities. With 45 people you can change the world with the right technology in the right business. Big organizations may struggle in this new world.

APPENDIX 2
Eve Poole

Eve Poole is a theologian, academic and consultant, and author of the recently published *Leadersmithing* (as well as earlier books *Capitalism's Toxic Assumptions* and *The Church on Capitalism*).

When you hear the word 'management', what thoughts come to mind? What does it mean to you?

EP: I think there's a suggested etymology, something to do with leading horses around, which is an interesting place to start. For me, 'management' has very practical connotations. It is about mobilizing people to do concrete things, then checking, reviewing and adjusting as required. So the reporting on it is also concrete – activities completed, the quality of them, the cost of them, feedback on them. Rinse and repeat. Task, process and relationships are really the holy trinity of management. So it is also fundamentally interpersonal, because getting people to repeatedly do excellent work requires exquisite people skills.

What distinguishes leadership from management? Do we worry too much about the difference, or risk over-emphasizing one over the other?

EP: Lots of nonsense has been written about this, and in many ways it is an artificial distinction that doesn't matter on the ground. But there are a couple of category differences that do lend nuance to one side or the other. First, the dynamic between people. If you are managed by someone, your relationship is more or less formally proscribed. You perform tasks for them, and if they like what you do, you keep your job and get rewarded for it. If they don't, you get performance-managed by them. The expectation is of a close relationship with lots of face-to-face interaction, and your manager is held accountable for your performance. This set-up lends itself to a focus on the day-to-day, and on quality and performance.

The second category difference concerns horizons. Of course, managers can look out and around as well as down, but for leaders this is a more crucial activity. Reputation, risk, stakeholders, shareholders – all of these externalities either in place or in time need to be wrangled well to protect the core business back at base. These necessitate an obsession with culture, key staff, key set pieces and other multipliers that effectively guarantee future performance because they in various ways summarize or distil the essence, the recipe, and the brand.

These together create the third category difference, which is about affiliation. Bluntly, you have to follow your manager. It's in your job description. But leaders have to earn their followers, and cannot meaningfully require or demand followership. So they have to create the right sense of travel and direction, the right culture, and behave in the right way, to attract the voluntary allegiance of others. Of course as the boss they have some powerful psychological tools at their disposal, but they deploy these at their peril and as a last resort. They also, and this would be my trite distinction, need to be masters of perception rather than reality. The latter may catch up with them, but they trade on the former. Which requires a sophistication in gesture and symbol which is highly complex and can easily backfire.

Managers can of course lead. They may need to, and their capacity to do so will make them valuable to the organization, and promotable. But their job, first and foremost, is to guarantee results, so their own bosses will tend to lose patience if they do more leading than managing, unless the results are also there. This is also true of leaders, of course, because if your organization does not perform on your watch you are also out on your ear, regardless of the whys and wherefores.

You've just written about 'leadersmithing'. What is that?

EP: Because of all of that, there is no way in which leading is a state of mind or an attained status, as suggested by the rather static and cerebral-sounding term 'leadership'. It is a craft skill, and it requires daily practice. I think leadersmithing is more suggestive of this sense of a dynamic activity. And the work I have done suggests that real leaders know this, and work with it, seeking out opportunities to hone their skills in order to future-proof their leading. Empirically, we do know what top leaders wish they had known 10 years ago, and how they learned it, so leadersmithing is about deploying this insight in the day-to-day activities of aspiring leaders to allow them to perform well in these roles in the future. It establishes the recipe for top leadership and sets out ways to learn this either through weekly exercises or by seeking out exposure to critical incidents under pressure, to cement the learning and enable consistent and sustained performance under pressure in the future. It is about layering on experiences, deliberately rather than at the hand of fate, to develop the character and muscle memory to lead in the full range of situations likely to occur in the future. If you know what you dread about the next role, it shows how you can domesticate your fears, by programming them in early, on your terms and at a time of your own choosing, so that you develop coping skills around them.

Is it getting harder to be a manager?

EP: Yes, because everyone wants to be a leader, which is seen as more glamorous (and better paid). Also managers have been de-skilled by the outsourcing of much of their remit to HR, and because of (legitimate) concern about litigation. I'd like us to get back to the idea of mastery and restore this relationship, and help managers to see that it is not about better/worse or senior/junior but about differing and crucial zones of activity which naturally overlap, blur, and move, but which each have a centre of gravity that must be honoured and protected.

Will management save us or be the death of us?

EP: Save us. It's perception versus reality again. Slightly chicken and egg, but if you don't have a product you can't sell it, and the leaders are the servants not the masters of the managers. Equally, good leadership de-risks management by stopping it from serving the wrong goals or masters and wasting valuable resource.

APPENDIX 3
Henry Mintzberg

Henry Mintzberg has long been the pre-eminent academic commentator on management as a practical activity. Since writing his first book *The Nature of Managerial Work* (1973) he has consistently debunked elaborate myths about the practice of management. He has subsequently published 18 more titles. Henry is Cleghorn Professor of Management Studies at McGill University in Montreal, Quebec, Canada.

What do you think when you hear the word 'management'?

HM: It depends on whether it's spelt de facto with a capital M or a small m. Capital M Management brings to mind all the distortions that too much management has become, people who sat still in a business school for a couple of years and think management is about reading bottom lines and deeming performance standards instead of rolling up their sleeves. That's capital letter Management.

Small letter management is plain old-fashioned personal engagement. Nothing fancy, nothing sophisticated. Just people who care, and get involved, and know what's going on. They're sympathetic to other human beings, not 'human resources'.

Have we lost sight of the essentials of what management is really about?

HM: Yes, absolutely. You know, when you see someone who is a natural in the job it's the most natural thing in the world, doing what they do. In fact, most of the revered managers never spent a day in a business school, except maybe to give a speech once they became famous. When you get people who've never managed thinking they've learned about management in a business school because they studied a lot of fancy techniques and did a lot of case studies and shot their mouths off about companies they know almost nothing about, then you end up with a very distorted view of the process. I call it 'management by deeming' – my granddaughter aged 12 could do that – 'I deem that you must cut costs by 20 per cent', 'You must increase profits by 36 per cent, or else I'll fire you.' That's easy.

And this sort of attitude has got wrapped up in something called Leadership with a capital L...

HM: Exactly. I think that good managers lead and good leaders manage. This idea that they are separated so that one does the fancy stuff and the other does the scut [ie routine] work is a myth out of the distorted minds of some Harvard professors. They are creating 'grand leaders'.

In 1990 there was a book called *Inside the Harvard Business School*. I looked at some of the stars mentioned in the book: most of them had failed, and only a few had done OK. Danny Miller, my first doctoral student from way back, did a startling study recently on the performance of what he called 'celebrity CEOs', who were on the covers of the major American business magazines. Not only was their performance worse than the non-MBAs but their salaries went up faster. [See Henry's blog: http://www.mintzberg.org/blog/mbas-as-ceos.]

Is it the quest for bigness and scale that makes life harder for managers?

HM: I would word it slightly differently. I am writing a blog called 'Enough of MORE, better is better'. What I mean is that you build a company, you care about your customers, your products, your services and your employees, until the day you do this famous IPO. And then it's all about MORE, MORE, MORE. To hell with your customers, employees, with anything human, it's just MORE, MORE shareholder value. And that is an utter distortion.

I think, frankly, if the stock markets were closed completely the economy would be one hell of a lot better off. There are other ways to raise money, you don't have to be beholden to that kind of short-term mindless investment.

Tata has publicly traded shares but the votes are controlled by family trusts. Same with Novo Nordisk. So there are alternatives to the stock market model.

Is management getting harder, with the arrival of new technology?

HM: I don't think management is getting harder, but people who deal mindlessly with those new technologies find it harder. I wrote about this in a blog called 'Managing over the edge'. Managing is hectic – it's always been hectic – it's a naturally hectic job. But throw in having to check e-mail every 20 minutes, and having to respond to everything instantly, and it could drive the whole process, and the incumbent, over the edge.

Does this make the human factor more important?

HM: Well, yes, it's back to Peter Drucker: 'Managing is doing things through other people.' Not through other electrons!

Are there any particular priorities for managers in the coming years?

HM: The subject matter of management always changes, but the process of management fundamentally doesn't change. There's always something to deal with, whether it's Donald Trump now or the oil crisis years ago, the subject matter is always changing. You never know quite how it's going to manifest itself. But managers will have to respond. But what that will be... your guess is as good as mine.

Do you think recent electoral shocks – Trump, Brexit – have anything to do with the leadership and management people have experienced?

HM: Some of it is certainly about the greedy grab of resources, of bonuses for bankers, and the like. It's not a one-sided issue. Those who supported Bernie Sanders had many of the same concerns as those who supported Trump. They just manifested them differently. Globalization is not holy writ. Globalization has some wonderful benefits and some awful consequences, not least of which is the outright attack on national sovereignties, which means on democracy.

Some of us were pleased when Unilever fought off Kraft a bit ago.

HM: Yes, as I understand it Unilever has been one of the more responsible companies.

Which parts of the world interest you most at the moment?

HM: I've been spending a bit of time in Brazil recently. My favourite question to Brazilians is: which country is more corrupt, Brazil or the United States? And I say, I'll give you a hint, it's not Brazil. And I mean it. In Brazil the corruption is criminal, and they are finally dealing with it. In America the corruption is legal. And they can't deal with it. The Supreme Court has legalized bribery. And the Brazilian court has recently delegalized bribery; the political donations of that nature are now illegal.

What is capturing your imagination in Brazil?

HM: There is always fascinating stuff going on there. Brazilians are the ultimate 'why not?' people. They are really interesting, although a lot is still on hold, because people are so discouraged by what took place [the ousting of former President Dilma Rousseff].

But in business they bring something different?

HM: They think for themselves. There is a good deal of social entrepreneurship there. Of course it is entrepreneurship too. But in fact it is really community activity, not just individuals. It's community initiatives, right across the country. The solutions they have found to social problems are often not-for-profit ones, and more creative than what we see elsewhere.

Can business schools do anything about the narrow orthodoxy?

HM: Well, there are a lot of people in business schools who worry about this. But as long as they are pretending to create managers out of people inexperienced in management, nothing will change. In our international master's for managers [impm.org] we take people who are managers and give them plenty of time to reflect on their experience and learn from each other.

I still teach at McGill, but half-time, I've been half-time for years. I'm probably more productive now than I've ever been!

APPENDIX 4
Herminia Ibarra

Herminia Ibarra is an expert on leadership development. Her most recent book is *Act Like a Leader, Think Like a Leader,* and previously she also published *Working Identity: Unconventional strategies for reinventing your career.* She is a professor at London Business School, having worked for several years at INSEAD.

What does the word 'management' mean today?

HI: Unfortunately, the first thing that pops into my mind is processes, compliance, things that you have to do that you don't necessarily want to do, the boring stuff, the bureaucratic stuff. Which in itself is a myth… I think we've grown so used to management being contrasted to leadership… leadership is the sexy, fun stuff, creating change, getting things done, and management is the bureaucratic routine, it's the pushing the ball just a little bit uphill, it's the incremental things you do, it's the meetings, and the performance appraisals, and budgeting.

It's unfortunate because management is the infrastructure that allows you not to have to do everything yourself. It's the thing that allows you leverage – so that then you can set direction and lead and do the sexy things. It's gotten a bum rap, I think in part because we're still using systems from way, way back that are not necessarily very agile or very suited to the world today. If you look at the whole controversy over performance appraisal and should it be done away with, well, maybe the way we do it isn't great but doing away with it opens us up to a lot of chaos and inconsistency, especially if you have any size of organization.

And, potentially, without management nothing really happens?

HI: You know, because of the whole 'knowledge work' revolution, we live in a world in which a lot of us as managers and professionals are also producers or also do-ers. Jobs get complex. There's the stuff you do – whether it's doing analysis or going after a client or writing a report – and then there's the strategic, leadership stuff, and then there's this area of work that often is imposed: you didn't come up with the forms or the processes, but it has to do with coordination, working across different units, and it tends to be no fun, and it tends to require a good bit of time and energy.

Managers are sometimes told to be themselves. Is that a good idea?

HI: 'Be yourself' is terrible advice, not because it's not good to be yourself, but what self are we talking about? We are as many different selves as the roles that we play, in a situation in which we have to perform. Situational leadership, which is one of the sacred cows, basically means that you tailor yourself to your audience: your tactics, your style, and so on taken to an extreme that can mean that there is no self there, you're just a tactic, or a set of influencing tactics. What's interesting to me is: when does authenticity become a problem? Ultimately, we shouldn't have to spend so much money on books and courses on 'how to be yourself'!

The reason we talk about it so much is that it's a problem. And it comes up as a problem in a couple of different ways. One way is when you feel you are faced with a trade-off between being who you are, or doing things as you would do them, and being effective. Somehow, being successful and effective requires something of you that is either not habitual or not palatable. And that's where you have to tease it out a bit. If it's not habitual, well, you know what, we've got to change, and it's very easy to get stuck in a comfort zone, and just because it's not habitual doesn't mean it can't become something you don't do quite well. And we've got to adapt. It gets a little trickier when it's also unattractive, it's not who we want to be. That starts to raise deeper questions.

I'm especially interested in the dilemma of authenticity at moments of transition, personal career transition. We used to define these transitions, 'what got you here won't get you there' moments, when people moved into a new role or into a new company and obviously it was a different culture or a different situation, and you had to adapt. Today you don't really have the luxury of waiting for a role-change moment because things are changing fast, and expectations of you are changing fast, companies are reconfiguring so your title could be the same but your responsibilities are different, and what all those situations have in common is that if you keep doing what made you successful in the past it's not going to work out as well for you. Because we overplay our strengths – it's the idea of 'fatal strengths', the things that you overdo. Now – overplaying your strengths, that feels hugely authentic. 'This is me!' – because our identity is based on the past, what we've been good at, what I'm the go-to person for, what people have rewarded. And so it really becomes an anchor in the good sense in that it's our mooring, it helps us make choices; but it becomes an anchor also in the negative sense of keeping us from exploring other strengths and learning to do new things. So at these points of transition, and particularly when what you're moving towards is actually unclear, what it requires – 'be a better leader': what is that? – or when there's some ambivalence, people want to move up, they want to have more impact, but at the same time when they look at their bosses or their former bosses they say, 'I don't want to be like those bozos...', it's not attractive, they think those people are political, they think they're manipulative, they think they're not transparent. They don't want to be that way, and they think maybe you have to be that way to be successful.

So sometimes you can be authentic by being aspirational. It's not who I've been but that's who I want to be. But in these cases you don't always have that because you're not so sure. Or you feel you are giving away the basis of your core competence, you're not working from it, what does that leave you, how do you add value? So the transitions are quite fraught with a lot of ambivalence – 'I don't know if I want to be that person'.

So if you take a more reflective approach – 'who am I, what are my strengths?' – that's only going to anchor you in the past. And that's not going to help you figure out how to move forward to a future version of yourself that has a core but that also has learned new things and grown and maybe been surprised, even pleasantly surprised. It's not a case of 'fake it 'til you make it', but it's 'experiment until you learn'!

And sense the situation...?

HI: Sense the situation, but also sometimes you really have to do things that are radically opposed to your natural inclinations. What if you come from a culture of consensus and all of a sudden you're in a context where you have to state your view forcefully and argue it to the ground; well, doing that feels completely a violation of your sense of self, yet you could learn a lot, and sometimes it's by going to the extreme that you find a way to come back to some middle ground that is part how you've always been and part the skill-set that it is necessary to adapt.

Authenticity has been so much in the public discourse that people use it as an excuse for anything – 'I don't have to change, I don't have to be a better listener, I don't have to worry about my rough side, I'm just being me', with the idea that people are happy just to get full transparency… no, people are not happy to get full transparency! They want you to behave like there's some kind of interdependence and that you have to work with people. It's not just about being yourself, it's about creating productive working relationships, and a culture and climate in which other people can be themselves and say what's on their mind. It's not just about you.

So you have to experiment?

HI: Because it's an iterative process. You don't go from A to B fully formed. You take some steps, you learn some things, maybe that was a little too aggressive, maybe that was a little too soft, let me watch how some other people do it, now that I've learned this I can try the advanced version. That's why it's act then think (book title), not that you should always shoot from the hip, but that you have to experiment your way into it.

People say, 'Oh yes, agile', but as soon as it comes to doing something that doesn't feel very natural they don't feel particularly agile. Agile is OK for a tool or a process, but if it's about them, 'that's not me'.

How about admitting to vulnerability? I heard Jeff Immelt say once that you can't tell the organization that 'I don't know what to do!'

HI: That's a classic, when people get put into a stretch role way in over their head, are you going to share the extent to which you don't feel confident? Probably not. Not at that particular moment. It's a lot easier to share a vulnerability after a success.

How can we develop better managers?

HI: Giving them some variety of experience is crucial. We still tend to let people grow up in silos. My favourite definition of professional identity comes from Ed Schein: the set of experiences, preferences, beliefs, values with which we define ourselves in a professional role but, he says, it develops with varied experience and meaningful feedback. But it's very hard for people in a corporate context to get either one of those! One thing that complicates this is that you may have a boss who is not in the same country. So those moments where you can have a casual discussion, instead of saving it up for a formal meeting, are few and far between.

Any other myths of management we should consider?

HI: I think it's a myth that leadership style matters. If you look around, you see people with all kinds of different styles being very successful. More or less interpersonally skilled, for example. More directive or more participative, more internally focused, more externally focused. You see over and over again a really wide variety. So one of the things I get my students to think about is not 'what's the right style?' but 'what is the right role for me in this context?' What is it that I can do most productively? Really effective leaders – whether they're nice or not, collaborative or not – they often play a really important role in bridging between their group or company and the external environment. They are always developing relationships with key stakeholders, with clients, with customers. Managing inputs and outputs.

You're not just there to manage the inside of a unit, you're there to manage the context of that unit.

What role can business schools play?

HI: Business schools allow people to step out of the fray and reflect a bit about the past as well as the future. Sometimes at work we can go through pretty intense learning experiences but we don't have the time to stop and process it. Working on that with a peer group who are also going through similar experiences is really important.

Also: exposing people to a different peer group and a different network, rather than the more narrow one at work, is valuable.

And the future?

HI: I'm not a good futurologist! But what I see in the large corporate context is that people's jobs have just become impossible. It's too much. The inbox, the demands on performance, the cost-squeezing, the growth expectations – without a lot of guidance, I don't know how far we can go with that, as human beings.

You see a lot of people just hanging on by their fingernails, but not necessarily happy to be there. A lot jumping off as soon as they can.

Managers now have to manage all sorts of external providers who don't necessarily have the culture, who don't have the commitment, or the informal glue, so maybe financially it's cheaper but the human costs can be high.

It seems to me that the way organizations operate now is very different from the way things were when there were big theories of the organization being studied and developed. Maybe we need to think about organizational structures again.

APPENDIX 5
Laura Empson

Laura Empson is an expert on the world of professional service firms. Her latest book, *Leading Professionals: Power, politics, and prima donnas*, is published by Oxford University Press. Among other publications she also wrote *Managing the Modern Law Firm* (2007). She is a professor at Cass Business School, City University London, and previously lectured at Oxford.

What do you think when you hear the word 'management'?
LE: I think the term management is essentially meaningless. You can only understand management in juxtaposition with other concepts like administration and leadership. What we would have called administration 50 years ago is now being called management. And what we might have called management 20 years ago is now being called leadership. In business schools, courses that were once called the management of something or other now have to be rebranded as 'leadership', in order to get people to sign up for them. If you add the word leadership to an executive education course you can immediately charge considerably more for it. So, just as personnel management has become HRM, and public relations has become communications, management is starting to morph into leadership.

It's terminological inflation – now the term leadership has been debased we'll have to invent another one.

Putting it really simply, I think management is about working with other people to try and get things done. It implies there's some degree of top-down hierarchical control, but not necessarily – we're all familiar with the concept of managing upwards, that is still management. People sometimes talk about management as 'doing things right' and leadership as about 'doing the right thing', or they juxtapose efficiency and effectiveness, or they talk about maintenance and change, but ultimately these are rather dull distinctions. I think we just need to understand that the terms management and leadership are used in a variety of different ways; no one can come up with a definitive definition, and it's a mistake to pretend that you can.

There's a nice quote in a great book by David Knights and Hugh Willmott called *Management Lives* – and they say: 'Management is part and parcel of life and how it's lived.' If you start with a definition as broad as that, you can take it anywhere you like.

A lot of people would equate management with an MBA, but the M does not stand for management – it stands for 'master's'. The BA stands for 'business administration' – which is funny because no MBA student would like to think of themselves as doing administration. So we still carry the legacy of this old terminology.

Some people agonize about the differences between management and leadership, but is that helpful?

LE: I've done a lot of research on leadership. It's very hard for an interviewee to explain when they're leading and when they're managing. And if they don't know, why should we try and impose these artificial distinctions? You can charge a lot more if you're giving a speech to practitioners about leadership. In fact no one ever asks me to give speeches about management, they always want me to give speeches about leadership, because it's sexy and cool. What I am trying to say is, there are a lot of business schools and academics who have a vested financial interest in promoting this premium concept called leadership.

How are management and leadership seen in the context of a professional services firm (PSF)?

LE: If management implies a degree of hierarchy, then to describe yourself as managing people implies that you think you're above them in some way. And in a PSF context that's quite a difficult distinction to articulate and sustain, particularly in a professional partnership where you have been elected by your peers. The partners have not really made you the boss of them. What they have done is allowed you to do some 'administration' on their behalf. So if you start behaving as though you're their boss they will be uncomfortable. But in the next breath they will blame you for being an ineffective leader.

So they feel like they want something called leadership which will be embodied in or characterized by certain quite purposeful decisions and announcements...

LE: ... but only if they are decisions and announcements that professionals agree with. In a professional context leadership needs to have an inspirational element to it so that professionals are prepared to cast themselves in the role of follower. In professional service firms management of other people is good, because other people need to be managed. 'I am led, he is managed.'

There are parts of our that life we want to be administered, parts of our life where we might want to lead or be led, and parts of our life where we need to be managed, though we might not accept that. Professionals tend to call that last bit bureaucracy.

In a PSF you don't want your high fee earners to get bogged down in management.

LE: It's about freeing up the time of the 'talent'. The talent chooses certain people to manage them, like a rock band has a manager. That's very different from saying 'I will follow you'. In effect the partners are paying the person who is leading the firm, because the person who is 'in charge' is taken out of full-time fee-earning work, to manage them. The most traditional partners would say that this person has now become a significant cost to the firm, and they are willing to accept that because it is important that other people get managed. But there's absolutely no acceptance that this implies a power relationship.

I actually try to avoid using words like management and leadership and I talk more in terms of the activities of senior executives, because that's much more neutral. Senior executives will be doing a mixture of leadership, management and administration, with different people at different times. The skill is to understand intuitively which to do when and with whom.

Some of the senior people you interview often seem to be reluctant to admit that they are in charge.

LE: And the question to consider is: do they actually mean that, or is it part of the game that they have to play, to imply a degree of modesty and diffidence? But in a crisis, partners want to believe the senior partner or managing partner is in charge.

So it's about having the sensitivity and subtlety to know who needs to hear what and when they need to hear it. Making these finely tuned judgements all the time.

Even in the big four accounting firms, which sometimes are regarded as being more corporate, the leaders may be frustrated because their partners can't be bothered to open e-mails they send them. There may not be active resistance, but the amount of passive resistance in a partnership can be phenomenal.

Of course, corporates are infinitely complex and subtle too. But my research has shown that politics are endemic in partnerships, it's a way of life, it is the lifeblood of these organizations. Professional service firms are designed to be inherently political environments. And the people within them play politics so naturally and so easily that they don't necessarily recognize that this is what they're doing. It's how you get things done and naturally exert influence, in an environment where authority is contingent and autonomy is extensive.

Are these still attractive organizations for young people to go and join and commit to?

LE: Well, 'commit to' is an interesting question. I wouldn't encourage any young person to commit to any organization, because organizations nowadays are not willing to commit to them. I think that's an important thing for young people to remember – much of what is said to them during the recruitment process is essentially garbage. People may be a professional service firm's 'greatest asset' but they are a very expendable asset.

That's just how the professional world is now. It wasn't always thus, but it is now.

The elite firms are very good at creating the impression of being very glamorous. These are the firms people want to work for. They do pay very well. They have great-looking offices. They are good at creating the sense that, if you've joined us, you've made it, you're part of the elite. And for many people that is hugely attractive and they are very happy to pay the price that goes with it.

Louise Ashley and I have done some work on this, looking at how these firms use signifiers of cultural capital to attract undergraduates. So during the recruitment and training programme they take the graduates out to glamorous locations, restaurants that their mum and dad might have heard of, saying: 'You can be a part of this one day. Come here and succeed and one day this will be your life.'

It's a sales pitch in a way?

LE: It's a very explicit sales pitch. And it's seductive. I was part of it – I became a strategy consultant straight out of my MBA programme. Before the days of Uber and Deliveroo it was amazing to work late in the office and just pick up the phone and order a taxi just to bring you your dinner – and then charge it to the client. It can take your mind off the fact you're working in the office till past midnight. That's a nice feeling when you're very young, and you haven't been born into wealth, it makes you feel like a special person if your client is paying £50 so you can eat chicken chow mein without leaving your desk.

Managing ambitious young people like this can't be easy, can it?

LE: There will be people who approach this in a very transactional way, who know what they want to get out of the firm. They want to get some money for a few years, and they want something good on their CV while they work out what they really want to do with their life. And then they go off and do it.

But it can go wrong. When I was a don at Oxford I used to get lots of young people coming to me with their job offers from McKinsey and Goldman Sachs, saying 'which should I go to, what shall I do?' I would give some extra advice to the male students: do it if you like, but don't settle down and have children quickly. Because I was aware of lots of guys who'd taken these kinds of jobs straight out of university on a temporary basis because it seemed like an appropriate thing to do, then somehow they'd got drawn in to the lifestyle, the money, and then they ended up marrying their university girlfriend, then the kids started coming, and 20 years later they were still doing a job they'd never really enjoyed, working for a firm they didn't like, but they'd put all their kids through private school. And I'd say, 'But you've always hated this job', and they'd look at me slightly sadly and say, 'Yes, but my children have had a good education.'

Then there is the phenomenon of the 'insecure overachiever', which I have been researching recently. The insecure overachievers are much more complicated and much, much more valuable to elite professional service firms. Many of these organizations deliberately set out to target and recruit them. They look for them at university, they look for people with a pattern of phenomenal achievement, but also underneath that, an underlying pattern of insecurity. And the deal they make with these people is: we will make you feel special because we want you, but in return we can ask you to do anything for us. The people then join the firm and are made to feel special but then they realize you don't get to stay unless you perform extraordinarily well. These organizations have very strict 'up or out' pyramids, so of the 100 people they take at graduate level only 10 will likely ever make it to partner – sometimes even steeper than that. Very few will make it to partner.

So the firms amplify the individuals' insecurity, they increase the insecurity so that people are competing with each other to make sure that they're the one that gets ahead. And this becomes a powerful control device which obviates the need for management. You don't need to manage people like that. The implicit message is: 'All your fears about inadequacy – we can assuage those by telling you that you are good enough to be a partner here, but we'll only continue to say that to you if you continue to out-perform.' That's what I mean by the insecure overachiever: people will drive themselves and drive themselves relentlessly in order to be allowed to stay. The insecure over-achiever has his or her own internal sense of what good enough is and that can never, ever be satisfied.

Lastly, do even the elite firms have to worry about robots and automation replacing them?

LE: The clue is in the word 'elite'. The elite firms will never be substituted by technology. But they will have to change to respond to it. Technology is never a substitution for brilliant people. Technology, typically, has been a substitution for essentially routinized tasks, and there is a lot of extremely routine work that is done within a lot of these firms, though they may be reluctant to acknowledge that. It's one of the reasons they need to hoover up so many graduate recruits every year.

Technology can replace that. But when you as a chief executive face a hostile takeover, if you want to raise billions of dollars to fund your expansion, or when you are worried you might be up in front of the SEC for some bad accounting practices, you are not going to ask a computer for the answer.

There will always be a place for truly professional work. I think what we may see in the future is a return to more traditional ideas of what professional means, which does convey expertise, status, income obviously, maybe even vocation. Along the way a lot of the expansion into fairly mundane, mediocre, less well-paid, certainly less interesting work will fall by the wayside as it starts to become replaced, not necessarily by technology alone, but by technology in tandem with less highly trained, less highly paid paraprofessionals.

So it's almost back to the future, the specialness will reassert itself potentially?

LE: Well, that would be nice.

APPENDIX 6
Lynda Gratton

Lynda Gratton is an expert on the world of work and how it is changing. She is the author of several books – including *The Shift, Hot Spots, The Key* and *The Exceptional Manager* – and most recently published (with Andrew Scott) *The 100-Year Life*. She is a professor at London Business School.

When you hear the word 'management', what thoughts come to mind? What does it mean to you?

LG: It seems like an old-fashioned word really, 'management'. What is it to be a manager, and who wants to be managed, how do you do it? It's not really a word I use very much. Which is not to say that everybody in an organization is a leader. I think organizations are becoming groups of specialists who are connected because they've got something they want to do together, or a mission, and the role of managers... I'm not sure what that is any more...

Because work is more fluid and interrupted, teams form and re-form...?

LG: Partly it's because conventional task management is different. What was the job of a manager, in the past? The job of a manager was to act as the funnel between the great words that had come down from the top and the people who are running around doing all the stuff, but actually, as we learn from companies like Tata Consulting Services (TCS), if you give enough information to people who are doing the work, they can get on with it.

You do need leadership in a project team. I don't think you can have leaderless groups. But that then is somebody who is making sure the whole thing is moving in the right direction. The role of the leader is to inspire, to engage, to mentor and to coach; and then with the most senior leaders their job is an external one, to look outside and link in with stakeholders.

How should we think of the people who are still 'sort of' managing?

LG: I think their job is to be part of a group, and to bring their own special-ist skills. There is a role for managers, but it's a much more sophisticated role than the one they had before. If you look back 30/40/50 years ago in organizations, teams were pretty simple. By simple I mean they were co-located, they were often men rather than women, they had the same speciality, nationality, same age… so managing them really wasn't that diffi-cult. Where management is really important is in complex teams. These are teams where people are 'virtual', the teams are big, they are multidisciplinary often, they are different ages, men and women… pulling a group together across the world is a really complicated management task, and that's a job that a manager has to do. In which case I would say that management is just as much a specialist skill-set as anything else. It really only kicks in when you have complex teams. Otherwise people can manage themselves, really. All the easy stuff is being done by robots and artificial intelligence. It's only the hard stuff that's left.

So people need to up their game, whatever we call it…?

LG: Managers are people who manage teams, it is an emerging role, a diffi-cult role. I wrote about this in my book *Hot Spots*: you've got to build a collaborative culture, you've got to think about networks, you've got to bring a purpose or a question – that's hard. How do you bring a group together: that is a proper management job. You have to be trained, you have to know how to do it.

Business schools don't necessarily teach this stuff.

LG: I think that's true. Of course we're very excited about leadership. We love looking at the CEOs and we love having them to speak to us. The students love having powerful people around. The role of management gets lost. That's why Julian Birkinshaw's work has been so important. He's iden-tified how important management is – but it's complex management.

Your latest book (written with Andrew Scott), *The 100-Year Life*, also considers how management has to change.

LG: Yes, it's partly based on the myth that people are finished at 60. It's a terrible piece of stereotyping. It's terrible for a couple of reasons. One is that as we live longer we have to work longer. We're going to be working into our 70s and beyond, we can't really be tossed out at 55, it's wrong for the individual. We also know that when people stop working their health deteriorates.

When I teach I say – I'm 62 but it's the new 40, and somebody stopped me and said – 'Lynda, it's the new 40, plus 20 years of experience'. That's the point – as people age, if they've learned anything on the way, they have more to offer.

That leads on to this myth about the generations. Gen X, Gen Y, boomers – there's very little evidence to support the claims that are made about them. People say, 'oh Gen Y, they love meaningful work.' For God's sake, I was a hippy, do you think we didn't want meaningful work?! Or they say, 'Gen Y, they're great at technology'… we're all perfectly adept at technology. It's really bad because it stereotypes age. Andrew and I in the book say, for goodness' sake, look at people for who they are. Stop being myopic about age. Some of the big accounting firms get rid of people at 55 – that's just ridiculous.

So another task for managers is to make the most of the mixed-age workforce?

LG: Of course. Andrew and I have been collecting data on our website (www.100yearlife.com), and one thing we have found is that there are very few differences between a 30-year-old and a 70-year-old, in terms of how they think about work. If you're 70, if you fill in our survey, you're just as likely to want to keep fit as if you're 30.

There are one or two things that could help with cross-age mentoring. In general, older people are more thoughtful about work–life balance. And are more able to put all that into context. So why not have cross-age mentoring when older people can help younger ones in that really frantic stage of your life in your 30s? The second thing is that younger people are much more attuned as to how to build a reputation. Why not get younger people to help older ones build a reputation, especially on social media?

Do we mix up leadership and management?

LG: Well, they are different roles. Leaders are looking into the future, and they're looking out. Leaders increasingly connect the organization with the outside world, in terms of stakeholders or investors or how people view the organization. And a manager is primarily looking down and across, and looking at the complex tasks that have to be achieved.

But they are fascinating jobs, these management jobs, and they don't need to be hierarchical. One of my children is studying medicine, he's becoming a surgeon, and he's told me that one of the things that happens now in complex surgery is that you have a group of people, they all know what their roles are, but the task is the complex thing, and that's the thing that they're adapting to as they go through. There are protocols, a list of 10 things you have to do, and those are rigorously adhered to. They have a whiteboard, and the person writing things down on it could be quite a junior nurse. And their job is to say, 'OK, you've already spent four minutes doing this, and at this stage you should now be doing X...' So who's the manager in that room? This is a group that works incredibly well together, and somebody is managing them, but actually if you were honestly to say who's the manager, you'd have to say, well, it's the lead surgeon, but it's also this nurse.

Another example: I was at the National Theatre last year, watching some top names performing, and as I was watching the stage manager walked on, and she closed the production down. There and then. Some elaborate scenery had failed and it was dangerous. Again: who was the manager there? Because she certainly wasn't the highest-status person. The famous actor had to stop in the middle and walk off. In any complex task somebody has to be able to say: 'This needs to happen now' – but it isn't necessarily a high-status role.

It's the same at the opera: a friend told me about a diva who was causing problems, complaining about the wig she had to wear, and the stage manager said: 'Tomorrow, on stage, somebody will be wearing that wig.' In other words, the show will go on with or without you. And it was the stage manager who was saying that.

In management we have tended to make everything so hierarchical. A manager is the most senior person. But actually the manager may be simply the person who is responsible for a task. That may be a more useful way of thinking about it. The role of the manager is to have protocols. If you're running a virtual team there is a set of protocols to follow. And the job of the manager is to take people through those protocols.

Are you talking about what we used to call a 'self-managed team'?

LG: I don't have much time for that label. Self-managed teams are fine when it's all straightforward, you don't even need a manager. But with complex tasks you need somebody who is managing it. People are all very busy doing the work, they don't have time to look up. First of all the manager has to make sure that the team knows each other.

What is it about opera that intrigues you in particular?

LG: It's just such a complex task. You've got the divas, you've got people who are sitting there all the time, the chorus and orchestra, you may have sometimes only one or two days to rehearse, it's astounding. And it's very complicated.

The other interesting thing is rehearsals – I've been sitting in on lots of rehearsals. And they are much more brutal than managers are. In management we've got into this ridiculous thing that everybody's got to be nice to each other. It's not that they are brutally cruel. They'll just say, 'Let's do that again', and 'let's do that again'. One of the things they do is that if the director is rehearsing them – if you're one of the singers, and I'm talking to you about your performance, my assistant is taking notes – and then they drop you a note saying 'this is what was said about you in that rehearsal'. And in the workplace we just don't have those disciplines.

I think management is a discipline. And it's complicated, and difficult, and what happens is we don't really think much of managers because they don't always do their job. How do you deal with underperformance? That's what people do in opera all the time.

It is partly about training – meaningful training. And the myth of the amateur. 'Everyone can be a manager, you just have to like people...' – no, it's really difficult to do it properly, and we underestimate what the job is and we underestimate how people have to make it work.

Can we bring this approach into the workplace?
The thing about the rehearsal room is that it happens in the moment. The director does not say, 'I shall meet you at four o'clock in six months' time to talk to you about the performance that you're just about to do.' They say I'm standing here with you, and they do it in a very thoughtful way.

They are really focused on the task. Watching, paying attention to what is going on, in the moment, watching people really carefully, and then they give them very detailed feedback in the moment, and then they write it down and send it to them... I don't know any manager who does that. But to do it you've got to be around.

Once the show is up and running, other managers – directors in this context – can keep an eye on the show and make sure things are happening correctly. Some management is about making sure there is that repetition of tasks.

So I suppose what I'm saying is either forget management, or make it sophisticated and do it really well. There's no in-between.

APPENDIX 7
Margaret Heffernan

Margaret Heffernan is a writer, businesswoman and consultant. In the past she worked in television and ran several IT companies. Her book *Wilful Blindness* was a bestseller, and was followed by her more recent titles *A Bigger Prize* and *Beyond Measure*.

What does the word 'management' mean to you?

MH: When I hear the word 'management' my mind goes in two directions. There are both positive and negative aspects to it. The positive aspects of management – which I think is how I've always attempted to run my companies – have been: hire lots of amazing people, and create the conditions in which they can do the best work of their lives. And it's a completely thrilling and wonderful thing to do. You know when it's working. It hums, people are happy. You see people grow, and you feel incredibly proud, and you think this is the greatest job on earth. And I'd like to think that every now and then, for one brief shining moment, it happens! A lot of the people who've worked for me have gone on to run their own businesses, and they've done it really well, and I think, well, they learned something that made them want to do this, and I feel very proud of that.

So simply it means hiring well and getting out of their way?

MH: I think it's more than that. It's about constraints, because creativity is about both freedom and constraints. It's tight and loose, being able to think about constraints that are provocative and inspiring rather than soul-crushing. I started my career at the BBC: if you're making a half-hour programme it does have to be 27 minutes and 30 seconds. What you learn is that great writers can do that and amateur ones can't. So I have a lot of respect for constraint as a creative driver.

So it's not just about freedom. It's about making sure the constraints aren't stupid, that they make sense, that there's a sense of context. It's often about seeing that people have more in them than they might think, or that they have something different in them than they think. I've had managers who saw that in me. So I like to try to do that where appropriate with other people. And it's about seeing opportunities, where people, markets and technologies intersect.

Some of the most creative people I've worked with were software engineers. I treated them like they were creative people and lo and behold they worked like creative people!

That's what I think of as the fun stuff, the good side of management.

But the bad stuff, which I've probably seen more of if I'm being honest, is what I think of as marking people's homework. So it's: here is the job description, in tedious, tortuous detail; here are the rules and regs, here are the standard operating procedures, here is the handbook, here is the culture, here are the reward structures, here are the incentives, whatever the heck that's supposed to mean, and here are the performance management scales and tools and all that nonsense, and I'm going to sit here and twiddle the knobs of this complicated machine and make sure that everybody does exactly what they're supposed to do. Which ensures that they won't do anything more. And it ensures that if the house is on fire nobody's going to say so because it doesn't say so in their job description.

And I think that form of management has been significantly perpetuated, I hate to say it, by business schools, significantly perpetuated by economists, and significantly perpetuated by people who prefer what I think of as a mechanical notion of management over what I think of as an organic model.

So this is an ultra-rigid approach?

MH: And if it can't be measured it has no value. Whereas I tend to think if it can't be measured it's probably the most valuable thing. It's a very numbers-driven approach.

When I ran software businesses in the States my companies had a lead investor who was really a mathematical whizz, and also a very creative, imaginative individual. And I had and have a lot of respect for him. And I once said to him: 'How do you know what is going on in your companies?' He had about 40 companies. And he said: 'I look at the numbers.' Now he's the most brilliant numbers guy I've ever known in my life, and I know he didn't know what was going on in his companies.

When I think of the bad form of management it really does believe the numbers tell the truth. And I have never been in an organization, a good one or a bad one, where the numbers told the whole truth.

So it's really the industrial revolution mechanical model versus an organic model. The organic model to me is really exciting – is it alive, is it flourishing? The mechanical one is – have we eliminated all the faults, are we producing perfect widgets? And what I think is really interesting is that you get companies – they don't often think of themselves like this – but they often have to have both of those. If you think of pharma, for example, they have to have the creative stuff, scientists are immensely creative individuals, but if you don't have the industrial get-rid-of-flaws management in terms of production, then what you're producing isn't safe. What's fascinating to see is when the two approaches butt up against each other. I have more often seen the industrial mindset infect the creative culture than the other way round. And I think one of the reasons pharma's in a mess is because the QA (quality assurance) mindset took over R&D. And so you have a great desire to do wonderful things, and people intellectually capable of doing wonderful things, in a machine that will not let them.

QA and manufacturing are about efficiencies, and creativity and innovation aren't. Can't be. Absolutely cannot be. And this is why the bigger world of organizational thinking is in a mess – these two things do have to co-exist but nobody can figure out what the API (application programming interface) is!

One of the people I've written about a lot, one of my favourite scientists, is a guy named Uri Alon at the Weizmann Institute. He talks about how if you're going to make a breakthrough – and his lab has made a lot of breakthroughs – you have to go through a period where you have absolutely no idea what you're doing. And if you don't go through that, then you're not actually doing creative work. You have to go somewhere you've never been before. But that's so frightening – emotionally, intellectually frightening, often financially frightening – it requires a gigantic amount of institutional social support, that a lot of organizations just think it looks like a mess, which it is. But they don't understand that it's a necessary mess.

Hence your stress on the need for a more collaborative approach – 'this could be nothing, it could be something...'
MH: Exactly – but you won't know if you don't keep going. Because if you fall back on what you know then you're not going to get anywhere you've never been before. It's got to be scary.

If you walk home the same route every day you can't expect to see anything brand new. If you go down the dark alleyway, it might be a bit scary but there's more chance of seeing something new.

In defence of efficiency, a firm like Toyota grew to dominance – before it slipped – through a relentless focus on improving processes...

MH: Yes. And let's be quite clear – you and I don't want to drive a car that was manufactured with the creative mindset. The reason cars have got so much safer over the years is because we got really good at this manufacturing stuff. But the crucial thing is recognizing what you are grappling with. My observation is that because the industrial mindset delivers all these numbers, and it's efficient, people feel a higher degree of comfort with that and think it will do everything. And it just won't.

Data will not solve everything...?

MH: I think there are two things here. I have sat in too many board meetings where we all pored over spreadsheets with masses of data. I don't think anybody understood what the data was saying. And so what they did was ask for more.

It's become this fantastic alibi. And we can now generate so much data we can all drown in it and mostly do.

Having said that, of course there's a lot of great stuff that big data can show us. But you have to understand how to ask questions. And I have not talked to a single, significant data scientist – and I've talked to quite a lot of them – who believes that it's all going to be done by machines. Nobody thinks that. The only people who are sending out that message, and there are people who are, are the marketing and sales people, who hope to terrify you into believing that I don't need people any more, I just need this piece of tech. You can call it salesmanship or propaganda, and as you'd expect it's part of the truth but it's not the whole truth.

What's the difference between leadership and management? Do we worry too much about that distinction?

MH: For a long time I was really allergic to the term 'leadership'. I thought it was rather pompous. And I had never ever thought of myself as a leader. The word 'leader' had never popped into my head.

I have changed my mind. It's partly about this tension between the tight and the loose, the industrial and the creative. Part of the job of leadership is to figure out where are we, what kind of problem is this and what do we need for it? To adjudicate those lines. But I also think increasingly the job of leadership has to be to understand, develop, articulate and monitor the relationship between the organization and the society that it serves.

There's always been this argument: does business exist to serve society, does society exist to serve business, is the business of business business, and

I'm pretty firmly of the view that business is there to serve society, because if there's no society business can't function, and because society is a greater and more complex thing than business in itself. But the person who has to own and negotiate and keep refining that relationship has to be the leader of the organization.

But when you were running tech companies you didn't have a big L for Leader on your door?

MH: I didn't have a door! I knew I was the chief executive but… my job was to do what was best for the business. That was my job description. And if that meant getting pizza for people because I can't write code, and people who can write code need pizza, then that's what I would do. And if it meant going round the country raising money for the people writing code, then that's what I would do. And if it meant explaining to investors what the heck we did, then that's what I would do. My job was to do what was best for the business.

Is management in the context of tech different?

MH: I have two contradictory views on that. The first is: you can't run a tech company if you can't really think through what the consequences of that technology are. And that means you have to be pretty imaginative. And there are some leaders in tech who are not – they just think about the technology, they don't understand what it means when people out there are using it. Pure technologists often make poor leaders. And people who are only leaders are often poor heads of technology companies. They can't see what the repercussions might be. So these are tricky businesses to run. This is also true in biotech.

If the bulk of the business is about building things nobody has seen yet, these are exceptionally hard businesses to run, by definition. You can't do market research, you have to have a high tolerance for failure. You have to have a really strong stomach. You have to have this tight/loose thing going on in your head.

Tech firms can't be run like traditional businesses. The risks are still huge. You can't make them grow up too fast. It's a mistake if your children grow up too fast, and it's a mistake if your company grows up too fast also. It can acquire middle-aged habits when it's still precocious.

It's hard for those businesses who are trying to become digital – they don't know what to keep and what to throw out, in terms of people and processes, practices.

Having said that, tech companies need people to run them who know, value and can communicate with human beings, who do think about ROI, and understand that there is a relationship between the company and the society it serves that has to be negotiated with finesse. And that isn't an optional extra. If you want grown-up money from grown-up markets you're going to have to have some people around you who can behave like grown-ups. Some careful stewardship is needed.

What about the emerging multi-generational workplace?

MH: I did some work with a huge construction company on this. They let me do some research. And one of the things I asked was – what age did people in the company want to retire? It bifurcated quite spectacularly: the young people wanted to retire at about the age of 50, and the older people wanted to retire at the age of 100!

So – a clash. But cross-generational mentoring helped deal with that. Because the veterans were incredibly wise people who had built immensely complex projects and were a great source of wisdom, and the young people were hungry for that, and hungry for mentoring, but also had a kind of edge and vivacity and openness that kept the veterans really young and sparking. It was the construct of history and values that was effective, not a personal intrusion.

The issue here really is justice, and equity. To me the big problem is: how come the older generation has pensions and security, and has enjoyed the benefits of security for a long time, and the younger generation is being asked to swallow zero-hours contracts and no pension and all that? The justice issue has to be resolved. Of course young people want security. They want choices of the kind that our generation had. They definitely want pensions, they definitely want some security in the future, they want to be able to live somewhere near where they're working. That doesn't mean they are going to stick in the same job forever, but I didn't, you didn't...

Michael Kinsley says that if the baby-boomer generation wants to go down in history as a great generation, it will have to start to pay for stuff. Relieve deficits, and pay for its own care. We have to relieve the younger generation of some of what they're going through.

Can we find a positive note to end on?

MH: I see a lot of good things happening, especially between the generations. I love working with younger people because they keep me young, and I think they like working with me because I know stuff, but also because I am interested in them, and listen to them, and have some time to be curious about them, and while I think I know some stuff I don't think I know everything.

Business, whether for profit or not for profit, has the capacity to solve the problems we are facing.

I can look back on times in my career, when I was working with utterly brilliant people, I don't think any of us ever felt we were being managed. We were together doing better work than we had ever done on our own. Sometimes in these situations I was a boss, sometimes I wasn't. But there is that moment of exhilaration when things really are working where you almost feel yourself grow, and that is when whatever we call management is really working. And it's fabulous when it happens!

APPENDIX 8

Rob Goffee
and Gareth Jones

As well as being a popular double act on the speaker and conference circuit, Rob Goffee and Gareth Jones have co-authored several influential books, including *The Character of a Corporation*, *Why Should Anyone Be Led by You?*, *Clever* and most recently *Why Should Anyone Work Here?*

GJ: [eyes digital recorder] But where's the tape…?
[Laughter]

What does the word 'management' mean to you?
RG: Do you want to go first?

GJ: It's the labour of coordination. In any society which practises an extensive division of labour there is what Karl Marx calls the necessary labour of coordination, which is often carried out by people who we've come to call managers. But whether that's the only answer to the necessary labour of coordination is an interesting question.

RG: I think management has had a bad press. It is about coordination, as Gareth says, but a lot of bright young people who come to business schools are interested in entrepreneurship, leadership, creativity, being a financial whizz-kid in the City, being a consultant… I wonder if anybody comes to business schools and says: 'I want to be a manager.' I think probably they did, and some schools still call themselves 'schools of management', but I think it's a word that's almost had its time, but that doesn't mean to say what managers do is unimportant, because I think it's really important.

A lot of corporate clients who come to places like this (London Business School) say they are interested in leadership development. And actually what they really need is management development. But it doesn't sound quite so sexy.

A lot of creative businesses – what they need is better management. They might need better leadership, but they certainly need better management. But that's the 'boring' stuff.

GJ: We've written quite a lot about leadership, but I often preface my remarks by saying, 'this is not to say that management is unimportant'. In fact Rob and I have probably spent the bulk of our lives helping people become better managers.

Take, for example, having 'difficult conversations'. You'd be amazed at the number of senior executives who can't do it. They find it very difficult to have discussions with people about performance issues. Not just Brits – all over the world. You can teach that. You can't teach people to go from awful to wonderful. But you can teach the mediocre to get good. There are management techniques and skills and practices which you can teach which make a big difference to organizational performance.

So I certainly wouldn't knock the word 'management'. But it's interesting, if you look at the popular discourse on things like the health service, whose fault is it? 'Bloated management structures' – which is almost certainly not the case. The health service is a highly complex organization which needs a lot of interface management, and the key players in it, the consultants, aren't very interested in management. So, someone has to do it.

RG: We wrote this book about the people we called the 'clevers', and if we're heading towards a knowledge economy with organizations containing lots of clevers, the last thing they are interested in is management. What they're interested in is their expertise and their individual contribution.

Drucker said management involves making it harder for people to get their work done.

GJ: Very occasionally I go back to the BBC [where Gareth was HR director under director-general Greg Dyke] for a retirement party or similar, and people wander up to me and say: 'You're Gareth Jones aren't you?', and I say yes, and they say: 'You used to be the HR director, didn't you?', and I say yes, and they say: 'You weren't too bad. You didn't get in the way.' And actually I treat that as a massive compliment. Too many HR directors get in the way.

In the context of the BBC you want great programme makers to make great programmes. And you need to clear out all the stuff that stops them making great programmes.

RG: This goes back to our first book, *The Character of a Corporation*. The sociability/solidarity stuff. Where do clever people want to work? Clever people want to work in what we called communal organizations that change the world – Apple, Google, religions. Or they want to work in what we called fragmented organizations – low on sociability, low on solidarity – investment banks or specialist firms. They want to work in these rather strange workplaces where they're either basically working on their own, or they're working with other really clever people, and they're going to change the world. The place they don't want to work is the place where most large organizations are, which we called network cultures – high sociability, low solidarity – which at their worst are political, cliquey, hierarchical, over-managed, under-led. And then the other kind is what we called mercenary – high solidarity, low sociability – stuffed full of measures, think of the NHS over the past 20 years, measures imposed by people who largely don't understand the work that the consultants and the medics are actually doing, and therefore the measures are inappropriate.

Most large-scale, complex organizations tend to be mercenary or networked. And that's where clever, talented individuals don't want to be. This is one of the reasons management has got a bad reputation, because it's largely associated with relatively dysfunctional, either political bureaucracies or organizations which over-control, over-measure, are short-termist and so on.

The unattractiveness of management has something to do with the unattractiveness of organizations.

GJ: Years back I was working with Glaxo, as it then was, with Dr Richard Sykes, who was head of R&D. And they were working on three cephalosporins, which are very powerful antibiotics. And all three failed in the last stages of clinical trials. They had spent a lot of money developing these drugs. And Sykes wrote the team leaders a letter, saying: thank you very much for killing the project. I thought that was inspired creative management, because it is intrinsic to the pharmaceutical industry that new products will fail in the final stages. You can't manage the innovation process in the conventional way, because drugs fail. All you can do is encourage people to carry on. The end of the letter was: what's next? What are we going to do next?

Same in the music industry by the way. My boss at Polygram, Alain Levy, used to say: 'I never fire people for signing bad bands, because if you don't sign bad bands you'll never sign great ones.' Absolutely right. You can't go up to people and say: 'I'd like you to sign the next Bob Marley please. You've got three weeks.'

So there's got to be legitimate, judicious risk-taking without fear of instant death?

GJ: Yes. But this is not, by the way, a recipe for anarchy. Because in the end if all you do is sign bad bands, you do get fired. And if all you do is develop drugs that fail, it's no good.

Sykes used to say: 'The most important person in this company is a good bench scientist. The only thing that matters is the science.' Although Sir Paul Girolami did treble the price of Zantac, which made a big difference too…!

Didn't Sir Paul used to go and talk to managers below his top tier to find out what was going on, to see which ideas had not got through to him?

GJ: Management by walking around was a good fad. If you don't do that, the information you get is sanitized.

RG: Being an executive – or manager – in a good organization offers you a wealth of development experience, which is massively under-marketed and sold by these organizations as something useful to do.

GJ: Years ago Rob and I used to teach on a programme for Unilever called the international management seminar. These were executives in their early 30s. You couldn't have had a more interesting group of people.

RG: The company had an ambition to push people outside their discipline, outside their business and outside their culture. Guess what, you ended up as a pretty rounded individual, with useful experience, and that kind of experience we know develops leadership.

GJ: Rich and varied early experiences.

RG: How do you get that – on sophisticated management development programmes. But companies don't make this sound attractive.

If you stand in front of a group of Nestlé or Unilever executives in their 30s and 40s they can be one of the toughest crowds to appear before, and the reason it's tough is they are bloody good! They're good because they have had management development.

GJ: I remember one marketing guy from Unilever, he was posted to northern Italy to run a factory. He'd never run a factory before. And as he was arriving in the taxi he was met by all the workers streaming out, going on strike. And he thought, 'Christ! I've never had to deal with this sort of thing before. We don't have strikes in marketing!' And he asked the driver what was going on, and he said, 'Oh, don't worry, they always do this when a new boss arrives.' But after a couple of years of this he had become a different kind of person… he ended up chairing a big part of the business.

When you meet really competent managers they have a tremendous array of skills. If you can sprinkle those sorts of skills on top of leadership then your organization is going to fly.

What about the problem of having too many rules in a business?

GJ: We say have as many rules as necessary, but no more. Safety can be critical in some businesses. But elsewhere you can get this proliferation of rules. I said to the DG at the BBC that there were so many rules it was impossible not to be in breach of them. And that means that most of them get ignored. Which of course can lead to all kinds of organizational excesses – dare I say it like the [Jimmy] Savile scandal.

RG: Organizations often try to get rid of rules but the evidence is they tend to come back. We have called for having fewer, simpler rules in our recent book [*Why Should Anyone Work Here?*] but the point about simple rules caused the most controversy. And of course excessive rules will piss your clever and creative people off.

It's a really hard one. Max Weber may have been right: when organizations get larger bureaucratic processes emerge. The issue is to have rules that people understand. Often they don't, hence the negative connotation of bureaucracy, which is not what Weber meant. But you do need systems.

GJ: Our distinction is between systematization, which big organizations need to do, and bureaucratization, when you don't know what the rules are for. They're just the rules. But that's hopeless. Our pragmatic advice is that every time you create an organizational rule you should eradicate two. Otherwise you will have rule accretion. A handful of shared values is worth a thousand rules.

RG: Yes, you could try trusting people first before you create another rule, which is a riskier option, but it might work.

Gareth, why do you think management still has this image problem?

GJ: Part of this has to do with the Taylorist hangover. Taylor divided work into the labour of conception – thinking – and the labour of execution – doing. And he concentrated thinking in the hands of managers. And many, many modern organizations still have a Taylorist hangover. And of course a lot of the really depressing data about low levels of engagement is actually a consequence of the application of Taylorist thinking about organizations.

One of the legacies of Taylorism is when you try and redress it you might meet with some resistance from the very people you've been telling what to do all these years. Donald Roy described all this beautifully in his wonderful, path-breaking articles in the late 1940s – 'Efficiency and the fix', 'Quota restriction and goldbricking in a machine shop'. He explains how people cheat the piecework system. He says: 'The men in my machine shop were canny calculators… The dollar sign fluttered at the masthead of every machine.' We now know that you can't devise a piecework system that people won't find a way around. You're much better off saying to the workers: why don't you devise a piecework system? Then we'll have something that we all agree about.

How can we drive the harmful instincts of Taylorism out of the workplace?

GJ: Donald Roy said: 'I donned a diving bell and took a trip to the bottom', which of course was a radical thought in the 1940s. It has to do with reconnecting the senior executives with what's really going on. One of the first businesses I worked with was Bass brewers. If you were on the board of Bass inns and taverns it was in your job description that you had to visit a pub every day – not necessarily a Bass pub. But you had to go to a pub, and you had to watch people consuming the product. The chairman said to me: 'You're the only bloody consultant we've ever had who likes the product!'

An Americanism I really like is: 'Be where the rubber hits the road.' If you think about head-office-type jobs, if you don't deliberately go to where the rubber hits the road, all you get is a kind of phantom version of the world. You get this sanitized, often quantitative, numerical account of what's happening.

RG: The difficulty is that managers don't always feel they have the time to get out and see what is really going on. They misguidedly think they can do it all from their computer. The pressure to meet short-term targets is overwhelming. In our book *Why Should Anyone Work Here?* the best organizations we looked at were not in the main shareholder companies, they had alternative ownership structures. Not all of them, but most. This allows them a longer time perspective. I think that unless you get that long-term commitment to make organizations and management better, you won't do it; you'll focus on the wrong kind of short-termist stuff, both individually and organizationally.

Can organizations stop themselves from failing?

RG: A good culture can drift into something bad without you knowing it, and by the time you discover it, it's too late. You slip into the negative but you have to work to climb out of it, manage your way forward.

GJ: Marks and Spencer would be an example of that. They had been one of the top retailers in Europe for a very long time. In the end senior executives didn't really know what was going on, and the ones who did really know what was going on weren't listened to. So there was no connection with the real world of work. There's a risk for business schools in this, obviously. Although everyone here is super smart, of course!

I had one student who was so bright, he used to put his hand up halfway through the case study discussion, because he had the answer already. After three weeks of this I said to him, listen, you stop ruining my class and I'll teach you to be a human being! And he was clever enough to go: 'OK, deal!'

RG: One of the things I say in classes is that leaders influence the evolution of the culture. People seem to like that. The next sentence is – but you can't manage culture. Leaders can influence the evolution of culture, typically through the example of their own actions. But culture is largely an outcome of behaviour. And behaviour can be managed.

The stuff you manage is behaviour. And that is an honourable contribution to how cultures change. But of course the management process doesn't seem to get the credit because we are focused on leaders influencing culture.

GJ: This is the labour of coordination. It's a coordination job.

RG: And in the knowledge economy, what organizations struggle with is managing these overlaps, and matrices. That is about the clever management of coordination.

GJ: Some call it supply chain management now. And that's a coordination task too.

APPENDIX 9

Tom Peters

Tom Peters is the original (and many would say best) management guru. He co-authored *In Search of Excellence* (with Robert Waterman) in 1982, has subsequently published over a dozen more titles, and there will be another one out soon.

What thoughts come to mind when you hear the word 'management'? What does it mean to you?

TP: I have disagreed with a lot of things Peter Drucker said – although that's not always permitted – but somebody asked him some years ago what he thought his greatest contribution was, and he said, effectively, I have reframed management 'as a liberal art' (he probably didn't use the verb 'reframe'). I think that's incredibly powerful, and it's one of the many reasons I think business schools are, frankly, messed up!

I'm working on a book myself at the moment. The context for this is: technology is coming at us like an express train. You've seen the forecasts saying how many white-collar jobs are going to go. If we're going to survive the onslaught we're going to have to do more than just learn how to install artificial intelligence, and arguably the people who'll survive will bring enterprises to life in an artistic fashion, or words to that effect.

I read a book recently, *When Breath Becomes Air* by Paul Kalanithi; it's by a neurosurgeon who contracted a nasty cancer and died. It's a wonderful book, and deservedly got terrific press. But I had this moment of recognition while reading it. Yes, he was a neurosurgeon who saved many lives and that's of profound importance, but any manager has an opportunity de facto to save more lives than any neurosurgeon. And the argument is: management is the arrangement of human affairs, and management is actually the highest of all human arts. Because we are attempting to help our fellows, whether it's three, six or sixty thousand of them.

There's a wonderful line from the late Robert Altman, the movie director. When he won an Oscar for his lifetime achievement he said that the role of the director is to create spaces where actresses and actors can become more than they have ever been before, more than they have ever dreamed of being. As far as I'm concerned the same thing is true of somebody running a small housekeeping department at the Four Seasons in London.

Management is a really big deal. It has the potential to be a really big deal. And business schools have reduced it to marketing formulas, and accounting formulas and so on. My thesis adviser said to me – it's very interesting, when the kids are here as 26-year-old MBAs all they want is finance and marketing; when they come back at 38 for exec[utive] ed[ucation] all they want is the people stuff.

What do you think of the distinction some people make between leadership and management?

TP: Well, I hope you leave this bit in: this so-called difference between leadership and management is a totally bullsh*t, useless, counterproductive idea. It's about human beings getting things done. The simple-minded way I put it is: a good manager has to be a good leader and a good leader has to be a good manager and, you know, get over it.

I adore Warren Bennis and will forgive him his leadership/management distinction, but reluctantly!

In the context of all this new technology, is management getting harder?

TP: Human beings are human beings, and though the context for management is changing, there is a human dimension that is not presumably going to change. I'm reading a powerful book right now called *The Distracted Mind: Ancient brains in a high-tech world*, and it basically says tech is really screwing up our brains. There was a wonderful book written a couple of years ago by Frank Partnoy called *Wait*, and what he said was [that] the biggest thing that differentiates us from other animals is the ability to slow down and think before we do something. Literally, pausing is what it means to be human.

Something is going on with technology that is going to require us to think about the world in a different way. That's different.

It's worth thinking about the difference between Artificial Intelligence (AI) and Intelligence Augmented (IA). Do we use this stuff to help us be more human, or do we get replaced by it?

I was at dinner with the head of one of the world's biggest investment firms, and he asked me: 'What do you think the number one problem is with CEOs?', and being a smart-ass I said, 'I could give you 50 but I don't know which one you would rank first.' But the reply I got back was startling – he said, 'They don't read enough.'

I effectively took a 12-month sabbatical a couple of years ago to read. I used to flatter myself that I was maybe a tiny step ahead of the crowd, but I looked up and realized I couldn't even see the crowd any more! Reading has not put me ahead of the crowd but at least I can see the tail end of it. I can have intelligent conversations with people who know this stuff well.

Driverless cars are coming, but they are not coming tomorrow. This will take time to implement. A lot of this is going to take 10–20 years and there is a lot that isn't going to change between now and then.

The other gross misconception that exists is that we are all working for FTSE 100 or Fortune 500 companies and it's just not true – 80 per cent or so work for small businesses. We ought to remember that.

Two key books for me in recent times have been Susan Cain's *Quiet*, about listening to the 50 per cent of us who are introverts, and Frank Partnoy's *Wait*. They've taught us a lot.

And yet there's a lot of talk about business acceleration, agility, pivoting and so on?

TP: Well my top investment banker told me CEOs should read more, and… I hate that 'agile' sh*t! There is no such thing as a process that automatically makes anything work. I wrote a paper once, never published it but it's one [of] the favourite things I ever worked on, and it's called 'Systems have their place: second place'. And fundamentally it says: 'culture first'.

Lou Gerstner and I were arch enemies at McKinsey because he was Mr Strategy and I was Mr Culture, even though we didn't use the word 'culture' in those days. And later he wrote his book *Who Says Elephants Can't Dance?* about his time at IBM, and in it there's a paragraph that caused me to start weeping copiously, because he says he would have avoided all the 'soft' stuff and focused on metrics and strategy, but culture is not part of the game, culture is the game.

Culture is not a speed thing. I did a speech last year for a project management group, and I started with a picture of me in drag, to attend a party dressed as Elizabeth Cady Stanton, who helped bring universal suffrage to the United States. My first slide talked about the 70 years, 8 months, 3 days, 6 hours people had worked on this, from the first meeting in 1838 to the day in 1920 when the suffrage amendment passed. I said: my idea of a project is an 80-year project.

When an idea is capitalized it has become a religion, at which point it is fundamentally useless. And that's what I feel about Agile! with a capital A! Agile training! Agile certified! Let's go back to Drucker and management as a liberal art.

Henry Mintzberg once cited some research that professional school graduates – engineering, business etc – get two or three times more job offers [than] and twice the starting salary of liberal arts graduates, but at year 20 the liberal arts graduates have left the professionals in the dust. So Henry asks what would be the best preparation for management? A philosophy degree. A non-trivial point. If anything, this stuff gets more important as you try to deal with the rate of change.

Time to reflect is important.

TP: I was with some bank executives recently discussing this. I reminded them that there is no legal document which requires you to respond to e-mails or IMs within 45 seconds. I know your boss expects you to respond, and you probably have to respond, but you don't have to mess with your people. Part of this is a million miles away for philosophy. What you really need is self-discipline, or a mentor, or a peer… we can slow down. I call it 'the sin of send' – wait five minutes before you press the button.

I had an editor, back in the days of fax machines, who said: 'I have a bad temper and I don't want to be able to respond immediately.' And that was in the days of fax machines. He didn't want anything to do with them.

What sort of interventions do make a difference?

TP: In my new book I've written a chapter on leadership but it's simply called 'Some stuff' – 29 things you can try. It's Howard Schultz going to 25 Starbucks a week, it's the former boss of Campbell's Soup in 10 years writing 30,000 thank-you notes. Get the hell out of your office and write some thank-you notes. Not profound but it will help.

Hiring. Here's a blinding flash of the obvious. I'm a great fan of Southwest Airlines. I asked their former President Colleen Barrett: 'What do you hire for?', and she said it was: 'Listening, caring, saying thank you and being warm.' Goes for pilots as well as flight attendants. And I've seen that working in practice for myself.

I've been preaching management by wandering around for 35 years, but I know the tasks pile up and some days you don't get out of the office.

Self-discipline matters. And a spouse or a best friend.

As always, I'm willing to blame the business schools for a lot of things. But they don't teach this stuff.

A friend at McKinsey once said to me: 'Who become leaders here? It's the least worst people people.' That's part of the answer. We hire for the wrong reasons, we don't hire for listening, caring, saying thank you. We hire wrong, we promote wrong, business schools teach the wrong things and emphasize the wrong stuff.

REFERENCES

Introduction

Birkinshaw, J (2010) *Reinventing Management: Smarter choices for getting work done*, Jossey-Bass, San Francisco, CA

McGrath, T (2017) *The Boss Baby* [film], Dreamworks Animation, produced by Ramsay Ann Naito

Myth 1

Collins, J (2001) *Good to Great: Why some companies make the leap… and others don't*, William Collins, New York, NY

Goffee, R and Jones, G (2006) *Why Should Anyone Be Led by You? What it takes to be an authentic leader*, Harvard Business School Press, Boston, MA

Hersey, P and Blanchard, K H (1969) *Management of Organizational Behaviour: Utilizing human resources*, Prentice Hall, Englewood Cliffs, NJ

Rosenzweig, P (2007) *The Halo Effect… and eight other business delusions that deceive managers*, Free Press, New York, NY

Myth 2

Kets de Vries, M (2006) *The Leader on the Couch: A clinical approach to changing people and organizations*, Jossey-Bass, San Francisco, CA

Marmot, M et al (1991) Health inequalities among British civil servants: the Whitehall II study, *The Lancet*, **337** (8754), pp 1387–93

Piketty, T (2014) *Capital in the Twenty-first Century*, Harvard University Press, Boston, MA

Myth 3

The Japan Times (2017) Japan Panel Proposes Capping Overtime at 720 Hours a Year, *The Japan Times* [Online] http://www.japantimes.co.jp/news/2017/02/15/national/japan-panel-puts-forth-proposal-cap-overtime-720-hours-year/#.WWSC-VGQyUl

Lansons (2015) Britain at Work, *Lansons* [Online] http://www.lansons.com/britain-at-work-event

Myth 4

CIPD (2015) From Best to Good Practice HR: Developing principles for the profession, *CIPD* [Online] https://www.cipd.co.uk/knowledge/strategy/hr/good-practice-report?_ga=2.123483656.245948691.1497960773-1662614946.1497960773

Goffee, R and Jones, G (2006) *Why Should Anyone Be Led by You? What it takes to be an authentic leader*, Harvard Business School Press, Boston, MA

Post, T (1973) *Magnum Force* [film], produced by Robert Daley and starring Clint Eastwood as Inspector Harry Callahan

Myth 5

Nobel Prizes and Laureates (2009) Oliver E Williamson – Facts, *Nobelprize.org* [Online] https://www.nobelprize.org/nobel_prizes/economic-sciences/laureates/2009/williamson-facts.html

Stern, S (2008) The challenge of straight talking, *Financial Times*, 20 Oct [Online] https://www.ft.com/content/755d8364-9eb8-11dd-98bd-000077b07658

Wise, H (1976) *I, Claudius*, BBC TV production written by Jack Pulman and starring Derek Jacobi

Myth 6

Bezos, J (2017) Letter to Amazon Shareholders, *GeekWire* [Online] https://www.geekwire.com/2017/full-text-annual-letter-amazon-ceo-jeff-bezos-explains-avoid-becoming-day-2-company/

Myth 7

Goffee, R and Jones, G (2009) *Clever: Leading your smartest, most creative people*, Harvard Business School Press, Boston, MA

Hamel, G (2007) *The Future of Management*, Harvard Business School Press, Boston, MA

Pfeffer, J (2013) You're still the same: why theories of power hold over time and across contexts, *The Academy of Management Perspectives*, 1 November [Online] http://amp.aom.org/content/27/4/269.short

Myth 8

Emerson, R W (1841) *Essays: First Series* [reprinted 2007 by digireads.com]

Myth 9

Gill, A A (2012) The parenting trap, *Vanity Fair*, December [Online] http://www.vanityfair.com/culture/2012/12/aa-gill-schools-ruining-our-kids

Koch, C (2016) Hiscox: The art of risk, *Director* [Online] http://www.director. co.uk/14550-2-the-art-of-risk

Monty Python (1979) *Monty Python's Life of Brian* [film], directed by Terry Jones

Myth 10

Kay, J (2003) Blog: The High Cost of ICI's Fall from Grace, *John Kay* [Online] https://www.johnkay.com/2003/02/13/the-high-cost-of-icis-fall-from-grace/

Kay, J (2014) Blog: Drug Companies Are Built in Labs Not Boardrooms, *John Kay* [Online] https://www.johnkay.com/2014/05/07/drug-companies-are-built-in-labs-not-boardrooms/

Kennedy, J F (1961) Inaugural Address of President John F Kennedy, *John F Kennedy Presidential Library and Museum* [Online] https://www.jfklibrary. org/Research/Research-Aids/Ready-Reference/JFK-Quotations/Inaugural-Address.aspx

Thinkers 50 (2011) Henry Mintzberg Interview, *Thinkers 50* [Online] http:// thinkers50.com/interviews/henry-mintzberg-interview/

Myth 11

Drucker, P (1984) Essay, in *Managing in the Next Society*, St Martin's Griffin, New York, NY

High Pay Centre (2015) Made to Measure, *High Pay Centre* [Online] http:// highpaycentre.org/files/FINAL_MADE_TO_MEASURE.pdf

Myth 12

Dweck, C S (2006) *Mindset: The new psychology of success*, Random House, New York, NY

Jacobs, C (2009) *Management Rewired: Why feedback doesn't work and other surprising lessons from the latest brain science*, Portfolio, New York, NY

Myth 13

Surowiecki, J (2004) *The Wisdom of Crowds: Why the many are smarter than the few*, Abacus, London

Myth 14

Hunt, V et al (2016) The Power of Parity: Advancing women's equality in the United Kingdom, *McKinsey* [Online] http://www.mckinsey.com/global-themes/ women-matter/the-power-of-parity-advancing-womens-equality-in-the-united-kingdom

Wittenberg-Cox, A (2010) *How Women Mean Business: A step by step guide to profiting from gender balanced business*, Wiley, Hoboken, NJ

Myth 15

Dannatt, R (2011) Bill Slim was an inspiration – and the greatest of our generals, *Daily Telegraph*, 8 April [Online] http://www.telegraph.co.uk/history/world-war-two/8436002/Bill-Slim-was-an-inspiration-andthe-greatest-of-our-generals.html

Myth 16

Bianchi, J (2014) The First 90 Days: Secrets to succeeding at a new job [interview with Michael Watkins], *LearnVest*, 10 June [Online] https://www.learnvest.com/2014/06/new-job-success

Freeland, C (2007) Transcript of interview with Andrew Liveris, *Financial Times*, 1 June [Online] https://www.ft.com/content/9ec78344-1061-11dc-96d3-000b5df10621

Neff, T and Citrin, J (2007) *You're in Charge – Now What? The 8 point plan*, Crown Business, New York, NY

Watkins, M (2003) *The First 90 Days: Proven strategies for getting up to speed faster and smarter*, Harvard Business School Press, Boston, MA

Myth 17

Fitzsimmons, A and Atkins, D (2017) *Rethinking Reputational Risk: How to manage the risks that can ruin your business, your reputation and you*, Kogan Page, London

Hancock, M and Zahawi, N (2011) *Masters of Nothing: The crash and how it will happen again unless we understand human nature*, Biteback, London

Myth 18

Birchall, J (2008) Transcript of interview with Wal-Mart's Lee Scott, *Financial Times*, 6 Apr [Online] https://www.ft.com/content/397effaa-028f-11dd-9388-000077b07658

Myth 19

Campbell, A (2012) Corporate Reputation: Alastair Campbell, Portland – Nine lessons in strategy, *PR Week* [Online] http://www.prweek.com/article/1152051/corporate-reputation-alastair-campbell-portland--nine-lessons-strategy

Kay, J (1998) Strategic advantage, *John Kay*, 5 Aug [Online] https://www.johnkay.com/1998/08/05/strategic-advantage

Martin, R and Lafley, A G (2013) *Playing to Win: How strategy really works*, Harvard Business Review Press, Boston, MA

Mintzberg, H (1994) *The Rise and Fall of Strategic Planning*, Free Press, New York, NY

Mintzberg, H, Lampel, J and Ahlstrand, B (2004) *Strategy Bites Back*, FT Prentice Hall, London

Rumelt, R (2011) *Good Strategy, Bad Strategy: The difference and why it matters*, Crown Business, New York, NY

Myth 20

Davidson, A (1995) UK: The Davidson Interview – Gerry Robinson, *Management Today* [Online] http://www.managementtoday.co.uk/uk-davidson-interview-gerry-robinson/article/410472#mRA4o0vBKbpPwee6.99

Red Letter Days for Business (2015) Lack of Flexibility Is Killing UK Productivity [survey], *Red Letter Days for Business*, 14 Oct [Online] https://www.redletterdays.co.uk/companyupdates/14-10-2015

Saunders, A (2017) Power Part Timers 2017 – Flexible Heroes, *Management Today* [Online] http://www.managementtoday.co.uk/power-part-timers-2017-flexible-heroes/your-career/article/1421373

Working Mums (2016) Mums Forced Out Due to Lack of Flexible Jobs [survey], *Workingmums* [Online] https://www.workingmums.co.uk/mums-forced-due-lack-flexible-jobs/

Myth 21

Fishman, C (1996) Whole Foods Is All Teams – Interview with John Mackey, *Fast Company* [Online] https://www.fastcompany.com/26671/whole-foods-all-teams

Furnham, A (2015) Executive Pay: Is it fair? *Chartered Management Institute blog* [Online] http://www.managers.org.uk/insights/news/2015/october/executive-pay-is-it-fair

Myth 22

Emrich, M (nd) Abraham Maslow (1908–70) [Online] http://www.muskingum.edu/~psych/psycweb/history/maslow.htm

Feder, B J (2000) F I Herzberg, 76, Professor and Management Consultant [obituary], *New York Times*, 1 Feb [Online] http://www.nytimes.com/2000/02/01/business/f-i-herzberg-76-professor-and-management-consultant.html?mcubz=2

Herzberg, F (1968) One more time: how do you motivate employees?, *Harvard Business Review*, Jan–Feb, reprinted 2003 [Online] https://hbr.org/2003/01/one-more-time-how-do-you-motivate-employees

Kets de Vries, M (2006) *The Leader on the Couch: A clinical approach to changing people and organizations*, Jossey-Bass, San Francisco, CA

Positive Psychology Center (nd) Martin E P Seligman [profile], *Positive Psychology Center* [Online] https://ppc.sas.upenn.edu/people/martin-ep-seligman

Myth 23

Arntz, M, Gregory, T and Zierahn, U (2016) The Risk of Automation for Jobs in OECD Countries: A comparative analysis, *OECD Social, Employment and Migration Working Papers* [Online] http://www.oecd-ilibrary.org/social-issues-migration-health/the-risk-of-automation-for-jobs-in-oecd-countries_5jlz9h56dvq7-en

Chaffin, J (2017) Farm robots ready to fill Britain's post-EU labour shortage, *Financial Times*, 25 Apr [Online] https://www.ft.com/content/beed97d2-28ff-11e7-bc4b-5528796fe35c?mhq5j=e2

Davenport, T and Kirby, J (2017) *Only Humans Need Apply: Winners and losers in the age of smart machines*, HarperBusiness, New York, NY

Dennett, D (2017) Philosopher Daniel Dennett on AI, robots and religion, *Lunch with the FT*, March [Online] https://www.ft.com/content/96187a7a-fce5-11e6-96f8-3700c5664d30

Frey, C B and Osborne, M A (2013) The Future of Employment: How susceptible are jobs to computerisation? *Oxford Martin School* [Online] http://www.oxfordmartin.ox.ac.uk/publications/view/1314

Jacobson, H (2017) A Point of View, *BBC Radio 4* [Online] http://www.bbc.co.uk/programmes/b08ns2m6

Masunaga, S (2017) Robots could take over 38% of US jobs within about 15 years, report says, *Los Angeles Times*, 24 Mar [Online] http://www.latimes.com/business/la-fi-pwc-robotics-jobs-20170324-story.html

Murgia, M (2017) Satya Nadella, Microsoft, on why robots are the future of work, *Financial Times*, 29 Jan [Online] https://www.ft.com/content/7a03c1c2-e14d-11e6-8405-9e5580d6e5fb

O'Connor, S (2017) Never mind the robots: future jobs demand human skills, *Financial Times*, 16 May [Online] https://www.ft.com/content/b893396c-3964-11e7-ac89-b01cc67cfeec

Taylor, F W (1911) *Principles of Scientific Management*, Harper and Brothers, New York, NY

Myth 25

Cable, D (2007) *Change to Strange: Create a great organization by building a strange workforce*, FT Prentice Hall, London

Erickson, T (2017) The Future of Work: Firms must 'mobilise intelligence', *Human Resources* [Online] http://www.hrmagazine.co.uk/article-details/the-future-of-work-firms-must-mobilise-intelligence

Myth 26

Bloom, P (2016) *Against Empathy: The case for rational compassion*, Ecco Press, New York, NY

Littlejohn, B (1998) *Hug Me While I Weep, for I Weep for the World: The lonely struggles of Bel Littlejohn*, Little, Brown, London

Obama, B (2006) President Obama's Visit to Northwestern: Commencement speech at Northwestern University [Online] http://www.northwestern.edu/newscenter/stories/2006/06/barack.html

Peralta, C F and Saldanha, M F (2017) Can dealing with emotional exhaustion lead to enhanced happiness? The roles of planning and social support, *Work & Stress*, **31** (2) [Online] http://www.tandfonline.com/doi/full/10.1080/02678373.2017.1308445

Myth 27

Bourdain, A (2000) *Kitchen Confidential: Adventures in the culinary underbelly*, Bloomsbury, London

Goffee, R and Jones, G (2006) *Why Should Anyone Be Led by You? What it takes to be an authentic leader*, Harvard Business School Press, Boston, MA

Scott, K (2017) *Radical Candor: Be a kickass boss without losing your humanity*, St Martin's Press, New York, NY

Sociology in Switzerland (nd) Georg Simmel: Biographic Information, *Sociology in Switzerland* [Online] http://socio.ch/sim/bio.htm

Myth 28

Goffee, R and Jones, G (2006) *Why Should Anyone Be Led by You? What it takes to be an authentic leader*, Harvard Business School Press, Boston, MA

Ibarra, H (2015) *Act Like a Leader, Think Like a Leader*, Harvard Business Review Press, Boston, MA

Myth 29

Gratton, L and Scott, A (2016) *The 100-Year Life: Living and working in an age of longevity*, Bloomsbury, London

Handy, C (2015) *The Second Curve: Thoughts on reinventing society*, Random House, London

Hill, A (2015) Part Generation X, part baby boomer: why products do not suit me, *Financial Times* [Online] https://www.ft.com/content/f5dca830-89d0-11e4-9dbf-00144feabdc0

Manpower Group (2016) The Can Do, Will Do Generation [survey], *Manpower Group* [Online] http://www.manpowergroup.com/millennials

Turco, C (2016) *The Conversational Firm: Rethinking bureaucracy in the age of social media*, Columbia University Press, New York, NY

Woods, D (2009) McDonald's proves the benefit of an age-diverse workforce, *Human Resources* [Online] http://www.hrmagazine.co.uk/article-details/mcdonalds-proves-the-benefits-of-an-age-diverse-workforce

Myth 30

CIPD (2015) What Employees Think of Their CEO's Pay Packet, *CIPD* [Online] https://www.cipd.co.uk/knowledge/strategy/reward/ceo-pay-report

Pink, D (2010) *Drive: The surprising truth about what motivates us*, Canongate, Edinburgh

Young, S and Li, W (2016) An Analysis of CEO Pay Arrangements and Value Creation for FTSE-350 Companies, *CFA Society United Kingdom* [Online] https://www.cfauk.org/media-centre/cfa-uk-executive-remuneration-report-2016

Myth 31

Clifton, J (2017) The World's Broken Workplace [survey], *Gallup*, 13 June [Online] http://www.gallup.com/opinion/chairman/212045/world-broken-workplace. aspx?g_source=EMPLOYEE_ENGAGEMENT&g_medium=topic&g_ campaign=tiles

Dahlgreen, W (2015) 37% of British Workers Think Their Jobs Are Meaningless [survey], *YouGov*, 12 Aug [Online] https://yougov.co.uk/news/2015/08/12/ british-jobs-meaningless/

McGregor, D (1960) *The Human Side of Enterprise*, McGraw-Hill, New York, NY

Queen Mary University of London (nd) Professor Rob Briner [profile], *School of Business and Management* [Online] http://www.busman.qmul.ac.uk/staff/ brinerr.html

Myth 32

Kahneman, D (2011) *Thinking, Fast and Slow*, Allen Lane, London

Royal Holloway University of London (nd) Dr Louise Ashley [profile], *Royal Holloway University of London* [Online] https://pure.royalholloway.ac.uk/ portal/en/persons/louise-ashley(0dd5ce07-ba2c-4eae-853e-e6cdd35b0719).html

Myth 33

Hilton, A (2016) HBOS whistleblower Paul Moore exposes badly designed corporate culture, *Evening Standard*, 12 Jan [Online] http://www.standard. co.uk/business/anthony-hilton-hbos-whistleblower-paul-moore-exposes-badly- designed-corporate-culture-a3154506.html

Luyendijk, J (2015) *Swimming with Sharks: My journey into the alarming world of the bankers*, Guardian Faber Publishing, London

Moore, P (2015) *Crash, Bang, Wallop: The memoirs of the HBoS whistleblower*, New Wilberforce Media, London

Seddon, J (nd) The Vanguard Method and systems thinking, *Vanguard* [Online] https://vanguard-method.net/the-vanguard-method-and-systems-thinking/

Stern, S (2007) Anti-guru of joined-up management, interview with Russ Ackoff, *Daily Telegraph*, 8 Feb [Online] http://www.telegraph.co.uk/finance/2803955/ Anti-guru-of-joined-up-management.html

Myth 34

Human Rights Campaign (nd) Website [Online] http://www.hrc.org/

Sandhu, S (2014) OUTstanding survey: Isolated, anxious and less confident – the damage that can be done by hiding who you are, *Huffpost United Kingdom*, 15 Mar [Online] http://www.huffingtonpost.co.uk/suki-sandhu/lgbt-diversity-in-the-workplace_b_6461636.html

Myth 35

Nayar, V (2010) *Employees First, Customers Second: Turning conventional management upside down*, Harvard Business School Press, Boston, MA

Williams, J C (2016) What so many people don't get about the US working class, *Harvard Business Review*, 10 Nov [Online] https://hbr.org/2016/11/what-so-many-people-dont-get-about-the-u-s-working-class

Myth 36

Stern, S (2009) Expert eyes on today's leading questions, *Financial Times*, 8 Jan [Online] http://www.ft.com/cms/s/0/5164884e-dd25-11dd-a2a9-000077b07658.html?ft_site=falcon&desktop=true#axzz4mRiRNF7N

Sutton, B (2008) Sesame Street simple: A G Lafley's leadership philosophy, *Work Matters*, 25 Sept [Online] http://bobsutton.typepad.com/my_weblog/2008/09/sesame-street-simple-ag-lafleys-leadership-philosiphy.html

Myth 37

Abrahamson, E (1991) Managerial fads and fashions: the diffusion and rejection of innovations, *Academy of Management Review*, **16** (3), pp 586–612 [Online] http://amr.aom.org/content/16/3/586.short

Taylor, F W (1911) *Principles of Scientific Management*, Harper and Brothers, New York, NY

Myth 38

Orwell, G (1946) Essay: Politics and the English language, *Horizon* magazine, April

Shaw, G B (1906) *The Doctor's Dilemma* [play] – Preface [Online] https://ebooks.adelaide.edu.au/s/shaw/george_bernard/doctors-dilemma/preface.html

Myth 39

Branson, Sir R (2013) Blog: Give People the Freedom of Where to Work [Online] https://www.virgin.com/richard-branson/give-people-the-freedom-of-where-to-work

Swisher, K (2013) 'Physically Together': Here's the internal Yahoo no-work-from-home memo for remote workers and maybe more, *All Things D* [Online] http://allthingsd.com/20130222

physically-together-heres-the-internal-yahoo-no-work-from-home-memo-which-extends-beyond-remote-workers/

Tarafdar, M (2016) Blog: Good Morning, Digital Co-Worker [Online] http://sbc-devwebsite.mj7.co.uk/business-advice/good-morning-digital-co-worker/

Myth 40

Accenture (2017) Liquid Workforce Website [Online] https://www.accenture.com/gb-en/insight-liquid-workforce-planning

CIPD (2013) Zero-Hours Contracts: Myth and reality, *CIPD*, 26 Nov [Online] https://www.cipd.co.uk/knowledge/fundamentals/emp-law/terms-conditions/zero-hours-reality-report

Office for National Statistics (nd) Labour Force Survey (LFS), *ONS* [Online] https://www.ons.gov.uk/surveys/informationforhouseholdsandindividuals/householdandindividualsurveys/labourforcesurveylfs

Myth 41

Cable, D (2012) Blog: Seven Questions to Ask Before Leading Change, *London Business School* [Online] https://www.london.edu/programmes/executive-education/content/7-questions-to-ask-before-leading-change#.WUmsUtQrJkg

Kotter, J (1996) *Leading Change*, Harvard Business School Press, Boston, MA

Kotter, J (2008) *A Sense of Urgency*, Harvard Business School Press, Boston, MA

Lewin, K (1947) Frontiers in group dynamics: concept, method and reality in social science; social equilibria and social change, *Human Relations*, **1** (1) [Online] http://lchc.ucsd.edu/MCA/Mail/xmcamail.2013_07.dir/pdfeF83xvxgaM.pdf

Myth 42

Jewison, N (1965) *The Cincinnati Kid* [film], produced by Martin Ransohoff, starring Steve McQueen and Edward G Robinson

Myth 43

Kellaway, L (2017) Apple has built an office for grown-ups, *Financial Times* [Online] https://www.ft.com/content/6e873378-5d68-11e7-b553-e2df1b0c3220

Society for Human Resource Management (2016) 2016 Employee Job Satisfaction and Engagement: Revitalizing a changing workforce, *SHRM* [Online] https://www.shrm.org/hr-today/trends-and-forecasting/research-and-surveys/pages/job-satisfaction-and-engagement-report-revitalizing-changing-workforce.aspx

Stern, S (2005) Loiter with intent, says Dr Goodnight, *Daily Telegraph*, 24 Feb [Online] http://www.telegraph.co.uk/finance/2906530/Loiter-with-intent-says-Dr-Goodnight.html

INDEX

Note: page numbers in *italic* indicate figures or tables.

100-Year Life, The 112, 195, 196, 197

A Bigger Prize 200
ABN-Amro 93
Abrahamson, E 140
Accenture 46, 151
Ackoff, Russ 127–28
Act Like a Leader, Think Like a Leader 108, 184
Against Empathy 101
Age of Unreason, The 171
ageism 112
agility 142, 216, 217
AkzoNobel 38
Alcan 175
algorithms 87, 162
Allen & Overy 21
Allen, Woody 15
Alon, Uri 202
Altman, Robert 215
Amazon 89
Apple 209
appraisals 45–48
    and distance 105
    employee ranking 46
    'growth mindset' 47
    and human nature 47
    targets, setting 46
Ariely, Dan 84
Arntz, M, Gregory, T and Zierahn, U 86
Arup 46
Ashley, Louise 124, 192
Ashley, Mike 67
authenticity 106–09
    career transitions 107–08, 185
    'dilemma of authenticity' 108
    'situation sensing' 107, 186
    and working relationships 109
automation of jobs 86–90, 95
    agriculture 87
    algorithms 87
    vs 'augmentation' 88–89, 215
    care sector 89
    routine work 88

autonomy
    of employees 11, 116
    of leaders 10

baby-boomers 111, 205
Barclays Bank 67
Barrett, Colleen 217
Bass 212
BBC 39, 90, 200, 208, 211
Bennis, Warren 215
Beyond Measure 200
Bezos, Jeff 25–26
Bianchi, J 62
Birchall, J 71
Birkinshaw, Julian 2, 196
Birt, John 39
Blair, Tony 74
Bloom, N, Sadun, R and van Reenan, J 2
Bloom, P 101
Bloomberg, Mike 165
Borough Market 87
Boss Baby, The 3
Boston Consulting Group 73
Bourdain, Anthony 104
BP 57, 69, 93
Brady, Chris 148
Branson, Richard 148, 149
Brecht, Bertolt 70
Brexit 11, 43, 133, 134, 161, 182
Briner, Rob 119–20
Britain at Work 13, 14
Brown, Craig 99
Brown, Liz 77
Browne, John 93
burnout 83
business process re-engineering (BPR) 38, 91, 141

Cable, D 96, 156, 158
Cain, S 216
Callahan, Harry ('Dirty Harry') 19
Cameron, David 134
Cameron, W B 162
Campbell, Alastair 74, 75

Campbell's Soup 217
Capital in the Twenty-first Century 11
Capitalism's Toxic Assumptions 177
Carlyle, Thomas 70
Cass Business School 137, 189
change, managing 155–58
    complacency 158
    engagement 157, 158
    Kotter's framework 156
    Lewin's three stage theory 156
    sceptical employees 156–57
    'urgent patience' 157–58
Change to Strange 96
Character of a Corporation, The 207, 209
Chartered Institute for Personnel and
        Development (CIPD) 17,
        117, 152
Chrysler 94
Church on Capitalism, The 177
Cincinnati Kid, The 162
Clarke, Philip 93
Clever 28, 207
clichés, using 143–44
Clifton, J 119
Clinton, Bill 39
Clinton, Hillary 134, 161
Coca-Cola 139
Cohen, Jack 92
Collins, J 7, 41
Columbia Business School 140
'command and control management'
        17, 58
conformity 95–98
    courage 97–98
    signature practices 96–97
    'strange' skills 96
    uniqueness 97
consistency 31–32
    vs development 32
    of purpose 32
    U-turns 31
consultative leadership 21
Conversational Firm, The 113
Cooper, C 84
Cope, Ingrid 77
Cseh, Arpad 77
Curran, John 161

Dahlgreen, W 120
Dannatt, Richard 59
data, using 159–62
    algorithms 162
    analysis 160
    vs human judgement 161
    margin of error 160–61
    and prejudice 162
Davenport, T and Kirby, J 88

Davidson, A 78
Davies, Rob 6, 157
Davis, Ian 8
decisions, making 25–26
    'disagree and commit' 25–26
    information, having 25
Deepwater Horizon 93
'delayering' 28, 39
Deliveroo 192
Deloitte 46
Deming, W Edwards 141, 159
difficult conversations 14, 208
'dilemma of authenticity' 108
Dimon, Jamie 22–23
Director 35
distance, keeping a 102–05
    feedback, giving 105
    intimacy, levels of 104
    larger businesses 104
    'social distance' 103
    tough empathy 103
Distracted Mind, The 215
Dixons Carphone 77
Dow Chemical 64
Downey, Myles 137
Drive 116
Drucker, Peter 3, 21, 42, 75, 87, 100, 138,
        141, 182, 214, 217
Dudley, Bob 69
Dunbar, Robin 173
Duterte, Rodrigo 18
Dweck, C 47
Dyke, Greg 39, 208

Economist, The 34
Emerson, Ralph Waldo 32, 163
emotion at work 99–101
    emotional exhaustion 101
    emotional intelligence 18, 99, 101
    empathy 100–01
    women in the workplace 100
empathy 100–01
Empson, Laura 21, 71, 87–88,
        189–94
Empty Raincoat, The 171
Emrich, M 83
engagement 118–21
    and business performance 120
    and change management 157, 158
    vs fear 121
    Theory X 118–19
    Theory Y 119
Enron 26
Equal Pay Act 1970 53, 81
Erdogan, Recip Tayyip 18
Erickson, Tammy 97
Escape the City 78

Evans, Harry 70
Evening Standard 127
Exceptional Manager, The 195

Facebook 164
fads, management 139–42
    agility 142, 216, 217
    'big data' 160
    business process re-engineering
        (BPR) 141
    holacracy 142
    leanness 142
    'Management By Objectives' (MBO) 141
    pivoting 142
    scientific management 140–41
    Total Quality Management (TQM) 141
failure
    'failure demand' 128
    learning from 138
Financial Times 64, 71, 87, 89, 93, 111, 164
first 100 days 61–64
    first impressions 62
    'listen and learn' 63–64
    preparation for role 62, 63
First 90 Days, The 62
Fishman, C 81
Fitzsimmons, A and Atkins, D 66
flexible working 76–79
    and caring responsibilities 77, 79
    job-sharing 78
    part-time hours 77–78
    see also working hours
Forbes 57
Ford 94
Ford, Henry 161
freelancers, using 151–54
    responsibilities, of employers 153
    zero-hours contracts 152, 205
Freeland, C 64
Fresh'n'Easy 92
Freshfields Bruckhaus Deringer 78
Frey, C B and Osborne, M A 86
From, Pål Johan 87
Furnham, Adrian 81
Future of Management, The 28

Gallup 119
Gap 46
Garnett, John 29, 52
Garrett, Katie 77
General Electric 38, 46
'Generation Cusp' 111
generations, differences between 110–13,
    196–97
    ageism 112
    baby-boomers 111, 205
    cross-generational mentoring 197, 205

'Generation Cusp' 111
    innovations 113
    millennials 113
    mixed workplaces 112, 197, 205
Gerstner, Lou 7, 216
gig economy *see* freelancers, using
Gill, A A 35
Ginsberg, Allen 64
Girolami, Paul 210
Gladwell, Malcolm 84
GlaxoSmithKline 42, 209
GM 94
Goffee, R and Jones, G 6, 18, 28, 103–04,
    107, 116, 207–13
Goldman Sachs 77, 193
Goldsmith, Marshall 107
Goleman, Daniel 18, 99
Good Strategy, Bad Strategy 73
Good to Great 7
Goodnight, Jim 164
Goodwin, Fred 65–66, 93–94
Google 164, 209
Granada 78
Gratton, L and Scott, A 112
Gratton, Lynda 96–97, 112, 132, 195–99
Graves, Robert 20
Grint, Keith 122
groupthink 34
Guardian 129

Haier 104
Halifax Bank of Scotland (HBOS) 127
Halo Effect, The 7
Hamel, G 28, 35
Hammersley, Ben 87
Hampton, Philip 42
Hancock, M and Zahawi, N 65
Handy, Charles 39, 104, 112, 171–76
Hanson, James and White, Gordon 38
Harvard Business Review 83, 134
Harvard Business School 156
Hayward, Tony 93
HCL 133
Heath, Dan and Heath, Chip 84
Heath, Dawn 78
Heffernan, Margaret 142, 160, 200–06
Hersey, P and Blanchard, K 6
Herzberg, Frederick 83–84, 116
hierarchy 27–30
    and authority 28
    and career paths 29–30
    'delayering' 28
    'holacracy' 28
    and information sharing 50
    'position power' 29
    and respect 28
hierarchy of needs 83

High Pay Centre 42
Hill, A 111
Hilton, A 127
hiring policy 33–36
    corporate culture 35
    diversity 34
    groupthink 34
    interview panels 34
Hiscox 35
Hitchcock, Alfred 118
'holacracy' 28, 142
Holmes, Peter 175
Hope Hailey, Veronica 133
Horton, Bob 57
Hot Spots 195, 196
How Women Mean Business 55
HR 97
Human Rights Campaign 130
Human Side of Enterprise, The 119
Hungry Spirit, The 171
Hunt, John 27, 29
Hunt, V et al 55

Ibarra, Herminia 106, 108–09, 184–88
IBM 160, 216
ICI 38
Ikea 96
In Search of Excellence 214
Industrial Society 29, 52
information and reporting 49–52,
        65–68
    knowledge as power 50
    listening 51
    micromanagement 66, 68
    openness of information 66
    'radical transparency' 51
    technology, role of 50
    whistleblowing 51, 67–68
INSEAD 10, 85, 184
'insecure over-achievers' 193, 194
Inside the Harvard Business School 181
International Institute for Management
        Development (IMD) 7
interpersonal skills 14–15, 18
intrinsic motivation 116

J P Morgan 22
Jacobs, C 47
Jacobson, Howard 90
Japan Times 13
jargon, business 143–46
    clichés 143–44
    examples of 145–46
    Orwell's rules 144–45
'job control' 10
job-sharing 78

Jobs, Steve 7, 8, 164
John Lewis 21

Kahneman, D and Tversky, A 123
kaizen 94
Kalanithi, P 214
Kandola, Binna 34
karōshi 12
Kay, John 72, 73
Kellaway, L 164
Kelleher, Herb 75
Kennedy, John F 38, 61–62, 64
Kets de Vries, M 10, 85
Key, The 195
Keynes, John Maynard 32
KFC 139
Kinsley, Michael 205
Kitchen Confidential 104
Knights, D and Willmott, H 190
Koch, C 35
Kodak 32
Korn Ferry 62
Kotter, J 156, 157–58
Kraft 182
Krugman, Paul 1

*Lack of flexibility is killing UK
        productivity* 77
Lafley, A G 137
Lancaster University Management School
        43, 112, 115, 149
Langan, Steve 35
Lansons 13
Lazear, E and Rosen, S 115
Leader on the Couch, The 10, 85
leadership vs management 37–40
    business process re-engineering (BPR) 38
    'delayering' 39
    shareholder value 38
    supervision, importance of 39
Leadersmithing 177
'leadersmithing' 7, 178–79
Leading Change 156
Leading Professionals 189
Leahy, Terry 7, 92, 93
leanness 142
'learned helplessness' 84
learning to lead 57–60
    authority 59
    'command and control management' 58
    luck, role of 58
    skills development 59
Levy, Alain 209
Lewin, Kurt 156
Lewis, Dave 69
Life of Brian 35–36

'liquid workforce' *see* freelancers, using
Liveris, Andrew 64
Lloyds TSB 127
London Business School 156, 174, 184, 195, 207
loneliness 20–23, 71
    asking for help 22
    consultative leadership 21
    succession planning 21
    and trust 20–21, 22
Luyendijk, J 128–29

Mackey, John 81
MacLaurin, Ian 92
'management by deeming' 181
'Management By Objectives' (MBO) 141
management consulting 141
Management Lives 190
Management Rewired 47
Management Today 77, 78
Managing the Modern Law Firm 189
Manpower Group 113
Marks and Spencer 213
Marmot, Michael 10
Martin, R and Lafley, A G 73
Marx, Karl 207
Maslow, Abraham 83
Masojada, Bronek 35
Masters of Nothing 65
Masunaga, S 86
May, Theresa 134
Mayer, Marissa 147–48, 150
McDonald's 112, 139
McGill University 180
McGregor, Douglas 118–19
McKinsey 8, 55, 73, 141, 193, 216, 218
Mencken, H L 7
Meyer, Marissa 78
micromanagement 66, 68
Microsoft 46, 89
millennials 30, 113
Miller, Danny 181
mindfulness 142
Mintzberg, H, Lampel, J and Ahlstrand, B 74
Mintzberg, Henry 18, 39, 40, 74, 126, 180–83, 217
mistakes, inevitability of 136–38
    human nature 137
    learning from failure 138
    message sharing 137
money as a motivator 43–44, 114–17
    vs autonomy 116
    intrinsic motivation 116
    vs mastery 116
    performance-related pay 46, 115

vs purpose 116
    unfair pay 117
mood swings 103
Moore, P 127
Morgan, J P 42
Morrisons 153
Mourinho, José 70
Murdoch, Rupert 55
Murgia, M 89

Nadella, Satya 89
National Health Service (NHS) 131, 173, 208, 209
National Westminster Bank 93
Nature of Managerial Work, The 180
Nayar, V 133
Neff, T and Citrin, J 63
Nestlé 210
Newhall, Steve 62
Norwich Business School 101
Novo Nordisk 181

Obama, Barack 100
O'Connor, S 89
Office for National Statistics 152
Office, The 3
offices, 'cool' 142, 163–65
    distractions and noise 164
    perks, providing 164
    privacy 164, 165
    time off, importance of 165
Ohno, Taiichi 1, 127
Oliver, Mary 117
Only Humans Need Apply 88
Open University 174
Organisation for Economic Co-operation and Development (OECD) 86
Orwell, George 144

Partnoy, F 215, 216
Pascal, Blaise 120
pay and rewards 11, 41–44
    equal pay 81
    high salaries, effect of 42, 43
    money as a motivator 43–44, 114–17
        vs autonomy 116
        intrinsic motivation 116
        vs mastery 116
        performance-related pay 46, 115
        vs purpose 116
        unfair pay 117
    pay gaps 42, 60
    pay transparency 80–81
Peralta, C F 101
performance reviews *see* appraisals
performance-related pay 46, 115

Pernod Ricard 77
Peters, Tom 137, 214–18
Pfeffer, Jeffrey 29
Pickavance, Norman 153
Piketty, T 11
Pink, Dan 84, 116
pivoting 142
Playing to Win 73
political correctness 131, 134
Politics and the English language 144
Polygram 209
Poole, Eve 7, 177–79
Positive Psychology Center 84
power 132–35
    of frontline staff 133
    'position power' 29
    'silent majority' 134
prejudice 130–31
    and data analysis 162
    political correctness 131
    quotas 131
    vs rationality 123
presenteeism 12, 78, 149
PricewaterhouseCoopers (PwC) 86
Principles of Scientific Management 140
Procter and Gamble 137
productivity 2
    and appraisals 48
    and engagement 119, 120
    and interpersonal skills 14–15
    and middle managers 39
    and remote working 149
    and skills development 59
    and work environment 164, 165
    and working hours 13, 14, 77
psychology, role of 82–85
    decision-making 85
    hierarchy of needs 83
    'learned helplessness' 84
    motivation 83–84
    stress and burnout 83, 84
Putin, Vladimir 18

Quiet 216

Radical Candor 105
'radical transparency' 51
Railtrack 57
rationality 122–25
    bottom line, the 122
    moral pressure 124
    vs prejudice 123
    system one and system two thinking 123
Reagan, Ronald 38
Red Letter Days for Business 77
Reding, Viviane 131

redundancies 9
Reinventing Management 2
remote working 147–50
    presenteeism 149
    supervisory management 148
    technology, role of 149
restructuring 9
Rethinking Reputational Risk 66–67
'right way' to manage 5–8
    'leadersmithing' 7
    role models 6–7
    'situation sensing' 6
    situational leadership 6
    telling, selling, participating, delegating 6
Rise and Fall of Strategic Planning, The 74
Robinson, Gerry 78
Roffey Park Institute 82
Roosevelt, Franklin 62
Rosenzweig, P 7
Rousseff, Dilma 183
Roy, Donald 211–12
Royal Bank of Scotland (RBS) 42, 93
RTZ Alcan 175
Rumelt, R 73

Sainsburys 42, 92
Salford Business School 148
Sanders, Bernie 182
Sandhu, S 131
Sandhurst 58
SAS 164
Saunders, A 77
Savile, Jimmy 211
Schein, Ed 187
Schultz, Howard 217
scientific management 1, 17, 88, 140–41,
    211
Scott, Andrew 196
Scott, K 105
Scott, Lee 71
Second Curve, The 112, 171
Seddon, J 128
Self-Reliance 32
Seligman, Martin 84
Semler, Riccardo 174
shareholder value 38, 175
Shaw, George Bernard 143
Shell 172, 175, 176
Shift, The 195
signature practices 96–97
Simmel, Georg 103
'situation sensing' 6, 107, 186
situational leadership 6, 185
Slack 149
Slim, William 58–59
'social distance' 103

Society for Human Resource
        Management 164
Sony 161
Southwest Airlines 75, 217
Sparrow, Paul 112
Spencer Stuart 63
Staley, Jes 67
Starbucks 217
Stern, S 23, 128, 137, 164
Stewart, Potter 120
strategy 72–75
        vs business planning 73
        execution of 75
        good vs bad strategy 73
        inertia 73
        inspiring 74
        luck, role of 73
Strategy Bites Back 74
stress 10, 83, 84
        and long hours 13
        of low income 11
        and prejudice 131
succession planning 21
supervisory management 148
supply chain management 213
Surowiecki, J 51
Sutton, B 137
Swimming with Sharks 128
Swisher, K 148
Sykes, Richard 209, 210
Symington, Rob 78
systems thinking 126–29
        'failure demand' 128
        targets and incentives 127

Tarafdar, M 149
Tata Group 181
        Tata Consultancy Services (TCS) 195
Taylor, Frederick 1, 17, 88, 140–41, 211
Taylorism *see* scientific management
Tesco 7, 69, 92–93
        Fresh'n'Easy 92
Thatcher, Margaret 16–17, 19, 33, 38
Theory X 118–19, 120
Theory Y 119, 120
Total Quality Management (TQM) 141
tough empathy 103
Toyota 1–2, 127, 203
Trades Union Congress (TUC) 13
transformational leadership 71, 91–94
        BP 93
        kaizen 94
        Royal Bank of Scotland 93–94
        Tesco 92–93
Trump, Donald 11, 18, 43, 131, 133, 134,
        148, 161, 182

Turco, C 113
Tzu, Lao 94

Uber 87, 192
UBS Asset Management 77
UK Labour Force Survey 152
Ulrich, Dave 137
Unilever 182, 210
'urgent patience' 157–58

Verizon 147
virtualization 91
vulnerability, showing 16–19, 187
        asking for help 19
        'command and control management' 17
        emotional intelligence 18
        interpersonal skills 18
        U-turns 16–17

Wait 215, 216
Walmart 71
Warwick Business School 122
Watkins, Michael 62
Watson Snr, Thomas 160
Weber, Max 211
Weizmann Institute 202
Welch, Jack 38
Wells Fargo 46, 115
West Wing, The 61
Wharton School 127
*What Got You Here Won't Get You
        There* 107
When Breath Becomes Air 214
whistleblowing 51, 67–68
Whitehall studies 10
Who Says Elephants Can't Dance? 216
Whole Foods 81
Why Should Anyone Be Led By You? 6, 18,
        103, 107, 207
Why Should Anyone Work Here? 207,
        211, 212
Wilful Blindness 200
Williams, J 134
Williamson, Oliver 21
Wisdom of Crowds, The 51
Wise, H 20
Wittenberg-Cox, A 55
W L Gore 28
women in the workplace 53–56
        ambition 54
        at board level 54
        domestic responsibilities 54–55
        emotion at work 100
        flexible working 77, 79
        gender pay gap 53, 55–56, 81
Woods, D 112

Woolworths 32
working hours 12–15, 76–79
    and fatigue 14, 78
    and health 13
    part-time hours 77–78
    presenteeism 12, 78
    and productivity 13, 77
    and stress 13
    see also flexible working
Working Identity 184
workingmums.co.uk 77
World Management Survey 2

Woudhuysen, James 145

Xi Jinping 18

Yahoo 78, 147–48, 149
Yes, Minister 97
YouGov 120
Young, S and Li, W and Li 115
You're in Charge – Now What? 63

zero-hours contracts 152, 205